WILD SHOT

WILD SHOT

*Struggles and successes
in biathlon and
cross country skiing*

By Andy Liebner

Copyright © 2011 by Andy Liebner.

Library of Congress Control Number: 2011918147
ISBN: Softcover   978-1-4653-7796-8
           E-book   978-1-4653-7797-5

All rights reserved. No part of this book may be reproduced or transmitted in any form or by any means, electronic or mechanical, including photocopying, recording, or by any information storage and retrieval system, without permission in writing from the copyright owner.

This book was printed in the United States of America.

To order additional copies of this book, contact:
Xlibris Corporation
1-888-795-4274
www.Xlibris.com
Orders@Xlibris.com
105228

INTRO:

I am Andy Liebner!
I am an American warrior!
This is my story!

I'm not a Marine. I'm not a member of a Special Forces unit. My battlefield does not lie in Afghanistan or Iraq. I'm an elite sportsman and my battlefields are the mountains and snowfields of the world's major skiing events. My enemy is not a guy in a caftan carrying an AK 47. My enemy is not even the other competitors. My enemy is inside my head and the thoughts of limitations it seeks to impose upon me. If I can master that enemy better than my opponent, then I win. That's the bottom line.

But this is not just a story about a sportsman overcoming obstacles, because, you see, sport is a metaphor for a deeper aspect of life.

Sport is a quest! To make it to the top requires a heroic journey to encounter and overcome external and internal barriers. There is something unique about America and American athletes, at least when I engage in this type of battle.

The way we Americans go about our task is different to the European champions and nowhere is this difference highlighted more than in Nordic skiing. We are not the best – they are. Consistently. Why is this?

That answer lies at the heart of what it means to be American. It touches on the role we play in the world today as the sole global superpower. My journey through the peaks and chasms of sport, on three continents, is more than one man's journey. As an American,

I am acutely aware of the role our nation plays in the world and how it is perceived by others. This creates a desire to uphold my nation's status in the world. My journey is a metaphorical quest to understand the American psyche and to come to terms with what makes us unique and great as well as the vulnerabilities and limitations that same role places upon each of us.

Come with me to Europe as I grapple to understand my journey and face the cultural challenges of being an American in another land. Enter into my world, a world of physical toil among stunning vistas shared with some amazing people.

TABLE OF CONTENTS

Chapter One 1
   The Unknown Calling

Chapter Two 11
   Europe Here I Come!

Chapter Three 27
   Inspiring Lessons

Chapter Four 57
   Opportunities and Barriers

Chapter Five 75
   Racing Begins

Chapter Six 107
   Work, Travel, Race

Chapter Seven 129
   Skiing World Championships

Chapter Eight 149
   Greece Here I Come!

Chapter Nine 173
   Skiing Down Under

Chapter Ten 201
  European Surprises

Chapter Eleven 225
  New Horizons

Chapter Twelve 243
  Follow-up

Chapter Thirteen 259
  Epilogue

CHAPTER ONE
The Unknown Calling

It is May of 2008, I am 25 years of age and I've competed nearly my entire life in the sport of cross country skiing. As skiing is my first passionate sport, distance running is second, and biathlon is third, but of high interest. It is the spring and I've just completed my second year of National Collegiate Athletic Association (NCAA) skiing. Because of an opportunity offered in 2007 to become part of a group of athletes to train with the United States Biathlon Association (USBA), I've departed my university and am interested in pursuing the sport of biathlon while still improving my skiing abilities. At my age I'm considered old by some in this sport, but I do not agree. The average age in the World Cup being 33, I'm still young, alive, and have plenty of energy to burn and will-power to spare.

But I'm getting ahead of myself because you don't know anything about me or how I came to be in this position, so let me step back a few strides and explain.

I'm from Alaska, so the snow and I have a familiar relationship, shall we say. I grew up in the small town of Soldotna and had a pair of cross country skis on my feet when I was only two. To me, skis are like extensions of my legs and poles are extensions of my arms. Making use of them comes naturally. My work ethic is to pour all my time and energy into life-enhancing progress and never give up when I set my mind on something.

I was a cross-country skier and runner when I was younger and skiing remains my real strength. A few years back I decided to try my hand at biathlon, which is a combination of cross-country skiing and rifle marksmanship. The shooting aspect utilizes a .22 caliber rifle that is shot at a distance of 50 meters. There are five targets at each shooting stage. Depending on the race there are either two or four shooting stages. There are two shooting positions: prone (lying down) and standing. The prone targets are of the size of a U.S. half-dollar coin and the standing targets are five inches in diameter.

As you can imagine, from the small size of the targets, to be a good biathlete, you need to be a pretty good shot. Now add in a hilly, challenging ski course — ski it — come in to shoot — try to lower your heart rate from maybe 200 bpm down enough so that the sights aren't jumping — and try to hit all those little targets — shoot as fast as you can, getting back to skiing again in less than 30 seconds if possible — if you've missed any targets, ski a penalty loop for each, in front of the fans, or lose a minute per miss (depending on the event). Speaking of fans, biathlon is to skiing what cyclocross is to road bike racing: it's a party time for the fans. Like Sprint skiing, it's easy to watch and is held at smaller, more compact venues. Because of this public popularity, biathlon is much more popular in Europe than cross country skiing and even alpine skiing. This is partly why I chose to pursue biathlon and enjoy competing in it.

Because each athlete must race while carrying the rifle on his/her back, biathlon rifles are specially made with a harness to facilitate getting it on and off one's back every shooting stage. This harness I have found to be greatly beneficial to improving skating technique, especially with preventing shoulder tilt and improving leg strength with the added weight of the rifle, about 10-12 pounds.

Biathlon is an art of finesse and mental concentration rather than one of brute skiing speed. This difference in focus generates tension between skiers and biathletes. Biathletes don't always like it when elite skiers, such as myself (even though I have never skied in the World Cup), enter their ranks. I'd like to use the current Austrian Biathlon Team as an example of skiers doing well.

After the 2006 Olympics, due to the disqualification of the entire Austrian Biathlon Team, the entire Austrian Ski Team made the transition to become the new Austrian Biathlon Team. This new team has done very well and quickly became one of the strongest Biathlon National Teams in the world.

You can think of it in comparison to the summer triathlon, where the athletes swim, bike and run. Some are top swimmers, and they'll come out of the water first, but then they have to ride, and the guys who are specialist cyclists often power past them. Same applies to winter biathlon, where strong skiers can often do well.

A guy who can hit all five targets gets a head start on someone who misses a few. But if that same guy is not an efficient skier then he is going to be caught on the ski leg.

I figure I have an advantage because I have a strong natural skiing ability and there is less than a handful of guys on the American biathlon circuit that I can't surpass on the ski leg. As for rifle shooting, well, logically, it's all about technique and routine. With the right coaching, determined application, and committed practice, that is always something that I can improve enough to be able to place in the mix. It is harder to convert a shooter into a skier.

Prior to any biathlon experience I had outstanding success within the Alaska High School competitions and earned a total of seven Junior Olympic medals and had a number of great performances in citizen races in the sport of Cross Country Skiing in the following winter months. Without snow during the dryland training season I'd placed well in every running race I entered. The intense mental pressure relating to my performances became so strong I decided to put my athletic career on hold and after watching the twin towers fall on television that cold September morning I join the U.S. Coast Guard and departed for basic training a month later. I break the 1.5 mile run record in basic training, which generates attention and my orders are redirected landing me in snowy Marquette, Michigan to serve my country.

My first experience of biathlon was in February 2003 after formal invitation to the U.S. Armed Forces Skiing and Biathlon National Championships held in Jericho, Vermont. I did well and finished in 2nd place, which qualified me to compete in Rovaniemi, Finland. Since most European-born males must choose between either a several-month obligation of community service or nearly a year of military service with many years following as a reservist, most of the world cup athletes end up competing in the World Military Championships to complete their countries military obligation.

After those races I bought my first rifle second-hand from a former Russian Athlete who was a U.S. Biathlon trainer. Over that summer while working full time at the Coast Guard Station I trained alone with no biathlon help, and had an old run-down (no longer in use) shooting range with only car parts and piles of junk to shoot at. I did the best I could with what I had. The running and rollerskiing is good there. I was able to make significant progress in fitness and strength.

That next winter I was granted special liberty to compete in many important events such as the U.S. National Championships. Half the races I competed in were cross country skiing and half were biathlon. It was a difficult season, but I prevailed with some great successes in both skiing and biathlon including a 5th and 6th place overall at the Biathlon National Championships.

A month after these trials I was able to take leave again to compete in the U.S. Armed Forces trials again; although in the first race one of the two bolts which holds the rifle-action to the stock came loose and I barely managed to hit one out of the ten targets. I skied my heart out doing nine extra 150m loops and came across the finish line with a story-filled smile on my face in 3rd place out of the fifty-plus other competitors. That's what extra skiing speed can do. Although this event was a military qualification, some of the juniors, selected ahead of me for the U.S. team, competed as guests and all but one finished behind me, despite my rifle problems. In the second race I made sure all bolts were tight on my rifle, shot half-decently, suffered a broken ski pole mid-race and ended up 6th overall. I again qualified for the World Military Championships in Ostersund, Sweden.

In preparation for this event I was able to spend five weeks training with the support of a coach. This preparation included travelling to Europe and competing for the U.S. Army National Guard Team in IBU (International Biathlon Union) Cup races. During my time in Europe I earned more IBU cup points than any other American that year, which raised my overall U.S. National ranking to within the top ten.

This success helped me appreciate that my vision of success at the top level was not just fantasy or testosterone-driven ego. Instead, it was an achievable goal and within reach. Given my European success I was surprised that no U.S. coaches demonstrated any interest in my development or to encourage me to continue in biathlon. I did not know it at the time, but this was to be the theme of my relationship with U.S. biathlon authorities. Without the support from the U.S. biathlon community I drifted back to cross-country skiing and kept training.

One of the spin-off implications of my biathlon race success was that the United States Anti-Doping Agency (USADA) placed me on its testing pool. Because of my geographical location it turned out that I was the only male athlete to be tested in that particular region. They were required to test a certain number of athletes, and I was the only available male, and consequently was being tested monthly. As these tests were impromptu, it placed a great strain on my working environment with the Coast Guard, as our boat sometimes had to come ashore just so I could be tested. At this time I had no support from any biathlon authorities and had already made the decision to focus on cross country. To avoid the hassles with work and the potential risk of being banned for missing a drug test I decided to retire from the sport of biathlon. This decision would come back to haunt me later.

Three years later, after a successful 2006-07 cross country ski season within the NCAA I was contacted by USBA personnel. They were frustrated by the lack of skiing speed of their developing biathletes and were recruiting athletes with skiing credentials who could be trained in the rifle aspect of biathlon. As I already had biathlon experience and had just concluded an outstanding skiing season I was high on their target list. The director had great things to offer, including the lure of a possible position on the U.S. team for the 2010 Olympics so I decided to accept. It was agreed that I'd spend one more year skiing with the NCAA and then commit to biathlon.

During that year I developed acute knee pain. According to my physician, I had a calcium deposit in the joint. At the end of March, 2008 I underwent knee surgery to remove the deposit and began the process of rebuilding my cartilage.

My knee rehab was progressing well and appeared not to

interfere with my training. I'd learned to live with pain, and I was not going to allow it to distract me from my goal of becoming the best I could be in the sport of skiing and biathlon.

And that is how I got to this point! My life stands at a transition point right now. I'm about to leave the University of Alaska, Anchorage, and head off into a new environment to commit the next two years of my life to the U.S. Biathlon Development Team. I'm excited about the challenge, but, as is usual, I'm also apprehensive.

I'm actually in the process of packing my stuff when an email arrives from the USBA. I cannot believe what I read. There must be a mistake. It takes several minutes for the reality to sink in – *I'm not going!* The invitation to move to Lake Placid and join the U.S. training squad has been revoked. The message consisted of a simple two-sentence email ended by wishing me the best for my knee recovery.

I feel as if I've just stepped off a cliff and am tumbling into a bottomless abyss. A chasm of unfathomable depth has opened in my bowels and I sense a demonic creature lurking there, waiting to swallow me in its gaping jaws. After all I've done both mentally and physically to prepare for this next stage of my journey, how can they simply sweep it away like this? No phone call, no personal explanation, just an email appearing on my computer screen.

This letter evokes buried memories of having felt blocked by people in authority throughout my life. I struggle to sit still and have a constant need to keep moving and the faster the better. That's why I love being out on the ski trails, running trails, and mountains – there is just me and the vastness of space, no boundaries, no rules, except the laws of nature and survival that I understand intuitively.

In the past the imposition of such constraints has caused me to slip into a dark state and I've had to fight my way out of it, usually with the help of intense physical activity. And right now the jaws of that demon are snarling within me, reaching out from some deeply buried inner dungeon, hungrily snapping at my heart. I've been rejected and it hurts. I can feel its allure, combined with the gentle caress of victim-hood. I want to lash out at someone, preferably the USBA. I despise them in that moment and in my hatred lies the seeds of salvation. I will not allow them to defeat me. I will not permit them to crush me. They will not be the executioners of my dreams. They will not condemn me to an endless slide into depression. I've fought against steeper slopes than this and I'll pull myself out of this one as well.

It's difficult, if not impossible, to understand one's true motivations in such times of intense emotions. It's easier to fight my way up a steep, snow-covered mountain during a marathon than to sift through the inter-twined waves of passion that sweep through me when I crash into myself. I'll never really know what drives me on this day, but something does. Perhaps it is the terror I feel at staying still, the dread that I'll succumb to the inner demon and lose myself. Maybe it is a combination of these and other forces that I'm not even remotely aware of. But what I know is that something emerges out of me, a greater will to continue, to defeat the odds that seem to be mounting against me. The unknowns to how soon I can resume the training hours to 100% of what's required to perform at optimal levels will remain a mystery. Until then, I enjoy entertaining the thought that I can use this down time to learn more about biathlon. Also lugging around an extra 12 pounds (rifle weight) on my back to make me a better skier seems like a good idea.

I think about what to do next as the world seems to open itself to me now. After some deep thought I decide to keep my focus on improving as a cross-country skier with an interest in learning all I can through experience in biathlon. I seize this golden opportunity to finally spend a winter in Europe examining what exactly the best skiers and biathletes are doing behind the scenes during the training months and how they mentally prepare for competitions. These aspects have always been a mystery to me. In America, I've always heard training was taught based on the ways the best Europeans are training, as if we must do it out of a fear that if we don't do those exercises we won't have a chance at rising to their level. I need to see what they are doing for myself and I am now excited to have that possibility. I have a feeling there is more to it than that.

The following day I sit down and draft a letter outlining my personal biography and send it to every ski and biathlon training center in the world I can find. I ask them for feedback on the possibilities of training with their local clubs with the aim of improving performance. With the emails sent off into cyberspace and my emotional state back on a more level footing, I have the chance to reflect about this decision. In a 24 hour period, my emotional state had gone from a bottomless pit, to a mountain top.

So now you know about my history with the sport establishment. You'll probably think either I am a young, head-strong fool, or you'll empathize with me. Either way, I cannot see myself staying in the United States and training with any of the established ski or biathlon clubs. Remember, the U.S. to date hasn't succeeded on the world stage. The mystery of what I feel I'm suppose to see, and learn in Europe to improve the most has such a profound call that there is no question I am going to Europe and I feel 15 months is about the right amount of time. What are they doing differently that sets them apart from us? I feel a thrill at the chance of going there and unraveling that mystery for myself. There is a part of me that likes the idea of being a little subversive, hiding out in Europe and improving before returning to the North American scene with a big splash. Yeah, that appeals to me!

My spirits are buoyed when responses start to come in with positive feedback and invitations to join them. Within days I would be accepted into an accredited biathlon club in Austria and a few weeks later would be on my way to Europe for the next stage of my adventure.

CHAPTER TWO
Europe Here I Come!

Now that I have made the decision to go to Europe, some of my friends and family have begun to express concerns about my future. I guess their questions are valid, reflecting the uncertainties of the life I am about to walk into. I'm not one who would claim to be spiritual and yet there is a sense of a "calling" about this trip, a kind of inner feeling that tells me everything will work out just fine.

Perhaps a psychologist would tell me that I am running from something, and there may be some truth in that. I feel stagnant in the life I'm in and that need to move is grabbing at me again. But it is more because, equally as powerful as that need, an inner force seems to be pulling me onward.

The other thing that some of my friends are suggesting is that I don't seem to care about them and the life I have here in Alaska. How can I just up and leave?

I can justify myself in the face of these arguments but the truth is they are right – I have not given a single thought to the people and life I am leaving behind. I'm aware that, to many people, friends and family are the most important assets in the world and they can find happiness and peace by culturing relationships and a social fabric. I'm simply not like that. I don't need friends to get by or be satisfied; what I need is a sense of challenge and a purpose that draws me into its grasp. It's not that I don't value friendship and relationships; it's just that many important things just do not sit at the forefront of my focus and personal needs right now.

Some people may see this as being selfish, putting my own

needs in front of those of others, but I don't see it this way. It's just the way I am; I'm driven by a sense of something greater than me. I see this world as a great playing field that I'm being called to explore and now I'm walking off into the mystery, driven by a desire to find out just how good I can become as a skier and what insight I can learn about becoming a better athlete by top Olympians directly.

Hassles and Creativity

One of the things that a skier has to deal with is the hassles of air travel that arise due to the amount of equipment we need to carry. The result is that we often have to pay substantial excess baggage as we travel. I had downsized my baggage from a full carload to two large ski bags but was still over the weight limit. While searching the Internet on Craigslist I saw an advertisement from a guy looking for someone to take his dog to Munich, Germany. I was flying into Munich as my coach had informed me this was the best entry point to get to Obertilliach, Austria even though it was in a different country.

At the time I still owned a three-bedroom home with property in Anchorage, Alaska and this guy was also looking for a place to stay for a while, so I contacted him. The match was perfect. I was able to give the guy a place to live for a week and take his dog to Munich with me, and he paid my overweight fees on my bags. The dog owner stayed a few days and was able to do some final house work repairs that I was incapable of doing because of my disabled knee. He successfully took care of the tasks and moved out before my long-term tenants were to move in.

The very friendly dog's name is Mable. In the airport after checking in and watching one of my bags glide down the belt, I have to check my long ski bag and Mable in at another area. They require Mable to be taken out of the cage and as I open the cage Mable darts out so quickly that I barely have time to grasp her collar by a few fingers. Her weight, strength, and momentum pull me off my feet as she drags me under the Security fencing and 15 meters through the airport lobby. I can't believe her strength and willingness to escape. She must have hated that cage or known what was coming.

After the bags are successfully checked, I say farewell to my mother at the Anchorage airport. It is my final hour in America and I can't wait to depart and begin an unknown adventure of learning, hard work, and racing.

A long international flight is the perfect place for reflection and I find myself thinking about my feelings and expectations for my looming adventure. Of course there is some apprehension as I am stepping into a world of complete unknowns. Despite this, however, the sense of excitement accompanying the trip is overwhelming. In fact I am more excited about beginning this new adventure than at any previous time in my life when I've made life-changing decisions.

Part of the excitement is certainly the allure of racing with the world's best in Europe. This is my chance to see and experience, firsthand, what real European skiing culture is all about.

As the plane heads across northern Canada I feel a deep sense of freedom, escape and joy at the chance of exploring the skiing and biathlon world. I smile to myself, reflecting on the similarity between Mable and myself. Like her, I cannot stand feeling trapped and this trip is like a flight from the cage of my existing life into freedom.

I don't really have many expectations as everything is just too unknown to settle on goals and plans at this stage. My mind is open and eager to learn the unknown secrets of these winter endurance sports that await me on the other side of the Atlantic.

There is a mystique in my country about the success of European skiers over the American skiers and I hope to peel back that mystique and be able to peer in on their secrets up close and personal.

What do these elite skiers do behind the scenes? What are their eating regimes, their training routines and their recovery habits? What are the little day-to-day things that set Europe's best apart from the rest? This is what I need to see and learn. Are there any secrets, are they doing anything different or is it the training locations that produce better biathletes?

On my previous trips to Europe with the US National Guard

team my memories are positive, but this is something different. On that trip I was part of a team and did not have the freedom to seek out the mysteries of the sport and of life on the continent that await me now so, in a way, it feels as if I am going there for the first time.

It is July 22 when I arrive in Munich only to find that my baggage does not arrive but Mable does. Little do I know this is a forewarning of the trouble I will have with luggage...and anything that can get delayed. I am greeted by Mable's family as well as my German friend, Raphael Wunderle. Raphael and I have spent the past two years as roommates and team-mates at the University of Alaska, Anchorage, (UAA). Raphael and I drive half of the day to arrive in Obertilliach, Austria, which I soon come to refer to as **O-town**. On the way in we stop at a meeting place that has been organized by my new trainer. His name is Joe Obererlacher and as we stand in the town of Kartich (outside of Obertilliach) it is fiercely cold and there are actually snowflakes in the air. Can you believe it? Snow in July! As Raphael and I follow Joe toward O-town, we can't help but notice that he drives excessively FAST! Our next stop is the Biathlon Center just 1 km from O-town and we learn that Joe is a police officer, which explains his driving.

O-Town

He shows us a little bit of town and leads us into a guest house that his family owns, and that I can rent. The guest house is next door to his parents' home in O-town. The next morning Raphael and I get some food and he helps me open a bank account at the local bank. Later he says his goodbyes and heads down the road back to Germany. He leaves me his bike and I am so thankful for such a great friend to help me out so extensively.

Once I am alone in O-town I finally start to think about the situation I have got myself into. I've set my sights on being away from the US for 15 months. I don't know a lot about O-town yet but there is an inner sense that it will become a base, a place that I can call my home and from where I can spread out around Europe.

The Academy turns out to be a little different from what I expected. It was originally set up as a partnership between the city of Obertilliach and Joe and his brother, created to work as one system. Problems had developed between the two parties, however, and the city withdrew its support, leaving Joe to take it on alone. This I only discovered after I arrived.

The result of all this is that there is no established team based at the Academy of which I will be a part. Rather it is a facility that people can come to improve as a cross country skier or to improve with the art of biathlon. I will not be the only one using the center as a base and am aware of some other athletes that are around my level. Leandro Ribela of Brazil is one of them. Joe also says there are many national teams that come and train here, assuring me that I will be able to train with some of the best in the world.

I immediately like Joe. He seems a kindred spirit in many ways; someone who speaks what he thinks, with a flexible attitude. He does not require me to enter into a formal contract but is willing to offer me coaching when he has the time with me paying when I have the money.

On my fourth day in O-town my bags finally arrive. For the past four days I've trained twice each day, all in the same clothes and now that my bags have arrived it is great to wear clean clothes again. I only had my running shoes and shorts, so all my workouts have been running along the trails and exploring the vastness of the Dolomite mountain range. It did snow briefly the day we arrived, but in the past few days it has been like full-blown summer, 60-75' F.

Joe had informed me that there are many competitions around the area and also many visiting teams who come to the Academy with whom I will be able to join in training. This proves to be true right from the beginning as during my first week, the Austrian National Biathlon Team (Men's A and B) is here training. I immediately began to absorb all kinds of different useful and powerful training drills, mental exercises, and ways to keep the spirit of sport fun and alive.

Joe explained that he would be busy at work for two weeks and had therefore pointed me in the direction of many far distant areas, encouraging me to explore the trail systems and mountain passes in those regions. It is an amazing experience, even for someone coming from a lifetime of living in Alaska. There are trails hidden within these dolomite mountains that seem to go forever in many directions and I can run freely without any worry about the wildlife eating me (i.e., bears and wolves in Alaska). The scenery is always green and the people are always friendly.

I had been aware that I was flying into the face of mystery and my first week in Europe has really reinforced that. I've landed in an environment that fosters a spirit of flexibility and my coach seems to be comfortable with that. There is a part of me that has been craving to do this but I cannot deny that another part of me is scared because I'm way out of my comfort zone, lacking structure and even a definite plan. I've left everything I know and own behind without a concrete plan and yet it feels so right to be here.

I guess I should really be thankful to the USBA because their rejection of me has opened up this new possibility and now I feel completely motivated. I've wanted to come to Europe for training and racing with the best ever since I've been skiing and so I am really pursuing my dream.

The Rifle – The Means to the End

After my early days of traveling as a biathlete I've always been thankful as a skier not having to travel with the most tricky legal piece of equipment, the rifle. The most critical piece of a biathlete's equipment is their rifle. As each rifle is slightly different there is a significant advantage in using the same rifle. You get used to the way it shoots and that can make all the difference when you're trying to hit a small target under stressful conditions. I have owned an Izhmash (Russian) rifle for years in America that I used in all my former competitions, but it broke, and so I sold it to Marc Sheppard and mailed it to him a year before I left on this trip with the plan to use the money to buy a new one. Marc is the only licensed biathlon rifle supplier in the United States, located in West Yellowstone, Montana owning a shop named Altius Endeavors.

I had ordered a new Anschutz (German) rifle early in the spring, but he was sold out. Marc informed me that he was going to be traveling to Ulm, Germany (city of the Anschutz factory) to select his next batch of rifles for the year. The current plan is that I will meet him there and he will attempt to make an arrangement with them to do the transaction, buying the rifle from them and selling it to me on the spot. I know there are some legalities involved but am optimistic they can be overcome with us both being there in person. In the meantime Joe allows me to use his rifle when I am in O-town so I have one to train with at least just to get started.

I'm into my second week and on the final day of July bike up a 2,000 ft pass and hike/ run along the ridge that separates Italy from Austria. While I am up there, a storm rolls and I am soon inundated in rain, lightening, and thunder. After this experience I know that the spine of an 8,000-foot high ridge is not the best place for protection from lightning. The chances of getting struck by lightning seem just as high when I get on my metal bike riding down the steep mountain slope. As I safely walk into my apartment I feel a deep sense of relief and am thankful to be alive.

Later that evening I go to the only real restaurant in Obertilliach. In the restaurant, the Italian National Biathlon Men's and Women's Teams are eating dinner. A moment after being seated, one of the Italian biathletes (Markus Windisch) rises from the table and approaches me, asking if I am Andy Liebner from Alaska. I am shocked! I'd never have expected one of these World Cup biathletes to know me. Apparently, he remembers me from competing against one another four years ago when I had competed in IBU Cups. He introduces me to the team and they invite me to compete in the rollerski biathlon time trial they were holding the following morning.

Rollerskis are what skiers use to keep their skiing muscles in shape when there is no snow. They are basically roller blades or skates designed to simulate the skiing action and used with a set of skiing poles. A rollerski is its own unit made of a ski like material about 1.5-feet long with a wheel on either end. A regular cross-country ski binding is attached to the top and regular ski boots are used. The speed of a rollerski is dependent on the wheel bearings, as they are made to roll at particular speeds, but all rollerskis are within the normal speed range of real skiing. The difference in feeling is directly related to the shortness and stiffness of the rollerski, the density of the wheel material, and the rolling surface.

Some rollerskis are made of ski materials, while others are made of aluminum. This makes a big difference in the amount of vibration and bumps felt in the feet, ankles, and legs. An average rollerski extends just a few inches forward past the toe of the boot and less distance behind the heel, which makes it easier to move over ground than a full length ski, but an odd-shaped rock or wet leaf can cause crashes. Up to this point, because of my knee surgery, I had only begun to rollerski after I arrived to O-town. This, in combination that I cannot run high mileage would mean that I am not exactly at my usual fitness level but I am excited to compete against these guys on the rollerski track and push myself to the limits as a skier. All of my abilities are going to be tested and am I ready? No! But it doesn't matter because I didn't come here to try and place well in a time trial, I came to learn and I feel time trials serve as a superb way to get real race experience with the guys from the big leagues to learn from.

The next morning I am very excited to be taking part in my first race, even if it is only a time trial. It would be very unusual for me to enter a biathlon race without any disadvantages, and this day is no exception. Joe has been out of town for the last five days including today. I mentioned that, before he traveled, he set me up with his rifle. What I didn't mention is that it looks like it's been through a war. He mentioned that when he was to return we would get some bullets and actually shoot it, until then I have been holding the rifle in the correct positions and dry firing only. So, this morning, when I show up at the range, I have to scrounge for bullets.

Armin, the head Italian trainer gives me some ammo and helps me zero my sights as I take a few shots in the prone (laying down) position. In normal circumstances only a handful of clicks up/down, left/right are necessary. Right away, he yells to take 20 clicks down. After that I shoot again and still have to add more clicks down to the rear sight. With an odd look on his face he walks over with tools and tightens the barrel-action to the stock because it is loose. After this I tell him that it is my first time shooting this rifle. All the other Italian trainers look at each other oddly. It is a beautiful day and I just smile, feeling happy to be here no matter what the condition of my rifle.

A section of the rollerski track looking toward O-town.

After shooting through six full magazines, the old, heavy, beat-up rifle is zeroed to my shooting positions. They give me a bib with the number 21 on it. My name is listed at the end of the 11-racer start list. There is one-minute gap between each racer's scheduled start. I have just shot the rifle for the first time, and just a few days before had my first training session on rollerskis because of delayed luggage by the airlines and my knee surgery. I have had to do other types of training. Skate rollerskiing and running is hardest on my knee. In this race I am up against the best biathletes in all of Italy while skating for my second time all year and carrying an extra 12lbs on my back (rifle weight).

In the race my first lap goes well and when I come into the shooting range I'm only 30 seconds behind the guy who started one minute in front of me. As for my shooting…I hit the first three of the five, which was pretty good under the circumstances. After only two penalty loops for my missed two shots, I am back on the rollerski track. The second rollerski lap covers a lot greater distance and over a tougher course. It has a hill that takes over a minute and a half to climb. Where the trails merge, I pass a guy who is on his 3rd lap while we are both V2-ing up a long gradual hill. I feel pretty strong and good throughout that second lap and come into the range right behind the guy who had started one minute ahead of me which made me feel good.

On the second shooting stage I hit four out of the five. It feels great only to have one penalty loop before heading back out on the track. Covering this third lap really hurts. I feel my lungs, legs, and arms burning. The altitude is around 4,500 feet and I haven't used these skating muscles this hard since the last ski season. I hang in there and pull through. The next shooting stage is standing and I shoot terribly. My arms, legs, and back are shaking uncontrollably. I only hit one of five.

That pretty much takes me out of the race standings. I do my four penalty loops and hit the track for another hard lap up that huge hill again. Many things go through my head when my body is pushed to its limits especially with the heat, altitude, and fatigue during this race. It is during these tough times that memories of past races in which I felt this tired come to mind. I also remember how I pulled through to finish strong and never quit.

When I come into the range for my last shooting stage I relax and do my best to hold steady. The aim is to hit each target while also shooting quickly so as not to lose time. Under the circumstances I am satisfied with my two of five hits on and off the mat under a minute, and do my three penalty loops before hauling around the last loop to cross the finish line, dizzy in the eyes.

It feels good to finish. The opportunity to race with some of the best in the world does not come along every day. I have only been in Europe for nine days and already I have had an experience unlike any other of all my years of training and racing in America. While I did not finish in the places here I take an enormous amount of positive energy from the race. I see it as a stepping-stone along the journey rather than needing to compare my results with the other competitors. I have always believed that, if I can maintain my mental balance and fierce determination that I'll be successful and this race reinforces that belief. I'm pleased at how positive I am able to be despite the setbacks that have been confronting me and the poor state of my rifle.

After the trial with the Italians it is time to think about a training plan. I feel that Joe's coaching style is fine for my training needs. Since returning from his trip he has been at the range three to four days per week and has written an excellent training plan that I follow and which allows me to do a lot of my training alone. This really suits me as I need a lot of freedom away from the center (sometimes a very intense place) where I can be in my own mental space. The opportunity to go exploring through the mountains, peaks, valleys, and anywhere I feel like going is a balm to my soul compared to the rigid constraints that are usually associated with being part of a team. With the biathlon range designed in partnership with the rollerski track, it is used by many biathlon teams, but there is also a great number of cross country ski teams who travel from all over Europe ranging from junior clubs to national teams. This serves as the greatest opportunity to see and learn the most from the diversity of coaching styles, lessons, and the team members themselves. The goals I have are coming true.

Training with the World's Best

Joe was true to his word when he said that there were many top skiers using the O-town Biathlon Center as a short-term training base. Over the three weeks I have been living here I have had the great opportunity to witness and train with the Biathlon National Teams from Austria, Belarus, Czech Republic, Germany, Italy, Slovakia, Slovenia, and Russia. On a daily basis between 20 to100 people are either rollerskiing or running on the trails.

Unusually, this Thursday morning not a single person can be seen at the Center. It is clear and sunny, perfect for training. I am nearly finished with my warm-up and waiting for my coach to arrive when *he* shows up. A vehicle arrives with Norwegian license plates and the only Norwegian known to reside in this area is Ole Einar Bjørndalen. After taking a closer look I confirm it to be none other than *the* Ole Einar Bjørndalen. Ole is 34 years old and known as the "Biathlon God" aka "King of the Sport." He's our version of Muhammad Ali, Michael Jordan, or Wayne Gretzky.

He is the absolute most-credited biathlete *ever* in the *world* of *all* time. He has won more world cup and Olympic Medals than anyone could ever deem possible. What makes him even more awesome is that at the 2002 Olympic Games, Norway allowed him to race in a regular Cross Country ski race. He not only competed against the best skiers in the world but won, adding another Gold medal to the three he already earned at those Games.

Joe had a hard workout planned for me and, after talking w

Ole, found that he is planning something very similar. Joe informs me that "Today, you'll be following Ole and doing everything he does." I can't believe it! My training partner is going to be Ole Einar Bjørndalen! Who could ask for a better training partner than Ole (The Best in the World)? The workout is totally hard, but it is the most exciting workout I have ever done. I follow him, roller skiing stride for stride on the rollerski track. Of all the world-class athletes I have previously trained with on the rollerski track I have never witnessed such a marvel. The way he floats on rollerskis, gliding up and down each hill while maintaining a steady speed, is incredible.

I also notice the shortness in length of his strides while in a V-2 on the up-hills and the long no-pole skating kicks on every downhill. He makes the rigors of rollerski tracks look easy. On the shooting range he always positions his shooting mat in a different direction to anyone else and will take over a dozen short quick breaths while on the mat and then hold his breath and shoot all five shots with spot-on accuracy. Just the overall way he goes about his daily training routine is of greater quality, spirit, and focus than of anyone I have ever seen. Obertilliach is awesome and the people who come here to train are even more awesome. Ole is good friends with my coach Joe, and when he comes, Joe usually helps him with clearing his targets, spotting his groups, zeroing, and anything else he needs.

Ole at his office.

I had seen Ole rollerskiing two other times, but the busyness of the range had always blocked any chance of meeting him. He seemed to arrive, get his workout in, and leave, with no time wasted. On this day he is much more relaxed and open to a conversation. I find Ole to be a well-mannered guy, very honest and respectful on the inside and of average human size on the outside. His physique seems rather small compared to many other professional biathletes and skiers I've seen training here. Ole even asks me questions and seems interested in my racing plans. On this day I became friends with Ole and will remember it for the rest of my life.

Ole and Andy taken January 2009

After the training session with Ole, Joe makes some observations about my progress. He says that my shooting has come a long way in the short time I've been here. He says that, based on my rollerski track times and fitness testing, if I continue to improve like I have, then I will have a great season in both cross country skiing and biathlon. As a result of the uninterrupted quality training I feel good, strong, and fast, despite my knee surgery in March.

A week later I am preparing to begin another vigorous training session in O-town. As usual, I find the shooting range to be completely full except for one shooting lane of the 30. I look on the assigned paper and find it has been paid for by an individual from Poland. It is past 10:00 and they have not yet arrived, even though most people begin training in O-town around 08:00 and finish by 11:00 so they can obtain a few hours' break and get a second session in later in the afternoon. It is common to share shooting numbers and mats so I help myself and begin to zero my rifle on that number for the day.

About an hour later an older man with a younger trainer shows up with the Polish flag on their gear. Once the man is rollerskiing and begins to shoot, my first impression is that he's not very experienced. He looks like an old man who is somewhat familiar with biathlon, but is way too old and slow-looking to be beginning training in this sport. I see him out on the rollerski loop and see neither finesse nor quickness in his form. It isn't until I ask his trainer the guy's name that I discover it is Tomasz Sikora! He had won his first World Championship title in 1995 (20 km event). He has competed in 4-Olympic Games and is now considered one of the best biathletes of all time. We meet and become friends, and he gives me an autographed photo with his credentials on the back.

Tomasz seems to be a real quiet, personal type of guy. One that you can look at and see he is intelligent, but only speaks when something important needs to be said. His calm personality is contagious when in conversation and he is relaxing to talk to. If there is anyone who is confident about their training plan, it is Tomasz Sikora. I learn and confirm that day that looks can sure be deceiving.

Tomasz rollerskiing in O-town. (from www.tomaszsikora.net)

CHAPTER THREE
Inspiring Lessons

After about two weeks in O-town I had become friends with a girl named Jenny, who worked in the most popular local restaurant. The relationship had developed and I spent a bit of time hanging out there talking to her. It was not that we were lovers, but we enjoyed each other's company and shared many smiles and laughs.

Jenny was also a close friend to another acquaintance, Viky Franke. Jenny and Viky come from the same town in Germany. If you are a keen biathlete you may recognize Viky's name as she is a reporter who covers all the World Cup Biathlon events and regularly interviews the top athletes.

Within a few weeks it became apparent that the restaurant owner was abusing Jenny's rights as an employee. He was working her ridiculous shifts, sometimes as long as 16 hours, and she was not getting any time off. On top of that, she was receiving no overtime. I found it hard to believe that her boss was pushing her so hard and I suggested she request a few days off.

His response was aggressive and forceful. He reminded her that she had a contract and was here to work. She translated his words from German to English as "You are here to work, not to have a boyfriend."

I tried not to get angry, even though his behavior was completely unacceptable to me. The boss and owner, named Andreas, appeared to be very controlling towards everything in life, not just his employees, and very focused on making money. At the same time, he worked extremely hard himself and was no doubt running on nervous energy half the time.

My frustration was compounded because I was not able to communicate adequately in German and so was 'forcing' him to speak to me in my native language. This probably helped reinforce his image of me as an interfering outsider.

There were two other waitresses working at the restaurant and they were given time off, but Jenny was more popular with the customers and so Andreas always wanted to have her working. A week after the first confrontation I encouraged her to approach him again but once more he reacted forcefully and negatively.

Finally, I devised a work schedule that would allow the work to be shared equally between the three waitresses. I brought the schedule to the restaurant one Sunday morning at 7:30. As soon as Andreas saw me he charged out of the kitchen and punched me right in the chest.

Witnessing the assault was the entire National Biathlon Team from Russia, who was eating breakfast. I threw up my arms and yelled "What's your problem?" He was setting himself for a full-on fight and I had only come in to give him a piece of paper. I made gestures to make it clear that I was not there to throw punches and I left the building.

I would have been justified in filing assault charges with the police and reporting work related abuse to the authorities. I did not feel pressing charges was necessary, but I did contact the worker right's authority with information about Jenny's work hours.

Traveling South

As the conflict in the restaurant reaches its climax my trainer, Joe, suggests that I take a break from training. I've just completed a strenuous three-week training block and Joe suggests I go travelling and see some of Europe. So, leaving the hassle of the restaurant behind me, I pack my large red backpack and hitchhike to the train station at Lienz, 40 kilometers away.

From Lienz, I travel south-west. It is exciting to feel the train rumble and to be on my own exploring more of the world. This is the first real trip I have made on the rail system in Europe. I am headed to Zagreb, Croatia where, apart from taking a break, I am hoping to find a cheap van to buy. I've been told it is much easier to purchase a vehicle outside of the European Union and Croatia is the closest country outside the border.

While on the train, I speak to many different people, most of whom are very different in their own cultural way. As the train approaches the Slovenian border I sit in a compartment with my bag when a hippie-looking lady comes and sits across from me. She has dreadlocks, is very thin, with a dark complexion. She is from Slovenia and informs me a little bit about the language and culture. She had been in a band that was a part of a circus and has quit and is running away back to her home.

As the train approaches the Slovenia-Croatia border, it stops and the Croatian government officials walk through, checking each passenger's passport. About two hours later the train arrives in Zagreb, which is my destination. It is 10:30 in the evening, dark, rainy, and the buildings look very old. Despite this I feel alive and excited to be in this new land and have the opportunity to explore. I walk around looking for a tree or a bench in a park to sleep, but I find no parks, just stone buildings and paved dirty roads. I do, however, stumble upon a hostel and stay the night.

In the morning I pack up and continue my trek. One of the reasons for coming to Zagreb is that a girl I had met on Facebook lives there and I think it will be cool to meet her. Her name is Ana-Marija and she is, you guessed it, a biathlete. When I was in the process of seeking out a European club to train with she had sent me a lot of information about the great training Center in Obertilliach and this had helped me make the decision to go there.

I cannot find Ana-Marija but to my luck I discover that there is a large used auto sale going on in a field a few miles out of town. I hop into a cab and soon arrive at the field. The cab is extremely cheap, equivalent to $2 USD. Walking around the auto show I see there are thousands of vehicles. The sale is not a dealer's sale but one where owners bring their cars to sell and haggle. I find a van that I like and that is relatively inexpensive but when I try to buy it they are not able to issue a title because I am not Croatian.

Suddenly, my search for Ana-Marija assumes greater importance. I only have her email address and not a phone number.

I borrow a cell phone to make a few phone calls out of the phone book, but it only leads to dead ends. As a last resort I hitchhike back into Zagreb and find my way to the Croatian Olympic Training Center, hoping they will know how to contact her. It is my plan to have her help register the van I want to buy, by putting the documents in her name.

When I arrive at the center I am surprised to discover the two people behind the desk consistently smoking cigarettes. You'd think a national Olympic training facility would be more health conscious. Still, they are helpful. They call her phone number in the registry, but we are only able to leave a message. After this I decide to forget about the van at the auto show and take in some local Croatian culture.

Walking around I find a real Italian pizzeria and buy a 14" pizza and coke for only a few Croatian lipa. In the evening I find my way back to the train station and wait on a bench seat. When my train arrives and the people are getting off the scene takes on a sinister atmosphere. High profile gang members must be getting off, because suddenly about 30 guys gather out of all different areas on the platform to form a mob and a melee begins. A few of them hold road flares in one hand and are punching with the other hand, using the flare to blind their opponent.

The mob turns into a free-for-all gang fight, or at least that is what I assume it to be. I grab my bag and run onto the train to duck under the seats in case bullets start to fly. I take the first opportunity to dart across the platform into the train, it departs quickly and only then I breath easily again.

I stop in the city of Ljubljana, Slovenia for two days and take in some local culture. It is a nice place. Then I hop a bus that takes me to a stunningly beautiful village named Bled. I camp in the woods along the waterfront of Bled Lake and swim to a nearby island and back in the morning.

A day later I begin hitchhiking my way back to O-town. It takes me 2 days and I enjoy the little villages I pass through, walking and talking to locals. I have to camp along the roadside one night because I do not get picked up on that stretch of road. But within two minutes the next morning, well before 6:00, I get a ride that takes me a long way. When I finally return to O-town I feel as if I am coming home from a month-long trip even though I have been away for less than a week.

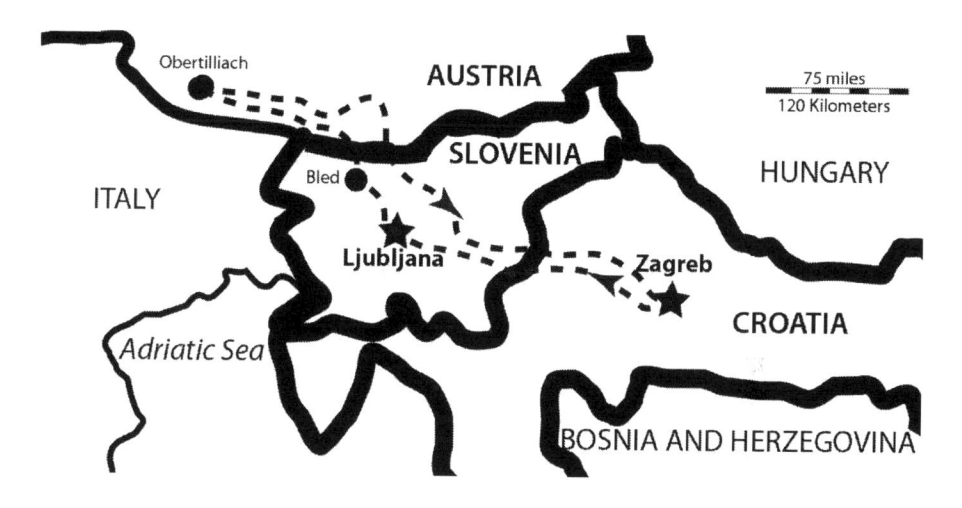

Back in O-Town

The first time I go to the restaurant after my return I get a hostile reception. Andreas chases me out the door wielding a butcher's knife over his head. Clearly he's pissed at me, but what I cannot understand is why Jenny seems equally angry with me.

It turns out that, while I was away, the restaurant received a visit from the work regulation authority, acting on the information I provided. Andreas is now forced to give Jenny one to two days off each week or he will be shut down. He also received a fine of 5,000 euros. For her part, Jenny assumed I had gone south on my trip to meet another girl and our relationship comes to an abrupt end. Oh well, I still feel good about being able to help her. She works at the restaurant for another three months, but I decide it is in my interest to stay away for a while.

One day Joe, his brother, and two friends invite me for a full-day road biking trip through part of Italy. The views are awesome and flying along the narrow roads is an incredible rush. During one long uphill section in Italy an Italian car honks and swerves at Joe, who is riding in the lead. Joe, being a lifelong competitor (13 years on the Austrian national biathlon team) stands up on his bike and charges after the car.

The driver sees him doing this and slams on his brakes, Joe nearly crashes but lands his hands onto the back of his car and begins to pound with his fist on the side. The driver in the car proceeds to accelerate fast and stop abruptly to make Joe crash. This goes on for a few short minutes. The others and I are behind observing in laughter as Joe, the policeman, fighting while on a bike, with a car. Who will win? It ends when Joe coasts and the car speeds away honking erratically. The driver was one of Joe's former acquaintances from his Law enforcement duties.

The Art of Bandit Racing

On September 6th, I hitchhike to Lienz to compete as a bandit runner in the Red Bull Dolomitenmann race. A bandit is one who is not officially registered, but who runs alongside the main field as an 'illegal' entrant.

The Red Bull race is known as the toughest relay race in the World. The first leg runs from the middle of town to the top of a mountain. The record for that course is one hour and twenty minutes. Racing up a mountain for anywhere near an hour is a long, hard effort. In Alaska I have competed in some mountain runs, but never in one of this magnitude. After the racers climb to the top of the mountain, they tag off a team-mate who parasails on a strict course down to the bottom of the mountain. They have to land in a designated area, run three kilometers with all of their gear up to a little cliff, then parasail to another designated landing zone where they tag off to a third team member who then has to kayak down a river through a slalom course. There are big poles hanging down over the river via cables that they have to go between. When the kayaker finishes, they then tag off to their mountain biker team-mate who has to pedal up the mountain on the other side of the valley and back down to the center of town to the finish. It is a huge event and thousands of people are here watching.

I begin running about a mile from the start line of the official race and just settle into my pace when the racers come along. I stay with the lead pack for a little more than half of the race but have to quickly act like a spectator at the checkpoint where they are writing down bib numbers. I want to actually compete next year with a team, so I don't want to get in trouble this year by being caught as a bandit.

I am very surprised while running through a thick forested part when a spectator from the sidelines recognizes me and calls out my name. It is Andy Schnitzer, a former University of Alaska Fairbanks skier who I competed against only one year ago. He is an Austrian, who is currently coaching a ski club in his home region of Austria. I continue on in the race, dodging the checkpoints and finish at the top a few meters before the actual finish line. It is a long ways up and I am one of the top 20 guys. That's not bad for a training run. The race is inspiring and exciting and I hope that I can come back next year as part of an official team.

After running all the way to the summit of this 5,000-foot mountain I find out that I will have to go down half-way by foot. My surgery knee has been feeling great for the past month and I dread hurting it again. When I arrive at where the transporting vans are parked to transport the runners back to town, they are all waiting for the required seats to be filled before departure. Fortunately I see a friend that I had met in O-town and he introduces me to Jonathan Wyatt of New Zealand, Markus Kroell of Austria, Helmut Schiessl of Germany, and few other guys that happened to be the top finishers. They end up inviting me to join them on the bus and I end up sitting next to Helmut on the ride down the mountain. He is a 7-time World Champion Mountain Runner.

We talk for a while and he tells me he has been in Alaska when the World Mountain Running championships were held at Alyeska. During the trip he gives me much useful advice on mountain running that I gladly soak up. Nothing beats a good mountain runner, he says, who instinctively knows the quickest path so it is essential to know your route. Other advice he gives is to practice your footholds and hand-holds along the most technically taxing areas in different weather conditions. It is important to know how to respond to the course in its various natural conditions, for example: wet, wet but drying, dry, dry but getting wet, snow, ice areas.

Crazy Antics in Italy

One calm, moonlit evening, a few days after the mountain run, I am invited by Viky Franke and Steffi Inwinkl to go to Antholz. As I've mentioned, Viky is the sports writer for both the German Biathlon Team and the U.S. Team and Steffi is her best friend, who also happens to be my trainer Joe's niece as well as the secretary for the Biathlon Sport Academy here in O-town. There is a world-class biathlon venue in Antholz, where World Cups are held each year.

As I ride in the front seat of Viky's little green car, I am not sure what we were actually going to do there, but Viky and Steffi have some random thoughts in mind. The first stop is at the home of one of the members of the Italian National Biathlon Team. Parking in the driveway, we are visually blocked by a large set of hedges, but we can tell there are people on the porch. Viky and Steffi instantly became too afraid to ask for their friend to speak with, so I volunteer to get out and make contact.

Not speaking a scrap of Italian, I stand behind the fence and yell loud enough down the rest of the entrance and through the hedges for someone to hear. "Does anyone speak English there?" I ask. Responses resound in my direction and I suddenly feel awkward as I don't even know the name of the guy I am looking for. I guess that is my way – to charge forward and work out what to do as I go.

I change tack and yell, "I need someone who speaks good English to help me with something." Luckily the guy they are looking for comes around the hedges and into view. We recognize each other from training in O-town and begin talking. Then he asked "What are you doing here this evening?" In response I turn and look at the car. Neither Viky nor Steffi are visible, as they are too embarrassed and have ducked below the window level. The guy is smarter than that however, and recognizes the car to be Viky's. As we walk towards the front window Viky rises to show bright red blushed cheeks and a big smile. She gets out and talks with him for about 20 minutes as I return to my seat in the car. At the end they hug and she returns to the car. "I owe you one for that Andy, you're crazy!" she says.

From there we go to the house of one of Steffi's Italian biathlon idols. Once there, they take a camera and walk around the house taking pictures through every window with a really bright flash. This is sketchy stuff, and I return the "you're crazy" statement immediately. Soon enough we depart and head to a pizza place. It is nearly 11 at night by this time and we then head to the world famous venue. With a pizza box in hand Steffi, Viky, and I walk around the stadium in the dark and start yelling really loud to hear the echo bounce off the grandstands. Viky then runs to the end of the range and rips off one of the paper targets that had been shot as a souvenir.

After that we go to a downtown area which is completely deserted. That being such a let-down we drive back to O-town to conclude the events for the evening.

With all the training and adventures on the side it is easy sometimes to lose sense of the bigger picture in life and perhaps that is just as well. I came to Europe partly as a result of the USBA's rejection but to also see how these great European athletes live and become a better athlete. I have contacted the United Ski and Snowboard Association (USSA) and asked to which International Ski Federation (FIS) races I can compete in. Their response was "All of them, if you want." All I have to do is send them a list of the races I want to compete in, and I will be in. *Now that's the kind of support that is positive for developing athletes and a good way to increase the level of American skiers!* I am very pleased to have this blessing and support.

Viky at the 2010 Olympics.

On the weekends that I have no ski races scheduled I've found biathlon races to take part in. Communicating through the same means, I ask the USBA for the possibility to compete to register me in the International Biathlon Union (IBU) Cup Biathlon events. They have told me that, in order to compete at IBU events, I must first qualify as one of the top two Americans in some of the early North American Cup races located in Canada and U.S. This would require me to fly back to North America to compete in those events.

To my knowledge there are no actual IBU Cup qualifying

standards set in writing, it's all up to their discretion, and so these constraints are being imposed by the authorities in the moment rather than being a pre-determined standard. The National Governing body of the sport, USBA, only has to submit a list of entries to the IBU. What makes their decision more galling is that there are 4-6 open race positions set aside for US competitors at IBU races and USBA is only sending two to compete. The vacant spots will go unused, one of which I could fill at no cost to the USBA. To make things even more perverse, for each entrant in any race, the IBU pays the National Governing body (in this case USBA) a stipend. So, by allowing me to run, the USBA would actually be paid and would incur absolutely no expenses.

The USBA snub affects my mental state and I feel I am in danger of sliding back into the abyss that has opened within me several times in the past.

The flexible and accommodating attitude of the USSA makes it even harder to understand and come to terms with the approach adopted by USBA. It seems they simply want to have nothing to do with me. First, they revoked their promise to add me to the National Development Team. Now they don't want me to even compete in the sport at all. I will not give up that easy, and the only option remaining to me is to get an endorsement from the USBA athlete representative to submit a protest of their decision to the USBA Board. In my heart I know where my real passion lies and that I still have much to learn and improve in within cross country skiing.

Once again, however, the inner battle rages and I push through the closing gloom of negativity to find a new motivation. I begin to research other biathlon races, not covered directly by the IBU, which do not require the USBA's approval. As I discover that such events indeed do exist, within relatively close proximity, the shadows of doom that threaten to reach out of some murky depth to strangle my life-force slip away into hiding and are replaced by the more positive outlook I like to view life through. I cannot help but feel, however, in some quiet corner of my mind, that these shadows have not gone, but are merely hiding, awaiting another opportunity to pounce and I suspect I'll have to battle them again in the future.

Friends in Ramsau

As mid-September rolls around I find a small band of intrepid skiers, much like myself, drawn together to train and share experiences. Two of these guys, who I become especially close to, are **Leandro de Carvalho Pinto Ribela of Brazil and Charlie Gombos of Hungary.**

Leandro Ribela is a skier and biathlete from Brazil. Coming from a country that does not get snow, he had only a few years of experience in these sports. He is also a part of the Biathlon Sport Academy in O-town. Joe provides training to both of us.

Leandro has a smooth attitude makes him easy to get along with. He's the type of guy that can always see the reality within current events. It's hard for him to pull off a joke without a big grin, but you can always see the honesty in his eyes.

Leandro in the 2010 Olympics.

His personality is very different from mine, however, in that he is very organized when it comes to planning and accommodations (stuff I really don't like doing). He will have an entire trip planned out day by day six months ahead of time. He knows exactly where he will be and what he will be doing every moment. Whereas I would much rather sort of plan out a rough sketch, buy a plane ticket, travel there, figure things out on the spot and see what life brings.

The other big difference is in the level of support he receives from his home nation. Leandro receives thousands of euros in financial support. It's frustrating to see a non-snow country supporting their skiers better than the U.S. does. Nations that are considered 'developing' within the sport, such as Brazil, have different qualifying standards than the 'developed' ones, such as the European nations, Canada and the U.S.

It is in the town of Ramsau, that I meet Charlie. I have decided to move to Ramsau on Joe's suggestion and also because Leandro is planning on being there during the pre-ski race season. The value of Ramsau is that it is the place where I can get on real snow early in the year. I will still keep O-town my home base, but am relocating for a few months. I am supposed to get my rifle from Marc during this time and our rendezvous point is only a few hours from Ramsau whereas it is about five hours from O-town.

Charlie on the glacier.

I first met Charlie when he walked through the front door of the Gletcherblick Hotel and we became instant friends. Charlie's situation is much more similar to mine. He is from Hungary and spent three months of the summer mountain bike racing in Egypt, of all places. He traveled directly from Egypt to France to compete in the summer Biathlon World Championships, where he successfully finished within the top 20 in all races. Charlie adds a flavorful spice to the mix of our growing little "team" and we become good friends right away. Like me, Charlie has spent the last few seasons in the biathlon world cup and has occasionally competed in the cross country skiing world championships as he is a great skier also. He has a conflict with the Hungarian Biathlon Federation and I think our joint training is no mistake.

A large glacier resides on the backside of the mountain that faces the north in Ramsau. It's only a 15-minute drive from my new home to arrive at the tram that travels to the top to the glacier. The place I now refer to as 'home' is called the "Gletscherblick" and is owned by a Hungarian man. When I had first arrived in Ramsau I had met Leandro and his girlfriend (also a high level athlete from Brazil) in the hotel car-park. After waiting 30 minutes for someone to arrive at the hotel, we walked in with our bags, picked our own rooms, and made ourselves at home. We lived there three days before anyone showed up. It's a small hotel, with lots of rooms, kitchen, bar, cafe, game rooms, fully-outfitted and operational.

Left to right, Leandro, István (of Hungary), and Andy.

The Dachstein glacier dominates the region. It's a large tourist attraction as well as serving as the world's largest preparation center for skiers to gain early time on snow before the ski season begins. There are two separate ski loops that are well groomed and maintained. One is a full 10 km and the other is 5 km.

It is a really cool feeling to be skiing on real snow in shorts and a t-shirt on a hot, sunny day. It is amazing to train alongside some of the best skiers in the World. Of the approximate daily +100 skiers on the Dachstein, at least 3/4 are on National Teams. Currently the National Ski Teams from Spain, Austria, Estonia, Germany, Japan, and Sweden are here, most have full Men's and Women's teams. Besides just skiing with the best in the world, each morning there is ample time to meet them and talk with them face to face while waiting in line for the tram.

Each tram can only carry 60 people at a time and the first 2-3 tram-loads of the day are at maximum capacity. Everyone packed in like sardines, skis and poles in hand. I am surprised by the size of some of the athletes (big and small) compared to how they look on World Cup and Olympic TV coverage. Post workout is another enlightening opportunity to speak with them and the different National Team trainers. Without being annoying, I take every opportunity to ask appropriate questions to gain the best insightful reasons behind the training of each nation. That alone is sometimes worth a trip up and down the tram.

In America, Nordic skiers are always watching ski videos to examine techniques of the best skiers in the World. It is really something to actually be skiing and in every direction you can see some of the best skiers in real life actually skiing! I have often tagged along at the back of a "ski train" of the Swedish men's ski team. Skiing with so many of the world's best, I begin to realize certain patterns relating to technique that these skiers are going through. What catches my attention is how their center of gravity is moving and at specific timing stages and I refine my experiences each evening.

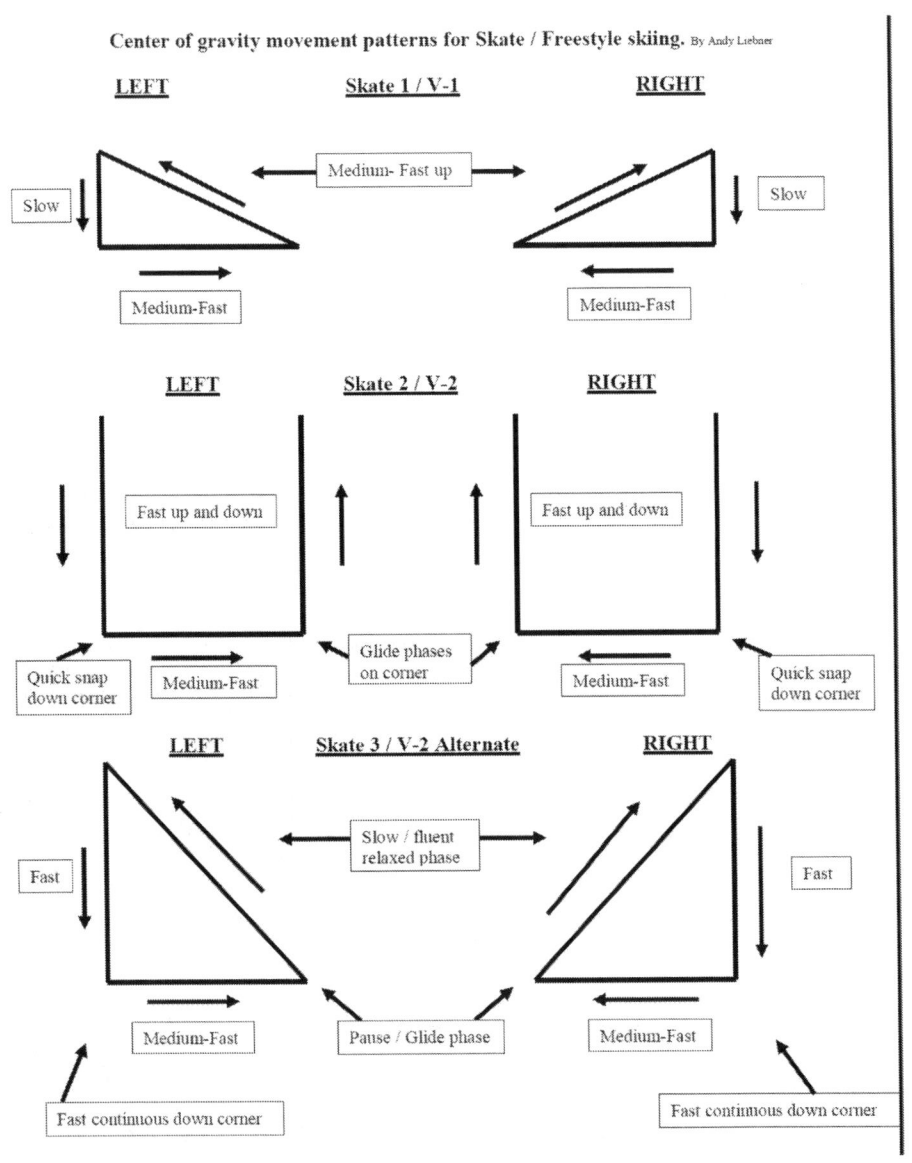

Center of gravity movement patterns for Skate / Freestyle skiing. By Andy Liebner

Skate 1 / V-1

LEFT — Slow, Medium-Fast up, Medium-Fast
RIGHT — Slow, Medium-Fast

Skate 2 / V-2

LEFT — Fast up and down, Quick snap down corner, Medium-Fast, Glide phases on corner
RIGHT — Fast up and down, Medium-Fast, Quick snap down corner

Skate 3 / V-2 Alternate

LEFT — Fast, Slow / fluent relaxed phase, Medium-Fast, Fast continuous down corner
RIGHT — Fast, Medium-Fast, Pause / Glide phase, Fast continuous down corner

I write an article with these shapes included for the Master Skier Magazine. It is published in the 2010-11 Issue.

Skate 1 / V-1
Starting at the top of the triangle, your center of gravity and majority

of weight should be on the ski on either the right or left side that you choose to be poling on. As you go through the poling phase think of where your center of gravity/ weight is, and where it is moving. Make your center of gravity follow the triangle in the proper direction. Once you have got the right flow and feeling down on the triangle, include the timing phases of each section. You should be able to recognize some sort of movement pattern that your center of gravity is going through. The overall rhythmic pace should be the same for each of the three sections of the triangle. They are of different lengths, but the time between each corner should be kept consistently the same.

If you are unsure about how the arms/ poles are used in this pattern, think about your power driving up the hill being implemented by the poles, while at the same time your leg is naturally compressing to the steepness of the hillside (the downward portion of the triangle. Once at the bottom of the triangle/ the lowest comfortable point of your compression, begin the weight shift onto the other ski and still using your poles with the same pressure to push your momentum onto to opposite ski. You'll now be at the sharp point of the triangle and it is time to immediately begin the weight shift again to the opposite ski but this time you'll lift your poles and body weight to re-center and begin the triangle flow cycle again. The most important part of skating Skate 1 is the movement pattern as that controls efficiency and the overall velocity of momentum carried over the snow/ trail.

Skate 2 / V-2
To best get started with the U-Shape, start by standing up straight, feet shoulder width apart and toes pointing outwards. Then let gravity pull your body downward. Let your knees bend forward to keep your hips ahead of your heels. Once you've reached a comfortable athletic position, raise your center of gravity up to the highest possible comfortable position and onto either your right or left leg (choosing your poling side). Once on **one** foot and high in the air, begin the "crunch" and bring your entire body straight down "together / evenly" as if you were executing a knee bend double pole. Once you've reached the lowest position, instantly shift your

weight to the other foot and begin the glide phase. The pushing leg should have a quick "snap" to it, as it has just transferred the downward gravitational force in combination with the poling power to the other ski. In the glide phase you should be able to "rest and recover" for a moment before rising to begin the next poling phase. If you're in question about timing of your hands, understand about 90% of the power is implemented only on the downward section and only when your hands reach your hips do you step on the other ski and begin the shift and glide phase, using the rest of the push with the arms and leg shifting across.

If done properly, you can spend less time "working" and more time "gliding." For example: if a stride (from the top of the poling motion, through, and back to the top) takes 3 seconds (2 seconds working down, 1 second up) you will be working 66.6% of the time. This U-shape movement pattern allows to work one second, glide/ rest for one second, and come up for one second (which is also resting). So you are only required to work 33.3% of the time and are able to rest 66.6%. In other words, if you divided up the three sections of the U-shape (down, across, and up) and assigned times for each section, then you can instantly see and control how much time you spend working -gliding.

Skate 3 / V-2 Alternate/ Open Field
*This larger triangle shape is used in similar context as the Skate 1 / V-1 as it follows the same directions of the triangle but the timing is to be executed in the **opposite** manor. It is also very similar to the Skate 2 / V-2 as the flow of downward force and glide phase are executed the same. Only after the gliding phase, you gracefully with swift force return to the same poling ski and compress on the same side again. The working to resting ratio is nearly the same as the Skate 2 / V-2 and can be modified easier as you can compress hard and fast for less than one second and spend 3-4 seconds gliding.*

Think of this being third gear as it is to be used at the highest speeds over the snow/ trail. Your arms/ poles are dropped at the top of the triangle over one ski (whatever side you choose) and the power is implemented exactly the same as the skate 2. You glide the same as the skate 2 and once you feel your ski is slowing then you shift your weight and forward momentum toward the opposite ski and lifting your hands/ poles to re-set the triangle cycle again. Think of this technique being the 'gliding' technique as it has been known to cover 15-20 meters of trail in-between strides.

College Friends

On the glacier skiing I have already recognized two people that I knew from college racing in America years before, one of which is Daniel Sonntag, former University of Utah skier/ competitor and the brother of one of my old teammates Ben Sonntag. Daniel has a van here and now drives us to and from the tram every day. I also ran into a former University of Alaska Fairbanks skier/ competitor, Vahur Tappan, who is now skiing for the Estonian National Ski Team.

Left to right: Charlie, István, and Andy.

In the town of Ramsau there is a good 10 km of rollerski track connected to a shooting range. Our daily routine consists of skiing in the morning on the glacier when the snow is harder packed and after 2-3 hours of skiing, driving to the hotel, wash up, eat lunch, rest, then later in the afternoons either run or rollerski. Every day for the past month it has been sunny and warm. I've trained more hours than I ever have during these pre-season training months, but mentally I have stayed fresh because of the awesome areas and the inspiring people around me.

Below is my Ramsau experience previously published on Ski-Post, America's most popular online Nordic skiing newsletter.

"Skiing with the Best!"
by Andy Liebner
Salomon Athlete Force
Posted: 18 SEP 2008

Who would think that in the peaceful little country of Austria most of the World's best Cross Country Skiers and Biathletes would come to for weeks and weeks to train each summer?

Since coming to Austria and training between the two cities of Obertilliach and Ramsau, I have not only seen, met, and talked with many of the World's Best, but actually trained with them on skis and rollerskis.

It has been absolutely amazing to live here and experience the hard work that goes on behind the scenes (summer training of the best in the world) of many National Teams and individuals.

My trainer knows many of the best in the biathlon circuit, so when athletes like Ole Einar Bjørndalen (the "Biathlon King") and Tomasz Sikora of Poland come alone to train, he ties in my training plan with theirs. It was awesome enough to be able to meet Bjørndalen, but ten-times more exciting when I was able to complete full workouts with him, 1-on-1. Training partners don't get any better than that.

The National Teams that I have had the honor to train with include: Sweden Ski, German Ski, Austrian Ski, Estonian Ski, Spain Ski, Japanese Ski, Norwegian Biathlon, German

Biathlon, Russian Biathlon, Belorussian Biathlon, Italian Biathlon, Czech Republic Biathlon, Slovenian Biathlon, and Slovakian Biathlon.

As for skiing at Ramsau, with many of the World's best skiers, just imagine skiing down a sketchy icy path leading from the tram to the groomed ski tracks in a crowd and watching Sweden's best skiers zoom past with all of their gear on their backs. Everyone laughs as some of them like Tobias Fredriksson, Bjorn Lind, Mathias Fredriksson, Mats Larsson, and Anders Sodergren almost wipe out at the bottom, barely clearing some rocks after blasting through a pool of glacial water and losing control over an ice patch. It reminded me of the times in high school when we did such things to be different, extreme, and most importantly to have fun.

Even though these guys are among the top in the World Cup, they still continue to do things apart from their training on skis that most people would consider harmful and dangerous. Why do they do such things? It makes them happy, sets the tone for the day, and as natural born competitors they need a daily competition, even if it is from the minute the tram doors open to the first one to ski on the trails each day. They love to ski.

Skiing on the trails among them makes training suddenly become a lot more exciting. Yesterday I classic skied for an hour with Tobias Fredriksson directly in front of me and Anders Sodergren directly behind. Their level-one pace can easily be maintained for hours. They ski easy enough to hold a conversation, even at a +9,000-foot elevation.

When the skiers from Sweden plant each pole in the snow, there is some serious power being expressed. They are SO STRONG, it is incredible!

In past summers, I had only been able to analyze the techniques of the best skiers in the world by watching videos from past World Cups and Olympics. Well, skiing at Ramsau in the summer allows the world's best skiers to be visible in every direction.

Technique is important to a certain extent, but not to be stressed. A huge advantage they have is to be actually skiing on snow and doing specific drills that are best done on snow. Trainers also spend a lot of time working 1-on-1 for hours on skis and rollerskis with each athlete, attuning to his or her needs, giving them time to do the right things.

From the many teams I have trained with, I have seen a wide variety of different techniques. For instance, when skating, the Russians are very strong, using mostly lower body power with their hands a medium distance from their chest, extending behind the hips when polling. The Norwegians (Bjørndalen included) plant their poles very near to the chest with a very short but explosive stride. The Germans appear to be utilizing medium ankle bend, but reach very far forward (lifting the elbows) when using their poles. The Swede's show signs of skiing with brute force. They plant their poles with their hands furthest from their chest. All National Teams' techniques have proven to work as they are the world's best.

The rollerski track at Ramsau is also something to appreciate. There is a good 7.5 km of smooth paved blacktop with each corner banked at precise measurements for optimum rollerski training and safety. Along with the great rollerskiing that exists here, there is a biathlon range located in the center of the trails. The entire experience is something that this skier will never forget!

Authority, Authority

After skiing 2-3 hours each morning and rollerskiing or running 1-2 hours every evening at Der Dachstein/ Ramsau for three weeks straight, I am ready to take a recovery break. I have found a deal on a van in Germany and finally discovered how it is possible to purchase it in my name. I bike to the train station, catch the midnight train and spend the night riding on trains across Austria and through Germany. I look the van over, find it to my liking, and pay cash. It is a 1997 Renault Traffic that has only 80,000 km on the odometer.

A few days later, after driving it around Ramsau on the temporary license plates I have to drive back into Germany to officially register it. That day I drive over 1,000 km across Germany, my trip not being helped by a 350 km detour as a result of using an out of date map. The most difficult task of the trip is avoiding police due to my license plates being expired and having no vehicle registration.

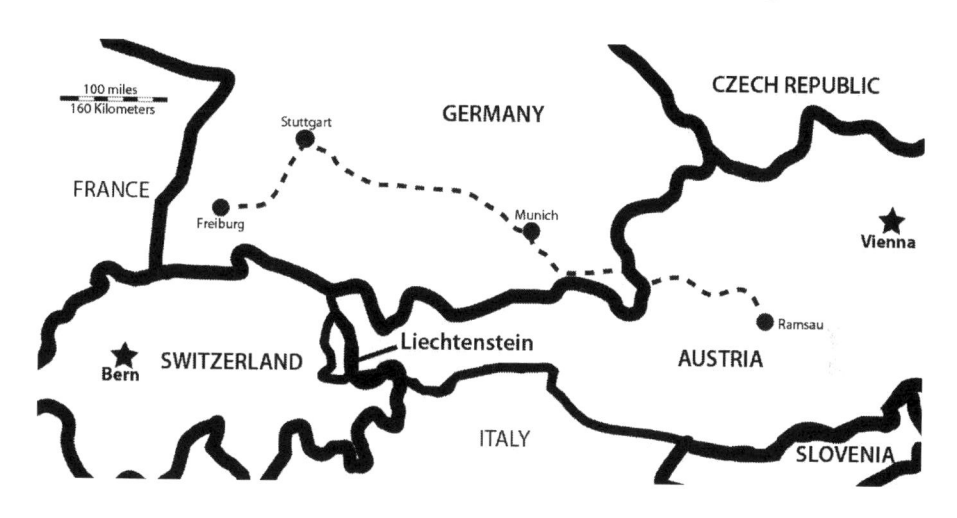

At the same time I have decided to apply for a German visa, so I'm entering into a potentially tempestuous relationship with German bureaucracy on two fronts: my van and my visa. I have tried every avenue possible to secure an Austrian visa but is appears as if my efforts are going to be in vain. As a result I have to register everything in Germany. It is not easy even to get the paperwork. The process begins when I arrive at my former roommate Raphael's home in the Black Forrest region in Germany, which is a truly beautiful area. Raphael's parents have kindly agreed to allow me to use their place as my 'permanent' German address. The law says I am supposed to officially establish an address in Germany within the first seven days of arrival from my home country, so I'm already in contravention of that one. With the address now established I am able to proceed with registering the van.

Next I have to have the vehicle tested for road worthiness at a place called a 'TÜV' (pronounced "*toof*") At the TÜV the officer performs all sorts of tests and examines every millimeter with a magnifying glass. The TÜV issues me a small list of things that need to be repaired before I can get the official license plate endorsement. Looking at the list I am confronted with a sense of failure, because there are a lot of things that would cost a lot of money to finish.

Once again I refuse to give in to this negativity and work with my mind to reverse the emotions of failure, using them instead to seek ways around the problem. I do this by focusing on how much I enjoy challenges in combination with working on cars. Solutions soon appear in my head and I go to work. A simple fuse added to the fuse box fixes one issue and some good ol' makeshift innovation fixes everything else. I am able to pick up a set of brake pads for the front brakes at a local shop. They are out of rotors, so I spend an evening and some of the night underneath my van with a metal grinder.

The next morning I drive the van back to the TÜV with all repairs complete and spitting old rusty rotor dust from my mouth and nose. The van passes all tests and the brakes…they are spot on even, perfectly performing to the same resistance, right from left, back to front. The guy is about to give me the good-to-go stamp when another guy raises the van up. After looking at the rotors and my grinding job, he says that I need to get new rotors regardless of how perfectly they work.

It does not make any sense to me, and I think he is making things harder for me because I am an American. Also the minimum thickness for a rotor to pass the test is 22mm and the thinnest point on my rotors is 25mm, easily passing. But what can I do in the face of the German system?

The repair shop has to order the rotors and the people at the TÜV will not let me drive the van anywhere so I am now confronted with another problem. I need to submit my visa application in person in the town of Freiburg, a "mere" 39 km away. The only option I can see is to borrow Raphael's bike and ride to Freiburg. I make it to Freiburg and find my way to the Landratsamt, the place where my visa application must be submitted. They are only open three days a week and for only four hours each of those days. I use the bike ride as my workout for the day. It is a nice ride, but a bit uncomfortable going through the tunnels.

I hand in the paperwork and they advise me that my application is not complete. I need a letter from my sport federation stating that I am here as an athlete and will be competing in specific events. All I must do now is send, via-email, the endorsements from either USSA or USBA about my purpose here and I should have my visa.

On leaving the Landratsamt I still have to make the 39 km return ride back to Bubenbach, where Raphael lives—and it is starting to get dark. I ride back through the first tunnel and am only about 2-3 km out from Freiburg when Raphael's back tire blows out. It sure isn't my day, but I keep moving forward, walking the bike through the tunnel headed toward Bubenbach.

After about 30 minutes and not finding any other way to get out of the inner-city highway cement channel, I am stuck walking along with cars and trucks whizzing by and honking erratically. Then I see an emergency exit and at that very moment a police car pulls up and the two officers approach me. They ask me many questions and I eventually realize that it is highly illegal for pedestrians to be in the tunnel or alongside this highway.

Luckily my residence paperwork was documented only the day before and I am able to claim that I just arrived here, giving them the whole story about how my van is not allowed to be on the road and that I only came here to follow the law by turning in my visa paperwork, etc. They give me a warning and safely help me out of the highway area. The usual fine for this offense is around 250 euros. From there I am able to find a train station and take the train to arrive 9 km from Raphael's house where his father comes and picks me up in the dark.

Andy with the van at the Gletcherblick.

The Crash

Five days later, as September rolls to an end, it is the last day before Leandro and I are planning to head back to O-town for a weekend training run with Joe. Charlie has gone to Germany to visit a nice girl that he met a few months earlier and the place is a lot quieter without him. Most days my sides hurt because of the laughter, hilarious jokes and pranks that unfold amongst us.

Living at the Gletcherblick with Leandro and Charlie has been the most fun I've experienced during any deep-training season. It is experiences like these that I feel are going to be the most memorable. Charlie's competitive spirit overflows to both Leandro and I and I believe he can motivate an entire group with just a few words. This personality I like and learn a lot from. The power of using optimism to its fullest potential and realizing how to obtain and hold an unshakable self-belief in my abilities come to the surface through Charlie. Also there is no question he has an attitude to always give his best effort no matter what his situation is or how bad the cards are played against him. I pick up on this and give my best effort to measure up to Charlie's high spirits.

This morning I have a really bad crash while skiing to the ski trails on the Glacier. It is really sunny and the conditions are very icy. I decide to ski on the smaller loop groomed on the east side of the glacier. When I have skied down to that trail previously, I have skied down the steep long hill on the right side of the rope tow for the alpine section because it is a straight downhill. But because of the icy conditions today I decide to use the trail on the left side as there appear to be three large lumps that I think will potentially slow me down and be safer than a straight shot down. The light is flat so the hill, from a distance, looks very different than up close.

Much to my surprise the lumps on the hill are actually jumps that have recently been made in preparation for the upcoming "Big Air Freestyle Ski and Snowboard Contest." I am hauling straight down this hill on classic skis with klister on, and after riding up the first jump, I think I can handle it and only lose touch with the ground for a meter or two.

Then the next jump comes and I am moving even faster. I am really cookin' over the second jump and am barely able to catch my footing with the klister doing its job, not to my advantage. The third jump really tests my skills. I still have my backpack on and it doesn't help. The landing of that jump sends me faster than I have ever gone on classic skis in my life. Klister is a special wax similar to a combination of honey and glue that is applied to the middle of a ski only for the Classic style of skiing. It gives grip, but ski jumping with klister can be a recipe for disaster!

I can barely keep my skis pointing in the right direction because of the freshly groomed corduroy lines and am heading directly for the middle of the ski tracks. As my life flashes before my eyes I think if my momentum and speed are reduced enough before I arrive at the trails, I might be able to maneuver onto one of the parallel paths and glide out. But it does not work like that at all. As I come near the first 2-meter wide ski-track I look in both directions frantically, not seeing anyone.

The rim-edge that the groomer left after grooming sends me airborne once again and I fly a lot further than I expected. I am terrified as I am now completely out of control. This time I am in the air for about a distance of 5 meters—yes, 5 full meters. I clear the entire un-groomed section in-between groomed tracks and another groomed trail, too, where I nearly collide with a woman from the Finnish National Team.

When my skis touch ground in the far un-groomed section, the klister grips like super glue and I plunge headfirst, and my head becomes tucked very hard forward. At the moment of impact I hear a loud "**crack**" from my neck, then feel the back of my head plow a path of snow for my body to follow on top of my face. I skid for a few painful seconds and come to a stop. I feel horrible and my head and neck are agonizing. My ear rocks are loosened inside the vestibules. I sit and stretch for a bit and try to ski that day but after 1.5 hours I have to stop because of dizziness and nausea.

On the positive side, the Director of USBA sent me an official letter to pass on to the German authorities. This letter does not grant me permission to race in IBU Cup events, it is only for the visa. In contrast, the USSA wrote a letter immediately, stating everything I needed while also signing me up for all the FIS cross country races. I pass both letters on to the German authorities knowing my chance of getting the visa is higher with two endorsements.

Despite the pain I still felt from my crash, I make it to O-town and am very pleased to have done so because Ole Einar Bjørndalen is there. I want to get a picture with him so I walk up and make conversation. He remembers me from previous conversations and training sessions, and comments on my recent haircut. I offer him a complementary haircut after the workout, but he laughs and respectfully declines.

Ole, the "Biathlon King," with me on his left.

He is amazing to watch in training and work with as a training partner. So fluent, focused, and exact, every movement turns into an art, an art that he loves and is passionate about. He's also a great person with a real wholesome spirit. It is not just his results that creates that higher level of respect, but his charisma and the happiness he demonstrates that is also very visible. I take note of his efficient routine and how passionate he is within athletics. I realize there is a lot to learn about sport beyond logging the training hours. Training in the emotional state of love holds an endless amount of power and energy towards the sport you are training in. Fear is the most limiting factor known to mankind. Fear of failure, fear of injury, fear of overtraining, fear of pain etc all are examples and although fear can motivate a good performance, love can inspire great performances. I see Ole as holding an endless passionate love for the sport of biathlon and skiing.

Unfortunately I cannot train this day because of constant nausea and dizziness from my skiing accident the day before, but I am still able to check-in with Joe and speak with him about the future training plan. This allows for the opportunity to observe in greater detail Ole's methods on both the rollerski track and at the range and I have the honor to reset his targets after he knocks them all down each time. The more inspiring part of being around Ole is not learning about those foundation principles which has made him into a national icon, but to see him living it. He is the real deal.

CHAPTER FOUR
Opportunities and Barriers

Holmenkol

At the beginning of October, following our weekend in O-town, Leandro and I drive back to Ramsau. We will not arrive home till the early hours of the following morning as we are heading to a meeting with representatives of wax supplier Holmenkol in Stuttgart. To get there from O-town we pass through parts of Italy, back into Austria, then hours north to Stuttgart in Germany.

The purpose of our trip is to attend a meeting with the CEO of Holmenkol, a man named Christian, which is to be held at their factory. Holmenkol is one of the largest wax suppliers in the world and sells a top quality product. I'd worked for them back in the States since 2002 and I knew the product line well. I also had emailed Christian a few times with special issues when I was the rep in Alaska, so it will be good for both of us to finally meet.

In the meeting Christian officially connects me to the World Racing Team as a European Race Rep, which is a band of wax servicemen who attend larger events. The meeting lasts three hours! Leandro also sits in on the meeting and contributes his personal knowledge of the market potential in South America, which is greatly appreciated. He gives Christian and Holmenkol the very insight needed to make educated decisions about sending a sales rep down there someday.

It was not my intention, when coming to Europe, to get work.

My priorities were focused on learning, training and racing. But with the uncertainties with getting a visa based on my intent on being here as an athlete only, this is sounding very good. A work contract with Holmenkol as a means of gaining approval to stay in Europe may be the solution. In addition, I enjoy the involvement with the business side of things: business type interactions and talking with people, teaching people how to wax. I'm a wax pro/perfectionist. Everything has to be done efficiently, in the right order, and correctly, with the right temperatures, and at the right times, pressures, and motions. Yeah, I deal with skis and their preparation a bit differently than my life. Or so I've been told.

The role of a race rep is to test waxes and hand out recommendations for the best wax to use on the day, which will vary depending on the conditions. They also sell waxes on site and through team orders, and give waxing clinics. The race reps are universally welcomed by skiers at races. Most skiers know that the right wax can easily make 30 seconds to 1 minute difference in time in a 10K race. Some skiers don't get into waxing knowledge and just don't care all that much about it as long as their skis are fast. Others care a lot and ask reps questions.

All in all the meeting goes very well and we leave in good spirits for the next part of the trip. This is to a city called Ulm where the factory of rifle manufacturer, Anschutz, is located. When I arrive I will be meeting with Marc Sheppard, who is the only Anschutz rifle dealer in the United States. Because of legal requirements this means he is the only person in the World from whom I can officially buy a biathlon rifle. Marc has traveled over to attend a clinic at Anschutz. Our intention is for him to buy a rifle from Anschutz and then sell it to me directly, on the spot, but when I arrive I discover that this plan is not going to work.

Because of the strict German weapons laws, Anschutz is not allowing Marc to turn the rifle over to me there. The law requires him to select the rifles for his U.S. shop and then they are to be shipped by post from Ulm to Montana, USA. It is very difficult for someone outside of the European Union to buy a firearm in Europe. We had thought that, seeing we would both be present in person, we could circumvent the need to ship the rifle all the way to the States, but this seemingly practical solution is out of the question. This all means that I still do not have a rifle of my own to race with for the season.

It has been over a year since I sent the rifle I formerly owned to Marc to have some repair work done. He discovered a crack in the chamber and, at that time, I decided to sell it to him intending to buy a new rifle from him later when the new shipment arrived. But the new shipment was delayed in exportation within the German customs and had not arrived before I traveled to Europe. It's okay though because I feel my purpose in Europe is to learn and progress the most within skiing, not biathlon. It's just disappointing to see a regulated process become in-efficient and stand incapable of adaptation, the essence of life.

When we are back in Ramsau I meet some of my friends from the Slovenian National Biathlon Team at the shooting range on the rollerski track. I discuss my interest in biathlon with them and their trainer allows me to borrow their team's spare rifle for a week. He informs me that Anschutz will be sending them 10 more rifles within a few days. Funny, Anschutz is able to give 10 rifles to a team in general, and I, standing in the Anschutz factory, cannot legally pay and register just one rifle with Marc (the only U.S. dealer) present. The rollerski track in Ramsau is very challenging and more so as a biathlete. The route leading into the range covers a very steep climb, so the heart rate is near peaking at the very most critical point, which serves as an extremely difficult range to shoot well at.

Great Training in Ramsau

Charlie, Leandro, and I are invited to take part in an uphill double-pole interval session with a Norwegian Biathlon Club Team. The Norwegian trainer picks us up at a ski shop called "Ski Willy" in Ramsau. He only has room for two more guys on the seats, and with a bus pulling in behind his van where we were loading up, there is no time to waste. Being the smallest of the three of us, I jump in the back and find myself sitting on a pile of rollerskis, poles, backpacks, and sweaty gear.

The drive down to Schladming from Ramsau is twisty, turny and after arriving, my head is spinning. My head was below the window level and the back and forth motion has left me feeling a bit sick. It takes some deep breaths and lying in a field before I can see straight enough to begin the workout. The plan is 4 x 15 minutes of intervals, double-poling the entire way up.

During the first interval I feel fine, breathing in control, and very strong. Pumping the arms hard feels good up these steep graded roads double-poling with this train of Norwegian guys. We all finish the first one well, and I am directly behind the two guys who are leading. After a 3 minute recovery of rollerskiing slowly and carefully back down, we start our second interval of 15 minutes. This time I follow a guy who leads alone, and after 3 minutes, I feel his pace isn't as good as I was capable. Taking the lead I move ahead and finish that interval approx 50m ahead, over 100m from the next guy in the white shirt, and even further back are the rest of them.

Then the trainer says to the guys as we take our 3 minute break gathering into a group again. "You can't let the Alaskan guy beat all of you." This will be a good test to see where I am with fitness, strength, and mental stamina at this time of the season. When skiing on the glacier, even though there are sometimes +300 skiers skiing around daily, it is 9,000 feet of elevation. Most skiers train real easy, slow, and relaxed. But today, down below on the road, it's only about 4-5,000 feet, so we are working hard.

As the third interval starts a different guy takes the lead by surprise. He only lasts a minute or two up that steep grade at that pace in front of me. We hammer our poles down against the asphalt and push harder, harder, and harder up the never-ending hill. My arms are really burning by this point but I keep the best technique possible. Then we come to a flatter stretch and a little down-hill, where he gains about 25 meters on me. The last 3-minutes I spend catching up to him and he spends it trying to not be caught. Another good interval!

The 4th and final 15 minute interval is really interesting. As we start together my internal fears creep into my mind with doubts if I can maintain the level that I have shown for the first three. The guy who had worked so hard to stay ahead is no longer able to keep pace with the pack. I am very tired and am tempted to join him as I do have a great excuse but I am not going there today. Two other guys come up and take the lead for the first few minutes, and I hang on. The climbing gets tougher and this is where the men are separated from the boys. With over 50 minutes of hard uphill rollerskiing behind us and 10 more minutes left ahead, I take the lead with the intention of crushing anyone who dares to think they can keep up, catch, pass, or beat me. This last interval becomes a fight from within: "How tough are you? How bad do you want it?" are my inner thoughts.

Near the end a guy tries to pass me before drifting back, and over the last two minutes one of the guys who has been far back in the pack for all of the intervals breaks from the group and is in full-out sprint mode. He is able to catch up to me, but climbing up the last hill he cannot keep up his high frequency tempo. We finish together and after I look over to give him a handshake, he has (what looked like) a liter of snot and drool oozing out of his face and dripping on the ground.

The rest of the guys are spread 25-50m apart and are glad to be finished with the double-pole intervals of the day. They nickname me "The Machine." It is pleasing to see that my training is working. I need days like this to help me see that my dream is not completely unrealistic and that the talent, desire, and mental resilience reside within me. I also realize that although this is not the national team or development team, they are aspiring to be the best they can be and there is no difference between me and them. In the past I have become a victim of my own obstructive mind backing off the intensity after reaching certain physical pain levels. This time I faced my fears and pushed through to prevail. The internal satisfaction I reap from challenging myself is indescribable and something no one can ever take away. This means that I must push myself into extreme levels of pain to fully enjoy physical activity.

Oil Change

By this time my van desperately needs an oil change and after I have visited "Das Auto" three times, and waited nine days for the correct oil filter to come in, I am ready to change the oil. Five quarts of oil cost between 50-100 euros. And that's not even full synthetic! If you buy it by the quart, it's "only" 25-40 euros each! A freakin' rip-off! The exchange rate was 30 Euro = 50 USD, so we are talking over $50 a quart.

With the expensive motor oil and correct filter in hand I dive under the van and with a carpenters knife, cut a hole in the skid plate made of plastic directly under the bolt. Much to my surprise, the bolt is "female" and to take it out, a special square-ended tool is needed. Not having one of those or an oil filter wrench, I have to drive down to Schladming to find a place to buy them. Apparently, people don't change their own oil here, because they don't sell those tools anywhere. I end up going into a mechanic shop, where they let me borrow them, but won't let me change the oil in their parking lot.

Driving down the street I find a random lot and park. The container I have to put the oil in is too tall to stand up under the van so I have to cut the top 2-3 inches off to make it fit. Unfortunately, the container is now not large enough to capture all the oil. As the extremely hot oil quickly rises to the top of the container, I desperately try to put the plug back into the oil pan, but it is way too hot. This black, hot, dirty oil completely covers my arm and now the container is over-flowing like a waterfall.

Being from Alaska I should know a thing or two about oil spills. I use the rest of a roll of paper towel and my T-shirt to absorb all that I can. It may have been better to pay someone to do it, but this day counts as the 25th day that I have been waiting on a money transfer from the United States and it still hasn't arrived, so I have no way of paying. I have been living off of 20 euros for the last week.

The rest of the process goes more smoothly, even though I get a few blisters from the removal of the oil filter and from slamming my hand against the extremely hot exhaust manifold. I clean up the oil spill mess as well as possible for the environment and the chance that the police will issue a citation for the offense. One more problem, my oil container has no lid and is now similar to a small bucket. If I put it in the van, it will surely tip over and spill. So I try to pour the old oil into the container that the new oil just came out of. Without a funnel or anyone to help I do my best to pour from a 10" hole into a 1" hole. The fact that I am also rushing does not help. Again, oil all over. When finished, I slam on the cap, throw everything in the van, and get the heck out of dodge. Mission accomplished!

Visa Problems – Shall I Marry?

On October 10 I receive official notification that the Austrian Government has denied my application that I submitted before I left Alaska. They inform me of my options to remain in the European Union (EU), and Austria I can either: Become a student of an Austrian University, gain employment with an Austrian company for more than 6-months with steady pay, or get married. First I had registered as a student, but then found out that I actually had to take classes and live near the University, which was not going to work. Then I tried getting a job with the city of O-town, but that didn't work because I am always traveling and it's not considered a steady job. So the only option left for me to be able to stay in any of the EU countries was to get married, or at least be engaged, with intentions of getting married within in a year.

My intention is to return to the U.S. in October of 2009 and it is now only mid-October, 2008 and it seems I must leave or get engaged. So yesterday, I wrote a message on Facebook (because I don't have her number) to one of my former Alaskan Ski Team members, Steffi Klocker, asking her to marry me! I did follow up the question with an explanation. She responded with an inquisitive message indicating that she would do what is necessary to help, but would not go through with the whole marriage thing, as it was a bit too much, as would be expected.

She is an Alpine skier who is Austrian and just recently graduated from UAA and has returned to Austria. It's not like I even know her well. Perhaps I spoke to her a dozen times, but there is a sort of kinship between athletes. We would not end up getting engaged or married in the end.

I guess this shows how desperate I am. In another way the decision of the Austrian government does not come as a surprise, which is why I've already put plans in motion to try to get a German visa, but that process is not necessarily going to have a different outcome. All of this makes the potential for a work contract with Holmenkol more important.

Fortner – The Godfather of Biathlon

Along with the visa situation my other pressing problem is attempting to secure my own rifle. While I have been able to scrounge and borrow a rifle it is essential for a biathlete to have their own custom-fit rifle. Each athlete has a different body size and the rifle is designed to fit perfectly within the structure of the athlete's physical form. In addition each rifle has its own 'feel' and it takes time to adjust to it.

When competing at the top level and trying to shoot small targets quickly, with an elevated heart-rate from skiing, everything has to fit perfectly. Every athlete I have seen has a custom stock made to fit their body. Exact measurements to the length of their arms, the forward grip more specifically is cut and carved down to the precision of millimeters making the rifle stock fit like a glove. It becomes one with the body, one unit functioning together and, like a Lego or a Transformer accessory; it just becomes natural to the body in a form-fitted way.

We have gone to train in Ruhpolding, a small village, but world renowned biathlon venue. We find the rollerski track to be in excellent condition and not as intimidating as Ramsau's but one that holds its own personality. At the venue I happen to speak to Walter Pichler. Walter is the head trainer for the Great Britain biathlon team and former U.S. Team trainer. He already knows about my rifle situation and suggests I go to Peter Fortner, the man who invented the "Fortner" action that is used in all Anschutz Biathlon rifles. Walter is good friends with Peter and was the first person to test/shoot/use the Fortner rifle action.

We drive to a little town in the middle of farm fields and ask a little ol' lady if she knows where Peter Fortner lives. She points across the street and we walk up to the house. There are no signs of any sort advertising the Fortner business. Above the doorbell, the name Peter Fortner is written in tiny letters. I press it and wait. His wife eventually comes to the door and invites us in.

This is their main office and home. Once inside we hear some machinery noises from the shop in the other room. Peter then emerges and offers to show us around. It is amazing to see that this world-wide company makes its products in a room that is the same space as an average bedroom.

I tell Peter that I need a barrel, action, and rear sight, and he informs me that he cannot sell it to me without a German waffenpass. We talk for almost an hour about all the ways of getting it in my name. He says that he once sold a rifle to an American named Jay and that he got into lots of trouble, almost losing his license and nearly lost his contract with Anschutz. I am soon to discover that the rifle I had arranged to buy from a girl named Janna months prior to me leaving the United States is the same rifle Peter had sold to Jay some years ago.

The deal was set between Janna and I, and two days prior my departure Janna informed me the deal was off. She had spoken with Jay and he talked her out of selling it to me. Knowing that rifle will be sitting in its case all year in some attic did not improve my mood. Apparently Jay told her that my use would wear out the barrel, by all the rounds going through it.

I ask Peter about the durability of the barrel on that rifle, and he assures me it would survive at least 8-10 years of hard use. It's only after about 160,000 rounds have gone through a barrel that it shows signs of inaccuracy. Jay messed up the purchase of that rifle in Alaska, and now the impact that he left here in Germany is disrupting my life again. Jay hails from Kasilof, and I'm from Soldotna, a small neighboring community, both in a semi-remote location in Alaska, so we could not get much closer and it is amazing to see this connection spread its tentacles across the ocean.

The only chance I have is to get a German waffenpass in order to buy a rifle from him. To do this I would have to drive eight hours across Germany (one way), take a two day German weapon law course (costing around 200 euros, followed by an exam), drive eight hours back (that's four days out of training), and then wait three weeks for me to be allowed to purchase a rifle. Even having done this the chances of a citizen outside the EU being issued a pass are not clear.

Due to the 2nd Amendment of the Constitution of the United States, Americans have the right to bear arms. Because of that right I have no need for a firearms license and so such a license doesn't exist for U.S. citizens. But European firearms dealers require a license and so none will sell a weapon to any American. I later walk into a waffenpass office establishment and after speaking to the proper employees, it is confirmed that only citizens of the EU can be issued such passes.

I hope, dear reader, that you appreciate I'm not one to give up in difficult situations, so I consider a different tack. I discuss with Marc the option of shipping me a rifle once the shipment arrives to his shop in Montana, but he is not allowed to mail rifles internationally. Another option I think about is to have him mail my rifle to someone within the U.S., then have them take it apart and mail the parts to me piece by piece at different times with other random objects in the packages and hope they don't look at the x-ray screen too closely. Yet another option I have thought about, which is a bit riskier, is to buy one from one of the many Russians who are non-EU and are currently skiing on the Dachstein glacier. There may be some biathletes among them and perhaps I can arrange to buy one from them.

I am becoming increasingly creative and desperate. My first biathlon races are scheduled for the end of this month, and right now is the most critical time to train the stance muscles to hold steady, train the eye to coordinate each shot with a high heart rate/breathing, and become confident in an efficient routine. Without a rifle each day that goes by is one less that I have to train properly. Although this frustration builds towards these restrictions trying to do more biathlon, I am more than satisfied with the ski training that I am able to complete.

You have probably noticed a recurring theme in my life: my struggle with all kinds of authority structures. First there was USBA, then the governments with the visa problems, then the rifle situation. Add to that the car-licensing process and even Jenny's boss and it must stand out like a big flashing neon sign. Living in the midst of it, however, it is not always so easy to see the repeating patterns of one's life. Even so, by this stage, I am beginning to wonder what on earth is happening in my life to make me continue to come up against this sort of resistance from authority structures. It is not a question I can answer at this stage but I have a growing sense that my journey is more than what it appears to be.

Climbing Der Dachstein

October 11th is a day of active recovery, a programmed part of my training and I decide to hike to the top of the Dachstein. Preparing for my hike as I always do, I put on an old retired pair of running shoes, cotton socks, surf shorts, and a T-shirt. Also I had gotten an email from a friend, Kevin Sadaj, in Michigan, who is having a Birthday Rock Party. Everyone has to bring a rock so he can make a rock garden in his yard. Since I can't make it to his party I decide that mailing him a rock from the tallest mountain in Austria will make up for my absence.

Leandro and Charlie are going skiing, as we normally do together, so I head out hiking alone. As I climb up the side of the glacier and parts of the rock wall, I can't help but notice that all the other people around in groups are wearing helmets, winter climbing boots (the kind with long spikes), ice axes, lines, and the whole set-up. It is a beautiful day, a slight wind, and so sunny that I'm sunburned from being up there, exposed to the reflection of the sun's rays off the glacier.

After going high enough to the point where I would need at least a carabineer and rope to continue, I grab a rock for my friend Kevin and head back down. Once I arrive at the snowy part, I enjoy showing off my native Alaskan skill of skiing on my feet. Meanwhile I pass a group of climbers who are all tethered together and are safely, and slowly (boring) making their way down the glacier to the main trail. It is great, I whiz past all of them, without any safety gear, enjoying every moment. Sometimes I think having all those sharp tools and equipment can be more dangerous than not to have any. If you were to trip, fall, or even one person lose their balance, all it takes is one blade to slice you and you'd have a real problem. I'll take my chances of falling into a mystery maze of the glacial underworld and enjoy the surface surfing in running shoes and shorts.

These are memorable times, when you know at any moment the ground in which you are gliding on could give way and you could find yourself somewhere that no human has been before. One day on the glacier (earlier in the summer) it was very icy and a guy from the Spanish team fell hard. His binding broke and his ski came off. The ski flew down the glacier and into a huge crack, never to be seen again. He was so mad.

Freedom to Be Me

When I arrive back at the 'hotel' I have time to reflect on why I take such risks and just how good it makes me feel. There is no doubt that there is some drive in me to push the limits, to defy the rules and fly into the mystery without all the support that normal protocol deems necessary. In some way it is an essential relief for me, contrasting to the struggles I have with authority structures. I mean, all these government authorities have the purpose to make people safe, to create a social environment in which we can all live in safety.

The gun restrictions in Europe, the visa system—they are designed to make people safe. Maybe they do, but in the end they also strangle the life out of someone like me who is daring to push themselves to the limit and find out just how far they can go. When I am up on the mountain there is no administrator telling me what I am not allowed to do; there is just me and nature and I can tell you which set-up I prefer.

The Physiotherapist

It is now two weeks since I crashed on the glacier and my neck still has some residual pain. There are also times when I feel uncomfortable vertigo symptoms. It took a solid week after the fall before my ear rocks returned to their proper locations. Finally I concede the need for help and locate the only physiotherapy/chiropractor type place in the area. I find him by searching the Internet and discover his name is Vincent. I also discover that there are many articles that come up in a search under his name.

Some of the articles relate to alleged illegal actions dealing with a big blood doping scandal at the 2006 Olympics. He was the doctor behind the work, providing all the illegal things involved, which in turn got a large number of biathletes (including the entire Austrian Biathlon Team), and some skiers, banned from participation in sport for many years. He is not allowed to help any National Teams leading up to or during the 2010 Olympics.

When I arrive for my appointment the doctor introduces himself as Vincent. *O-MI-GOSH*, this is the guy. He seems like a nice guy, talkative and tells me about the former U.S. Ski Team athletes he knew (mostly in the 80's to mid 90's). He is a former athlete from Denmark and competed in many World Cups, World Champs, and Olympics as a cross country skier. He cracks my back, does some other chiropractor-type moves, checks my right knee, finds a little bit of excess fluid around the surgical area, but assures me it is normal. He only charges me 30 euros. Away goes all neck pain. Thank you, Vincent.

Finances to the Front

When I left Alaska I thought money was not an issue. I had a buyer lined up for my home and investment funds that could be cashed in. Now it turns out that, due to more rules, I'm not able to access the money from the investment fund I was planning to use. On top of that the buyer of my house encountered some 'unexpected financial dilemma' and is not able to proceed with the deal. So here I am, in the middle of a foreign continent, with no legal status, and my money supplies dwindling rapidly.

This has a devastating impact on my self-esteem which has plummeted like a skier falling through one of those glacier chasms. I am confronted with the very real possibility that, if I do not come up with any more funds, I may be on my way back to Alaska much sooner than anticipated. As if I need any more issues to deal with and distract me from my training! But it seems I am not controlling this game of life as much as I would like to think and now, to add to my gun and visa challenges, I'm confronted with an increasingly tenuous financial situation.

In times like this the best course of action for me is to get out into the fresh mountain air and push myself to the limit. Out there, alone, I gain a fresh perspective and clarity of mind. I also think much better when moving than when I'm penned up inside a room.

After two hours of skiing several possibilities have opened up in my mind and I return in a much more positive state of mind. Once again, movement and the clarity of nature helped me pull myself from the brink of a chasm of self-misery and back onto the forward trail. My financial problems have not been resolved, but at least I no longer feel as if my future has slammed shut as I did a few hours ago.

Crazy Little Thing Called Fun

One of the stand-out differences between the training I have witnessed here among the World's best, compared to that which I experienced in the States, is the crazy little things the athletes will do to make their training fun and add some variety and laughter. Today Charlie and I engage in a little bit of that approach ourselves.

For years Charlie has dreamt about double-pole rollerskiing up Der Dachstein Strasse (The Dachstein Street) from the hotel to the main road where the lift begins and this afternoon we decide to take on the challenge. It is similar to the total of the previous week's interval training from Schladming. It is tough. I'm running while Charlie is rollerskiing. We end up training the last 30 minutes in the dark, but luckily we end our last interval with less than a kilometer to the finish. Charlie double-poles while I run backwards uphill and we make it to the top. It is crazy but a lot of fun and it is these sorts of experiences that keep my training feeling alive, dynamic and enjoyable.

We are training on the glacier in the afternoons now due to the cooler weather. In the mornings it has been windy and cold, but the afternoons are calm and sunny. Three days ago, during the morning, it was so windy on the glacier that some people had to be rescued by snow machines. The entire team from Turkey looked like an ant trail as they crawled on their hands and knees back to the building to take the tram down.

All in all, my training has been going well, tuning up for the season. The most intense training occurs in the months leading up to the race season. Once the racing begins it is necessary to allow more recovery time so that the athlete is fresh on race day and able to push themselves to the limit. If we are training too hard in between races there is nothing extra in the tank on race days. This means that perhaps the most important months in an athlete's year are actually the two or three leading into the race season where skills, strength and endurance capacity are built and fine-tuned. To give me one more 'push' Joe has written another intensity block, which consists of four hard days in a row, 1-2 days rest, and repeating that for three solid weeks. This will be the second intensity block I have done in Europe.

Part-way through this intensity block I find some relief from rifle problems as I am thankfully able to borrow a rife again from the Slovenian Team for five days. Surprisingly, for not having shot for so long, I shoot pretty well. The five day period coincides with the ending of the final intensity block for the fall season. This means during most training sessions my heart rate reaches near maximum levels. This, in combination with the uneven shooting surface in Ramsau, I feel, makes for the best conditions to make up for the lost time from not having had a rifle. Many of the athletes who come here commonly say "If you can acquire a solid stance here, you can acquire a solid stance anywhere."

Not having a rifle to train with leading up to the races is probably the worst thing a biathlete can experience. It is essential to practice with a rifle to improve efficiency, training the body to quickly drop its heart rate, mentally prepare, get into each shooting position fast, and shoot each shot quickly and accurately. A good shooting time, from the time you step on the mat, shoot five shots, and step off, is between 15-30 seconds. That's including taking the rifle from your back, getting into perfect position, opening two optic sights, a magazine exchange, and taking five single shots with a high heart rate. Fortunately, during my first six weeks at O-town, I was able to borrow Joe's old rifle and that has proved to be the foundation of my shooting.

The only positive aspect to not having a rifle is that my training has focused on skiing, which has its own meticulous details. In recent days the Dachstein glacier has had the best skiing conditions in all of Europe, except for the northern parts of Scandinavia. Within the past few days hundreds of freestyle snowboarders and alpine skiers have arrived for the "big air" event. The groomers have carved up some wicked jumps and added a lot of platforms to do tricks off of.

One day during my interval training program, I see (and hear) a large number of dogs running around on the glacier. At the end of my training session I ski over and ask the guy about his dog team. He tells me he is training his team to compete in the Iditarod, which is a race held in Alaska. After telling him that I am from Alaska he becomes very excited and asks that I pet every dog on his team for good luck. It's a shame I have spent the majority of my life living in Alaska, but have never actually witnessed the event. Later, I have the opportunity to ski with the dogs, under their trainer's supervision. The groomer had groomed a path just for dogs and skiing with them is like Rocky Balboa running down the streets of Philadelphia, with everyone following behind with high excitement.

Since I've been living in Ramsau I've visited the Nystad house where Trond and his wife Claudia live. Claudia has been, and still is, a member of the German Ski Team. Trond was formerly the head coach for the U.S. Ski Team until he recently moved back to Europe to be closer to his wife and take a new position as the Sprinting trainer for the Swiss National Ski Team.

Trond is the type of guy you feel comfortable around right away and I am not surprised he succeeds in coaching, as he can easily relate with athletes on different personal levels. Claudia is a real spark of energy and a lot of fun to be around. She has been operating at the highest level of ski racing so long that she values her family and friends to a greater degree than I've seen with many athletes. They are always very welcoming and accommodating when I come over, and I really enjoy being there and listening to the endless crazy stories of athletes getting themselves into all sorts of predicaments. These moments serve as great confirmation that even long-time elite athletes like Trond and Claudia are not hermits and enjoy the company of others.

During one of my interval sessions, at the rollerski track in Ramsau, I see Trond and his team gathering. I stop and he invites me to join them for a similar interval training session. I enjoy jumping in and had a great training session. It's one thing to meet athletes and ski along with them at an easy pace on the glacier, but you acquire a much stronger bond when you work really hard side-by-side, challenging each other's strength, speed, and straight-up mental endurance.

USBA Remains Unyielding

It is now early November and I've received the final word from the USBA athlete representative. He refuses to endorse my requested entry into any IBU competitions. He stated that it's his job to protect the guys who follow the selection process (i.e.: the trial races in the U.S.) against people like me who, as he put it, try to "circumvent the system."

That is it in a nutshell, right there. The USBA is not interested finding, welcoming or encouraging athletes to represent our nation internationally; it is about protecting the guys who play within the system. It makes me want to scream out in rage and in pain and anguish. How can this be happening? I'm an American, I'm an athlete, I'm giving everything I have to become the best I can be, and I want to represent my country in the proudest manner, and yet they see me as someone who wants to "circumvent the system." But why am I circumventing the system in the first place? Because that same system rejected me; it did not want me, it cast me out, wishing me well. What choice did they leave me?

I can't let it go at this, and so I sit down and draft a response to the representative...

> Dear ****,
>
> Maybe you misunderstood my request. I am NOT asking for any special favors. I am only asking permission to compete in the IBU cups in which the U.S. race entries are NOT all being filled. In other words, if the U.S. is not fielding a full team there, and the open race positions are going to be unused, then I would be allowed to compete.
>
> I will be at all the IBU Cups with my teammates anyway. If the U.S. has all positions filled, I understand, no big deal, I won't compete. But if there are open entries for Americans and USBA would rather have no athlete compete instead of me....That is the ultimate question. Would it be better for USBA to let Andy Liebner compete, or no athlete at all?
>
> Comments about your (the representative) last

response: You wrote that it is your job to protect others who follow the selection process from people like me. Where were you last spring when the selection for the Development team was made? As of last summer and winter, ***** and ***** led me to believe I would have a position on the U.S. Development team depending on the previous year's ski results, and especially at the NCAA skate race. I was the second actual American at the NCAA's in the skate race. All year my plans were to dedicate the future 2 years to biathlon and was shocked to read the team announcement with two of the selectees coming from the same collegiate circuit, not even qualifying for the NCAAs, and both of them having less biathlon experience than I. So please tell me again that it's your job to protect them from me. I don't mean for that to be a direct stab at you, but please understand, I feel like the victim, not the enemy. - Andy

The only positive thing I can say about USBA is that the head Director offered to personally transport my rifle with him as he travels to Germany on December 5. The problem is that Marc is still waiting for the shipment of rifles from Ulm to arrive so he can send it to the Director. If the shipment arrives in time, the Director's act will be the first supportive thing that anyone associated with USBA has done for me on this journey. I am very thankful for that. The ski training continues.

CHAPTER FIVE
Racing Begins

The Cave

I've decided to move back to O-town for a week before the racing season begins at the end of November. On my final day in Ramsau there is a blizzard on the glacier making skiing rather challenging. Charlie and I ski together for two solid hours with the entire trail to ourselves. Afterwards, while walking back to the tram on the top of the glacier, we notice the doors are open to the cave entrance into the glacier. We have never entered the cave but have seen hundreds of tourists going in and out all fall. We enter cautiously and see two ticket machines (like at a train station). There is no one around and so we climb over the three pronged metal rotators and run inside.

I have a camera with me and am ready to snap off a few quick shots of whatever is inside. There are lights in random places and even music playing throughout the cavern. After we are 25m in the tunnel the music stops. Throwing caution to the wind we hurry further into the cave, running, still in our ski boots with plastic bottoms, which makes it hard even to walk on the solid glazed-over ice. I pose next to an ice sculpture of a Lion that reminds me of Aslan from "The Chronicles of Narnia" as Charlie takes a picture.

A minute later all the lights shut off. Charlie says, "They surely know we are in here now," but the unspoken fear that hangs between us is that they don't and are about to lock us in for the night. We are immersed in absolute darkness and have to slowly back track our steps using the handrails. Eventually we spot some light reflections from the mouth of the cave and begun to run. Hurdling the gate near the entrance is a challenge in our skiing gear, but we clear it and race back into the freedom of the glacier without ever seeing a single person.

Camp Alaska

Sometimes to make things work you have to make sacrifices from time to time. To save some of my dwindling money for the more important times later in the season, I decide to sleep in my van when I arrive back in Obertilliach. "Camp Alaska," as I call it, is established in the parking lot of the Biathlon Center. Some of the luxuries I am giving up include heat, a bed, lights, and showers. The great thing about it is that I can go skiing right from the moment I wake up.

Some nights I read using a candle that is taped to the wall of my van. I will never forget what it looks and feels like to see my breath as I blow out the candle, lay down and listen to the snow land lightly and dance off the windows and roof as I drift off to sleep. In the mornings, it's a little rough with everything being frozen. Water, toothpaste, contacts in their solution, and all my food is frozen solid.

After 3-nights/ 4-days of camping, I decide to investigate where I could purchase a heater, and the possibility of plugging it in to a nearby building. The closest appliance store is 20k away and driving down about 2,000 feet in slick conditions is not an easy task. The other thing I have to do is to collect my summer tires and summer training gear from the basement of the housing complex I lived in during the summer. It was a nice place but the rates during the winter are triple what I paid earlier in the year. The owner only rents it during holiday weekends and special events in winter, and it costs a fortune to heat the building for just one person the rest of the time, so staying there again is out of the question financially.

Joe's niece, Steffi, who is also secretary of the Biathlon Sport Academy, has offered the shed and attic at her house for my summer stuff, and they live in the same town as the department store where I hope to buy a heater. After dropping my stuff of at Steffi's house and leaving for the store, her parents question her as to why I need a heater. Upon my return they inform me that they will cover my housing costs for the week. Steffi's mother is the niece of the owner of the house where my stuff had been and where I lived before and she says that they will work out an arrangement. I tell them I can't possibly accept their offer that they were being too nice, but they insist and invite me in for a wonderful warm, home-cooked meal.

That evening I cancel Camp Alaska and move into the room I first inhabited when I arrived from the States. It is only when I return to indoor living that I realize all the little things that I might have taken for granted.

Secret Training

I had run for my morning workout before leaving for my daily tasks and had planned to do a ski-sprinting workout during the daylight hours on the ski trails in the afternoon. By the time I am moved into my room and am ready to ski it is getting late and I wonder whether to go or not. As usual, the part of me that desires to be out in the open air, pushing my body, is victorious over the part that is cautious. By the time my warm-up is complete it is completely dark and my headlamp visually reminds me that it needs new batteries. It is so dark that the trails are difficult to follow. On top of this, there are many ruts from the daily ski traffic.

This training session has turned into something I like to call "secret training" because it is training in difficult conditions with low visibility at high speeds that provides the best opportunity to improve abilities in areas such as balancing on slick uneven surfaces, depth perception, and the free feeling of movement over ground. I especially like the cool snowy air breeze whoosh by my face as I move down the trail as fast as possible without crashing.

Shortly after arriving back in O-town I meet Mark Raymond, a skier from Australia. He is their best biathlete and goes by the nickname "Ramsey." He will turn out to be a great training partner and we are kindred spirits of sorts, both being a long way from home and receiving little support.

We soon begin doing lots of speed drills together, working to challenge both aspects of skiing and shooting. One day, when we set out to do some basic intervals, we discover that the longer ski loop is closed because the trail workers are adding more snow to the areas under the trees. This means there is a lot of traffic skiing on two shorter loops. Even with many close crash encounters Ramsey and I continue to fly past all the other athletes training.

As we enter a downhill S-turn I am in front and have to quickly decide how to pass the two skiers in front of me, side by side, skiing down the trail. Go to the right, left, or my favorite.... the middle? The middle looks the best until the guy on the left takes another stride and his pole tip almost jabs me in the eye. He then goes into a tuck, spreading his poles are spread wide, leaving no room. I grab the basket of his pole just as it is about to pierce my chest and give him a boost by pushing it forward. Then the guy on the right moves over to let me past and I shoot forward.

When we are finished, Ramsey describes the scene: "He looked back after you passed. I tried to tell him to look forward but he didn't understand and flew off the 3-meter drop at the edge of the trail. All I could see was snow flying and I heard a loud shout." For Ramsey, it was the funniest thing he had ever seen on skis.

Swiss Cup

I've signed up on-line for many of the Swiss Cup biathlon events. These are not official IBU events and are being staged as part of the selection process to determine the Swiss team for the IBU series of races, and they are open events that anyone can enter.

In biathlon, besides the Olympics, which is only once every four years, the elite competition is the World Cup. Below that in the hierarchy are the IBU events, and then there are regional events, of which the Swiss Cup is one series. The way they structure them is that two races are run over a weekend, which when combined make a Cup. In the case of the Swiss, they are staging two Cups over successive weekends so there will be four races and I am planning to compete in them all. This is where all my training comes to the fore and I get to see just how capable I am.

The competition at these events is seriously strong by American standards, but still short of the World Cup or IBU events. Most guys I'll be racing against will probably be considered to be level two or three racers, where the elite are level one. In Europe, however, there are so many skiers that level two guys are still very good.

I pack my stuff in O-town and head west toward Switzerland. Most of the day is spent driving on a vast range of roads through several tunnels. There are autobahns right through to narrow country back-roads. I take a short cut through Italy, western Austria, and the little forgotten country of Liechtenstein to arrive at the tiny village of Realp, Switzerland, population 25.

The town of Realp surprises me. It reminds me of the two abandoned Alaskan villages of Kennecott and Hatcher Pass. Only, in Realp, people are still living in this snow-inundated village. Half of the stone buildings are falling apart and the ski trail reminds me much of the courses in Utah and Colorado.

It is after sundown when I arrive only to find that there are no places open to even find out if they are renting. This does not bother me as I was figuring on re-establishing Camp Alaska anyway, at least for this first night. Finding a hotel online in some of these remote villages is nearly impossible due to their lack of websites or internet. Sometimes even if they do have websites they are not always in English and are not reasonably priced. Conveniently, there's an Info center located in nearly every town.

I really like the village of Realp. It is very quiet—until the train comes through and the church rings its bell. During the first night I hear the train come through about every hour, stop, load and unload cars, then take off. This town is located way up in the middle of a mountain pass and the road for cars ends here. Many drivers drive their cars onto the trains that take them the rest of the way through the pass. In the morning I wake up to the church bell clanging away. It is so loud that I decide to count the rings, thinking it will indicate the time of day. After counting to 50, however, I turn over and go back to sleep, thankful I'm not a light sleeper.

After getting up and preparing for the day, I ski over the trails hoping that someone will eventually open the shooting range. It isn't long before I meet Marcus, the Swiss Development Coach. He gives me info about reasonable places to stay and briefly describes the loops of the race course. The range here is interesting, only 10 shooting places instead of the usual 30, but all have the latest technology with electronic targets. Also, all the ski trails are lighted for night skiing.

The first race is on Saturday, November 29th and I have a really good race. Despite my high confidence for skiing and fears revolving around the range due to the lack of consistent marksmanship training this fall, I ski and shoot like a champ, overcoming all the odds. I'm using Joe's rifle, which I had been training with in O-town earlier in the season. After my race I am happy inside, having enjoyed a good race experience. Moments later, however, my euphoric mood is shattered when I discover I've been disqualified. It turns out that I missed an entire loop.

We were supposed to do the same loop two times in between the first and second shooting stage, and I only did one not knowing that I had to do two laps at that stage. It is so frustrating when you cannot understand the language of the race announcers. Because we all start at different times it is not immediately obvious where I would have placed, but I'm confident I would have finished on the podium, and now it is all over.

When I hear of my disqualification my mind nearly snaps. I don't know what to think or where to turn. All the time and money I have spent in Europe and now, in my first race, it is blown. Why am I doing this to myself? What stupidity and stubbornness drive me on in the face of so many obstacles? In moments like this my self-confidence, that gift that allows me to confront whatever barriers are put in my way, evaporates. Without that belief in self I begin to doubt that I can ever make it in either sport.

I cannot allow these thoughts to consume me. A deep fear lurks within me that if I allow them to gain root, to have one little tentacle establish itself in my mind, then my quest will be ended right here and now and I am not willing to permit that to happen. I have to resist them, to gain mental equilibrium and restore the fire of competitiveness that drives me onwards.

I ski the cool-down in my racing bottom and a cut-off T-shirt, without any hat or gloves, using the cold to dislodge the negative thoughts from my mind so I can begin to prepare for the next race. I really want to succeed in this Swiss Cup overall and I have blown it on day one, so I better get into the right mindset for the next one tomorrow.

That evening I go for a lonely run in the dark. I decide to park in the large parking lot next to the train station, to ensure I can get out safely, which turns out to be a bad move. During the night it snows nearly half a meter and the plow that clears the train station parking lot pushes snow up against my van in all directions. There is a sign that reads "Public Parking 24 Hours." Maybe they were trying to be funny, but I have a heck of a time digging it out, which makes me late to pick up my bib at the race registration office. My shoes, socks, pants, and jacket are soaked before I arrive.

First Result

The second race is a Pursuit event. The Pursuit builds on the race from the previous day. The results of the first race, which was a 10k sprint, dictate your start position, meaning how many minutes you start behind the winner to begin the pursuit. In a 12.5k pursuit, which we are racing today, those individuals who finished within five minutes of the winner in the previous race will start the same distance behind the leader as they finished the day before. Those who finished more than five minutes behind the winner the day before, did not race the day before, or, as in my case, got disqualified the day before and therefore have no time, all start five minutes behind the winner as a group (mass start).

The other challenge for me with the Pursuit is that it is a 12.5k skiing event with four shooting stages, whereas the sprint is 10k with only two shooting stages. Obviously the pursuit is more of a shooter's race, because there is a greater ratio of shooting and given my problems with rifles and my greater confidence and speed over the ski portions, I am at a significant disadvantage.

By now, however, the mental destruction of the night before has morphed itself into a searing fire from which emerges a source of inspiration, motivation and willingness to push my body in order to defeat as many skiers as possible. The sense of injustice at being disqualified and having to start so far behind now acts as fuel to the inner flames of passion that compel me to compete. I am also better prepared today and have done a better warm-up and spent more time confirming my zero.

Riding on the wave created by this fire, my first lap in the pursuit is excellent and I have already advanced many positions in the field. Even though I had to start in last place I am skiing well (smooth, strong, and in control) and I can see I am making up big distance on the guys that started minutes ahead of me. Each shooting stage I come to I enter like all the times I have practiced over the past few months. But ironically, I only hit one in each of the four shooting stages. I cannot believe what is happening as I slowly move back, back, and further back into the field after every shooting stage.

After my first shooting stage, Marcus yells to me in the penalty loop area that I should move my rear sight four clicks to the left, which I take as I come in for my second stage, but the wind has suddenly changed directions, making his guidance worthless. Also the time I used Joe's rifle and the hundreds of rounds I have shot with it, I have only had one practice bullet misfire on me. In this single race, I have two misfires and I have to manually load two separate bullets.

On the beginning of my third ski loop, I am passed (meaning I have been lapped) by the leader and I keep up with him for the entire loop, so I know my skiing speed is great and feel good about my skiing.

A Fan Club, Whether I Want it or Not

To add to my sense of embarrassment I have developed a fan club, who gather near the penalty loop area and cheer for me by first name (even the officials there know me well by now).

I finish second to last and while I am skiing my last lap, the officials are already taking down the course markers, which is a depressing notion. After it is all said and done, I have skied more than a mile worth of penalty loops. I just cannot believe all this can keep happening. At least I finished with an actual result listing a time and I am satisfied with my skiing.

Once again my mind spirals into negativity and I have many thoughts of quitting biathlon and simply packing up to head back to Alaska. A less extreme part of my mind encourages me to drive back to O-town to continue training with Ramsey and the convenience of Joe as my coach. It's been literally a disastrous trip so far and I've only been here three days. Am I really going to stay through to the following weekend and race in the second Cup?

Toothbrush Repair

After investigating all of the many reasons for the rifle malfunctions I'm shocked to discover that the butt plate has broken and the lower "hook" which keeps it from slipping up my shoulder is totally missing. How didn't I notice this? Still, it's always nice to uncover facts like this so the result can be blamed as an external force instead of an internal one (my error). This helps me find the energy to look ahead to the following week's races with greater hope and enthusiasm and prevents the desire to flee from all of this hardship and chaos from gaining control.

Living on the road leaves no room for excess stuff, so to repair my rifle butt plate I have to do some serious brainstorming. The best solution I can come up with is to take an old tooth brush (that I use to clean my rifle) and tape it securely in place, where the metal bracket was previously, holding it in place with a bolt that I manage to force into the wood. It now looks absolutely hilarious, and I have already seen some younger athletes pointing at it and laughing while my rifle is sitting on the rack near the range. One asked, *"Does this mean you are sponsored by Oral-B?"* Despite its comical appearance it's holding up.

Judging the Wind

In the week between the two Swiss Cup events I seize the great opportunity to pick up some useful knowledge from Marcus. The most important thing we spend time on is keeping an eye on the amount of wind in the flags around the stadium, and knowing how many clicks to take in the right direction on the rear sight with a quick, keen sense.

This is one of the shooting factors that is really important, which nobody has ever really explained all the variables for me so that I can understand and be confident enough to make changes to my sights in the middle of a competition. After the first session I decide to write down the facts and label them with arrows on a little piece of paper which I then tape carefully directly to the side of my rifle. Knowing how many things go through the mind as one is pushing their physical capacity to the maximum, it is easy to forget the proper meticulous adjustments during the most critical time.

Marcus is a great help. He does not have many men under his guidance, most of his athletes being women, and as they are racing at different times to the men, he is happy to help me, all the more so because he is a friend of Joe. He seems to be a genuinely nice guy at heart, the type that just flat out likes to see people succeed at anything they work hard for. He saw me working hard and has done what he can to discern and provide those extra supportive things matching my energy to learn. I also have a sneaking suspicion he is using me as sort of an example to some of his athletes, because in a lot of cases those who make teams kind of sit back and don't strive as hard. Here I am on my own, making every effort to be the best I can possibly be.

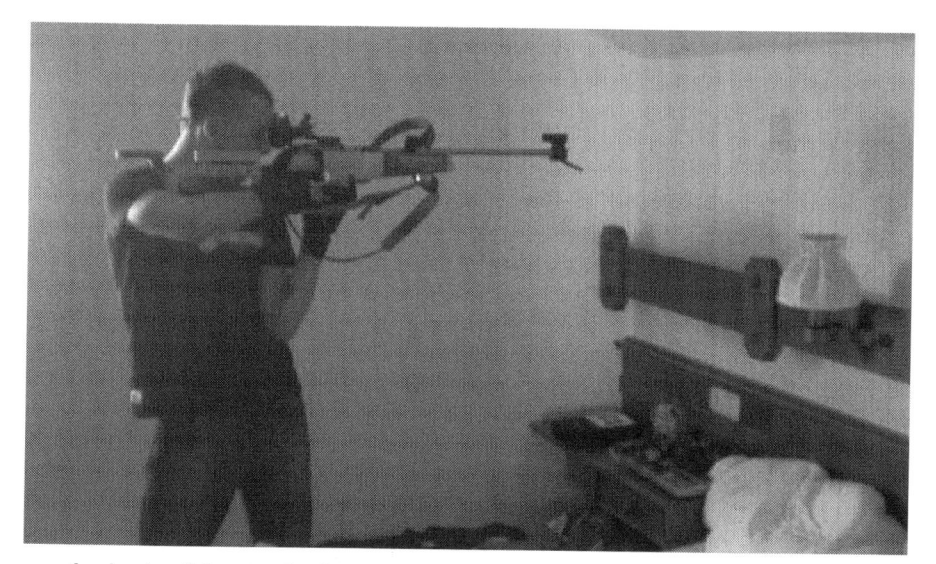

Andy dry firing in the hotel room preparing for the next competition.

A New Day

It's a week later and I hope the dreaded biathlon jinx that seems to afflict me will stay asleep or disappear to wherever it goes when it is not tormenting me. Once again the first race is a 10k sprint and I come well prepared having done everything the best I know how to physical warm-up, rifle zero, and prepare mentally. I have even gone over the course with Marcus three times and recited it back to him to ensure I understand it, so there will be no error from my side. Even though these races are at the same venue, there is a different organization with different officials, thus changing the course from last week's 10k sprint.

I start out very strong and mentally decide to keep my pace under steady wraps, so that I have more control of the amount of lactic acid and the state of oxygen supply. The first loop of skiing goes very smooth and as I come into the range for my prone stage I pay close attention to the wind, taking two clicks to the right. The weather today is probably the worst I have ever competed in for Biathlon. The wind is very strong (flags are completely horizontal) and to make it a bit more challenging, it is snowing.

Unfortunately I should have taken more clicks than just the two.

Marcus is watching my shots with his scope and tells me later that he thought the wind was pushing them just outside one edge of the sensor. The prone targets are the size of a U.S. half dollar coin and our shooting mats are 50 meters away. Marcus also says that my shooting group was all within the half dollar size, but because of the wind, my sights were slightly off (same as last week).

Even though I only hit one out of those five, I jump off the mat and get back into the race. Surprisingly, as I head toward the penalty loop, I find it to be almost completely full. I think to myself: *"Everyone seems to be having a hard time shooting today; this means it's more of a skier's race, look out, it's my time to shine!"* I cruise around that penalty loop area passing nearly a dozen people. The next part of the course is a full 5k of skiing; half of it more difficult because of the strong headwind with snow pelting directly in the face.

Then it is time for the standing shooting stage. I take another two clicks on my rifle and relax. In biathlon, there are so many things going on around you and so many noises, that the only way to shoot well is to block out everything and put yourself mentally in a separate zone.

This moment is often called "flow"—you are so engaged with what you are doing that you lose track of time and your surroundings. Getting in and out of flow while shooting is something that one acquires through experience and over many years. Since I have no years, barely months, of experience, I often can't hold this state for all five shots. I believe I am in the zone for the first three shots (which I successfully hit) but then, unwillingly, I start thinking about how nice it was to hit those last three. There are also some people talking in the background and their conversation catches my ear, which also acts to take me out of the flow zone, and I miss the final two shots.

Extra Half-Kilometer?

From there I scamper through two penalty loops and hit the course for my final loop. I can't quite believe it; so far so good, nothing is going wrong for once. I hammer out the last loop of solid headwind followed by really fast tailwind which carries me into the finish. I cross the line and am surrounded by the officials who are checking my rifle and are about to collect my bib. I ask for confirmation that I did the loops correctly, speaking to them in German and using my hand to demonstrate all the loops that I skied. They say I did everything correctly, but I want to make sure, so I ski back near the finish line. It is then that I notice some of the guys who had started behind me, are not finishing, and I yell over the orange plastic fence to the race director about the last loop. He tells me that there is an extra half-kilometer loop still remaining that I have not actually completed.

Racing back out of the finish area and onto the course I cut in behind the guys who were still racing and had started between 30-seconds to 2:30 minutes behind me. I am back in the race I guess but, not even knowing where this extra loop is, I have to follow these guys to see where it is that Marcus forgot to mention when he was explaining the course to me. The extra loop actually has a sign pointing for "Juniors only" and even though I don't think we should be skiing on it I follow along.

After finishing I check the map again and find that the extra half-k loop was not even on the map for the seniors, but after further investigation I hear a very familiar explanation: The Organization Race Director states *"We host this race every year and everyone knows the final loop has this extra half-K."* Emotions of frustration, disappointment, and a strong feeling of a worthless effort flow within me. I think to myself: *"I skied my butt off and am fed up with getting disqualified for stupid crap like this."* The officials could disqualify me for finishing too soon and for skiing backwards on the course, but because, as he stated *"Andy was correcting his mistake, use his second finish time."* I guess that is better than another DQ, but I lost approximately two minutes while standing in the finish area. So my result is 3rd to last. One place better than last week! Wow, what an improvement!

Still, I suppose it has been a real learning experience. With the largest hills on the course located on both sides of the range my ability to ski hard and drop my heart rate has been really challenged. Also, the inconsistency of the wind, as it gusts through the mountain pass here, makes it very challenging to determine the right shooting set-up.

In my hotel room that evening I sit staring at the wall, frustrated and angry. I know I have the choice of changing my mentality and how doing so will affect the next day's performance, but I just cannot forget all that I have been through over the week. I know to be successful in biathlon I must hold a successful image of myself in biathlon, and the memories of three disasters in a row are threatening everything that holds that image together. In the end it is all I can do to stop my mind and try not to think about biathlon until the morning. The walls in my room could use repainting!

Swiss-Cup Finale

The fourth and final race here in Realp is a 20k. The very first biathlon race I ever competed in was a 20k and I haven't done one since. It was in Feb 2003 and I was disqualified four times in the event. A lot of improvement has been made since so let's hope I can get through this one, although recent form and fate would caution against any great optimism. In this race, even though I am misled within the first kilometer by an official to ski down the wrong trail (due to the combination of me leading the field and them not being ready) everything else happens satisfactorily.

I have had a week between races here and I have been able to do a lot of wax testing and ski testing to get the most out of my equipment. I decide to try a different strategy here-ski at my 75% level, keeping in control, with the intent to keep the heart rate slightly lower and to keep my thinking patterns more regular when it comes to the transitional stage from skiing to shooting. The first half of the race goes okay. I shoot a lot better than the race on the previous day, but I know I can still shoot better and faster. There are four shooting stages and instead of having penalty loops in races like these, they add one minute for each shot you miss. The course they decided on is the absolute hardest they could possibly make it.

If you don't know the phrase "high marking" it is commonly used in Alaska when snow machines (also known as snow mobiles) run straight up the side of a mountain and each driver tries to go higher than the previous one then turn and streamline the down route. Well, I can almost hear the Piston-Bully driver with one of those mischievous laughs as he high-marked the trail 200 meters before the shooting range and again immediately after it. Absolutely ruthless!

There's nothing like a mega-steep climb straight up the side of a mountain that takes two minutes, followed by a hairpin turn (180' around a flag at the top) and a screaming fast downhill that gives you about 10 seconds to bring your heart rate down before shooting. Then after shooting in a hurry, before you can even think, you are back to climbing up a solidly steep wall of mountain at the start of the loop. (Piston-Bully is the main brand of trail-grooming machine, like a Zamboni at ice-rinks.)

Race Reflections

After five loops, four shooting stages, and skiing up and down the side of that mountain a total of 10 times, the finish line finally arrives. Solid skiing and decent shooting earns me 4th place overall.

It has been a very interesting trip. Dealing with all kinds of mental factors, coming from a skier's background, there are so many more "little mental things" in biathlon that can easily mess up a good day.

For instance, you can dry-fire for hours, spend months doing combo drills at the range, shoot thousands of rounds in training. But what you cannot practice for is what the fans do while you ski, and especially shoot. Yeah, there are times during training when the range is full and there is a lot going on in the background, but it's completely different in a competition. I'd say that is one of the most difficult things that I am learning to deal with.

I have done a lot of intervals, training hard coming into the range and shooting quickly. Physically I can pace the shots, take the shots in-between every two gasps for air, and successfully hit them. But when you have guys you're catching on the ski trails there next to you shooting, and you can hear the guys come into the range that are trying to catch you on the slinky effect, it adds something that you really can't practice. It's another one of those things you just have to experience and learn to deal with.

One thing that the crowd started to do today when I came in for my first prone shooting is commenting on every one of my shots. My first shot is a hit, I then hear a loud "*Yyyyaaaaa!!*" my second shot comes directly after and is also a hit, I hear again the chant "*Yyyyaaaaa!!*" I know they are just being fans and it's a part of the sport but then I start to think stuff like, *"Wow they're calling out my shots, sure wouldn't want to disappoint them,"* while taking my next shot and so I then miss it. Stuff like that is unexpected and can't be practiced or trained for no matter how much time you spend at the range.

It doesn't bother me when there is a lot of noise, because it all meshes together and is easier to block out. But when you're the first to come in and shoot for the day and you're the only one shooting, and the entire crowd is focused on your every move, it's absolutely nerve-wracking. Yet, it's absolutely critical to experience these types of scenarios and the best place to get that experience is in Europe. If I were in America, first, it would be hard to find an actual biathlon race; second, even if I found one, there wouldn't be any fans. So in a way, I came here for these types of nerve-wracking, mind-twisting experiences, which I will hopefully benefit from later.

After racing the 20k in the morning, in the evening I venture out for one last classic ski in beautiful Realp. They have more than enough snow here and it makes for great classic skiing. Since biathlon only uses skating technique I really enjoy getting out on my classic skis during some training days. Classic skiing utilizes many of the same muscles, but the motions are different, which allows recovery in a way from the skating muscles. There is a lot of great cross-over benefit between the two skiing disciplines.

Hochfiltzen World Cup Venue

I drive from Realp to Hochfiltzen, in Austria in order to meet with representatives from the USBA in the hope of a better understanding towards why it is so difficult for the USBA to allow me to participate in IBU events. I am watching for the border patrol stamping my passport. Thankfully, on the way into Liechtenstein and Switzerland, they did not stamp my passport. The German government has not yet approved my visa to stay in the European Union and the rules state that you can only stay in the EU for three out of every six months. Since the Austrian border did not stamp my passport on the way out, nobody can verify how many days I actually spend in or out. For five months prior to racing in Switzerland, I have been what we Americans consider an "illegal alien." If I had been caught, I would have most likely been incarcerated then deported to the U.S.

The day-long drive gives me time to think and reflect. At one fuel station I walk in the building to pay and feel like a normal average everyday human again, the sense that I'd lost touch with the reality of life come to the front as I see more people around. Realp is a nice place, but with so few people around, I had unconsciously removed myself from the world, much like we U.S. skiers often experience after a full week in West Yellowstone over Thanksgiving. On the road I spend a good deal of time reminiscing what my thoughts and expectations were over a week ago while in route to Realp. The four race experiences within those 10 days certainly changed my perspective and challenged me mentally beyond anywhere I could have expected. I enjoy the return drive as it serves me well.

On the way to O-town after driving most of day, I arrive at the little farming town of Hochfilzen. I then followed the signs to the biathlon stadium to find out that the two officials I need to meet have had schedule changes and are not at the venue. I spend a chilly night sleeping in the stadium parking lot with temperatures dipping down to -15° C. In the morning at 6:30 am, I wake up to a loud noise and feel the van quake. Less than a minute later I am outside standing in the cold parking trying to convince the tow truck that I will willfully move my van. They were clearing the space to set up the party tent for the world cup events taking place and I was parked right in the middle of the lot. I wash up and thaw out in the stadium bathroom, then wait for the two USBA representatives to complete their work as course and stadium inspectors.

One of the men is the Director of USBA who had offered to bring my rifle from the States with him. Unfortunately, my rifle is still going through U.S. Customs and has not made it to Marc

Sheppard's shop yet, so the director was not able to transport it. The director sits with me to discuss my situation and he expresses genuine concern at the way the rules of engagement are preventing me from qualifying for the IBU cup races. Although I feel his sympathy, he assures me there is nothing he can do to directly intervene in the process. If the USBA board approves my request then I can compete. If they refuse then I am in the same position I am currently in. Our conversation is calm and unemotional and he suggests I continue to compete in as many ski races and local biathlon events as possible to make the most of my experience and time in Europe.

Wax Tech Extraordinaire!

After the meeting I head back to Obertilliach. Only kilometers before the city I get that old-fashioned feeling of "I'm almost home." It feels good to be back, and with the second IBU Cup race scheduled in a few days, there are hundreds of athletes from countries around the world occupying the village. Over 40 nations are in attendance. The U.S. is still not allowing me to compete, so there is no chance I can even get access to the trails because of the event—or is there? With a lifetime background of finding ways of doing things after being told no, I find a way. Holmenkol!

Through them I receive the credentials granting me access to the trails, trainers/ officials areas, and also giving me a place in the wax area. It could easily be said "Typical American, abusing work rights for personal use." If the U.S. would let me race instead of letting two of the 4-6 U.S. entries go unused, I wouldn't have this problem, plus I do use the time on the trails for testing waxes, and I will later post my wax recommendation for the day on the board at the wax area entrance.

At this point I realized that there weren't any wax reps following the IBU Cup circuit. Wax reps only seem to follow the World Cup circuit. I quickly learn how fast someone in my position can come to be needed on the spot, to either sell wax right then, or be of urgent service to many athletes who are needing fluoro applied to their bases moments before the start. Fluoro is an expensive powder that has the ability to greatly increase the speed of a ski.

Comparing the numbers of athletes competing in the World Cup to the number competing in IBU cups there are about 40 more on average in the IBU and yet no wax technicians. As a result of my personal presence I have numerous trainers come to me asking how much I'd charge to wax their athlete's skis. It is not in my job description to do this service, but I don't mind it. I like helping out, and the money turns out to be good. Having a strong skiing background, I am able to go far out on the trail and test different waxes to find the one that suits the snow conditions best.

Dobbiaco

At the IBU cup I meet two brothers, Trevor and Matt de Freitas, who are skiers from Australia and we strike up a friendship. They don't have any transportation and so after the event I offer to drive them from O-town into Italy to the town of Dobbiaco.

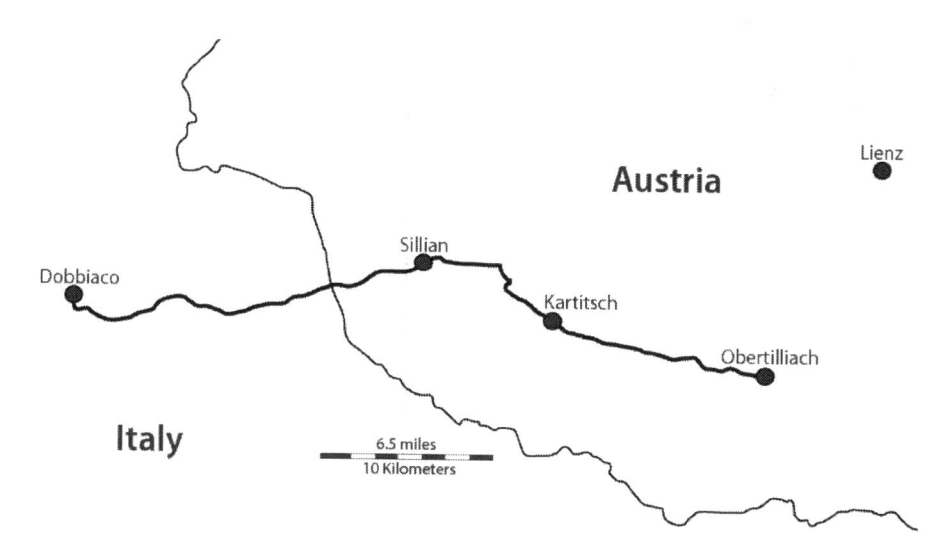

Dobbiaco is the place where Ole Einar Bjørndalen is based for living and training. His wife's family owns a hotel resort there.

Matt, Andy, and Trevor (left to right).

The ski trails in Dobbiaco are excellent. There are lots of wide, well groomed, twisty, turny, up- and down-hills. It's a really fun course, but challenging. The three of us cruise the loops then head up a famous scenic ski trail that runs directly, down a steep-walled rocky ravine. From the trail head it's mostly uphill. It is after we decide to turn back that the experience goes from relaxing and enjoyable to exciting and hazardous.

Since there are no designated directions on the trail, and some sections where they are necessary, it makes for an interesting return. Trevor, Matt, and I end up racing most of the way back, since there are so many downhills. The hazardous part is mostly fear of crashing into the touring skiers who are either coming in the opposite direction, skiing in our direction, or have crashed and are trying to get on their feet. We have three close calls but manage to stay accident-free.

The following day after returning from Italy I devise my own time trial to mirror the IBU cup event, which took place the day before. I time trial the same course and format as the 20k individual biathlon race. It is really tough due to the continuous snowfall and skiing all 5x4k loops alone. I tough it out, skiing strong, solid, and swift. I also shoot incredibly well, hitting 17 of 20. Two of the three misses are the last and final two shots when I am most fatigued near the end. I use my stop watch result, including the three minutes added to my time (for three penalties) to compare to the final results from the race the day before. I would have placed within the better half of the field, which is really a confidence booster, considering I had no one to chase, pace with on the trail, or draft behind on the downhills.

Having Fun, Remembering Roots, European-style

While I am out there I see some of the Norwegian men's Biathlon National Team exercising their "extreme skiing" skills through heavily forested areas on their classic gear. They are flopping all around in the deep snow, head over heels, causing mini avalanches, while the rest of the team (including the trainer) is laughing hysterically. It reminds me of high school in Alaska, especially after the races held in Seward out at Mile 12, or in Valdez. The meters of fresh untouched snow makes for fearless skiing and tumbling fun. After my session is complete, I stand at the bottom of the hill and watch the remaining guys tumble down the steep, wooded slope and contribute to the team's roaring laughter.

I am really coming to see that one of the major differences between the elite in Europe and those in the US is the amount of fun and camaraderie they share in training. When we were kids (most elite skiers and biathletes start skiing when they're kids) we played around on our skis, going off of jumps, shooting down dangerous hills, laughing in the face of danger, and when you crashed everyone laughed and there was often an unwritten competition: the bigger the crash the more glorious and fun it is.

With the massive amount of snow that has dumped this week it is pretty safe to dive head-first into any snow pile, which makes ski jumping and cliff skiing a blast because the chance of injury is low. There might be a high chance of breaking a ski, but low bodily-injury risk. Also, these guys work hard and when there is snow like this, it's a way of remembering the 'good ole days' when they had three-pin bindings and skied their hearts out making their parents force them back to the car or into the lodge because skiing was so much fun. Now, with the heart rate monitors, strictly-followed training logs, and results expectations, where is the fun in skiing? In this case the trainer seems to remember his roots and he takes part.

My sense is that such a "child-like" approach to training enables Europeans to retain a youthful approach and enjoy their training, allowing them to continue in the sport longer than most Americans while remaining mentally refreshed.

I have also noticed that I am among the younger competitors over here whereas in the US I am generally considered old. The average age of competitive athletes in Europe is definitely older than in the States and I am sure this contributes to their dominance. Not only do the older athletes have more experience and greater mental capacity to deal with the peculiar challenges within the Nordic disciplines, but they also have years of training to build their muscle strength and cardiovascular endurance. This is what gives consistency within these sports. Yeah, there are the athletes who shoot to the top quickly, but their results have greater fluctuation. One weekend they may be racing really well, finishing at the top of the results and the next weekend finish mid-field or near the bottom, whereas if observing the older, more seasoned world class athlete will finish with a decent result in all events.

I've thought about this difference a bit and while the fun element of training will certainly contribute to longevity in the sport, that is surely not the whole picture. In the US the way the system is set up it goes, high school racing, college racing, then either quit or if you are good enough a professional club/factory team. Only rarely are new people added to the U.S. Ski Team squad. So, basically, most American skiers retire from the sport between age 21 and 24. But in Europe, based on my living in O-town and seeing so many different national teams coming and training, there are lots of athletes on both their A-squads and B-squads (development team) who are in their 30's.

The sheer numbers of athletes in training from each country who are held in reserve, improving and preparing for their chance at the World Cup is much greater than in the U.S. There are good quality support systems in these other countries and a level of faith in each athlete that they will improve, which is also important. In the U.S. we only have a handful of guys, or fewer, on a development squad, and their status can change from year to year, so they are also training with a sense of fear and competition with each other, rather than a sense of camaraderie. On the Glacier sometimes there are as many as 80-100 Russians, many in the national team gear, all training hard!

This is a sport of endurance and it's biologically proven that we peak in these sports between ages 27-33. If trained right, the body can become very strong, with much stamina, which allows athletes in their 30's to rise to the top of the World Cup. This is possible through the European countries' national team funded support systems, but the U.S. government does not support any sport, so we are left to fend for ourselves. Our sports have to find private sponsors to stay alive. We just don't have the money to have bigger development squads. That causes athletes to quit because they cannot manage the financial burden and training/racing motivation on a yearly basis.

In just this one week in Obertilliach the snow-fall set a new 50-year record for the whole month of December. Two nights in a row a meter of snow fell and I had to dig for 30 minutes before I could even get out of my parking space and that is with chains on the tires. Over the past seven days it has snowed five. For three days the roads were closed within 1k of both exits because of the many avalanches and trees that have fallen on the road due to the heavy snow-fall. Some of the teams who are living outside of O-town have to actually ski to the race, and some of the trainers show up wearing snowshoes. My trainer, Joe, couldn't make it to the race because of four avalanches between his house and the range. It was a winter wonderland and will make a very beautiful Christmas Holiday.

Andy beginning to uncover his van.

Winter Lodging and Klister Chaos

Since the racing season has begun I've found reasonable lodging in O-town, where I continue stay every time I return to my home-base. It is called Haus Gatterer Obertilliach, owned by a nice young couple with two little kids who also live there and do all the cleaning and maintenance. It is a huge place with about 24 rooms. It also has several wax rooms in the basement, and it is booked all the time with skiers and biathletes. I pay rent to them but also solicit my wax service in the basement to teams. That wax service business has turned out to be a great financial support, allowing me to keep myself in a warm room with food on the table.

One night in the hotel a "classic" experience unfolds involving klister. Klister is designed for and works best for classic skiing in wet and icy conditions. It has such strong sticking properties however that it can also be used for such things as temporary glue or tape and it works like "stop leak" in plumbing emergencies. On the more sinister side it has been used for many practical jokes such as applying it to the bottom of a friend's ski pole baskets when they're not looking. When your joke victim uses them next, they have snow constantly sticking to the bottom of their poles.

The incident at the hotel is actually an accident which involves my ski (with a fresh layer of klister) falling onto a cushion seat on a chair. Right after it happens I leave the hallway I am applying it in to get the base cleaner/ klister remover. Upon my return to clean it off, a British skier named Alan Eason (in his boxer shorts) has found the seat unoccupied and decided to sit down. He thinks I am kidding when I tell him he has sat in a bunch of klister, but when he stands up and his boxers almost come off because of the stickiness he becomes a little upset with me. I'd always check my seat before sitting down around ski season.

Time Trial with the Brits

The day following my own private biathlon time trial, I compete in a classic race/ time trial with the best British Army biathlon team named "1LSR." There is good energy on their team, and sometimes I have to hold back a smile listening to their strong

English accent. Much like many American teams and races like this, the trainers race also. The way the trainer, Marc, sets it up is that each person is scheduled to start in 20-second intervals with Marc himself going first to make sure that he will finish first to record each athlete's time as they come in behind him. Seconds before Marc takes off he puts the clipboard with the start list in the snow and sets a stop watch on top of it.

I am scheduled to start second-to-last, and as my time approaches, I stand looking down at the ground waiting for the stop watch to read my start time. The format is a full-on 7.5k, with 20-minute recovery, followed by another 7.5k race the same course as the first. I hammer the whole 7.5k as hard as I can, passing all the athletes and finishing strong. I am feeling great, despite the hard effort that I put forward the day before racing the 20k in deep un-groomed snow.

When it comes time to race the second 7.5k I am ready and this time I lengthen my stride and glide out even more. It is working like a charm and again I pass all their athletes long before the finish line. It sure feels good to get out and ski hard on classic skis again. After doing so much skating for biathlon, my skating muscles are pretty worn out. In the results, there are almost two minutes in between me and Marc, who was the best of his athletes. And Marc was more than three minutes ahead of all his athletes. It's a lot more fun to train like this with a team rather than alone.

Sharing Christmas Globally

Our Christmas dinner is shared by 4 Aussies, 3 Greenlanders, 2 Brazilians, 1 Estonian, 1 New Zealander, and 1 Canadian/ New Zealander…and 1 American. Many different languages and dialects are flyin' across the table. Some of the Aussies and one of the Brazilians have never been in a place with snow during Christmas before. All of them are here for one reason…to ski.

Later that evening Trev, Matt, and I decide to take in some local events and, to our surprise we walk all over town and find it to be completely silent until we stumble into the Catholic church cemetery. I don't know what we are doing hanging out in a cemetery at 11 on Christmas eve, but we are here. The church bell rings non-stop for 15-20 minutes so we meander around to take a peek inside. None of us are Catholic and this is the only church in town. As we walk near the door we notice that there are lots of people entering and so we walk in with them and sit in the cathedral. It is absolutely freezing cold in there and it looks like the church is under renovation due to its old age. We end up staying for the entire service and not really understanding all that is going on or much of what is talked about.

Italian – Swiss Trip

The next morning I pick up Leandro, Mica (pronounced "Meeka" (both of Brazil) and Ben Falconer (New Zealand) at 7:00 am in O-town and we begin our trek out of Austria, driving halfway into Italy. They are scheduled to start in a FIS sprint race in Fiera di Primiero. The route is only 150k, but takes a solid four hours due to the narrow, slick, windy, mountain Italian roads. At one point we have to put the chains on and use them for over an hour just to keep moving forward.

The route reminds me of an elongated roller-coaster. But we arrive with just enough time for the three of them to get their stuff on and test out the course before the race. The race is in a downtown area with lots of trucked-in snow to form a 400-meter loop crammed between tall buildings and local shops.

They have to individually ski three loops as the preliminary round. Only the top 16 finish times for men and women will continue on to the elimination heats. Unfortunately for my friends they do not ski fast enough in their prelim to qualify. As soon as the results are posted we pile back into the van and continue our trek west toward Switzerland. We drive for the majority of the day, only stopping for fuel and one stop for real Italian Pizza.

We decide to stop at the 4-Star Hotel, a few hours shy from reaching our final destination and rest. Leandro and Ben believe it is a real 4-Star Hotel, but I think the name is a joke. The sign along the Autobahn had four stars in a line with the word Hotel under it. Real 4-star hotels have a real name. After pulling off the Autobahn in the town of Milano Italy, parking, and entering the building, I think everyone is surprised. It looks like a cheap imitation of a nice hotel. The receptionist tells us they have only two rooms available. We are the only vehicle in the parking lot. From the parking lot the hotel looked to be somewhat large but the hallways and number of rooms tell a different story. In the morning we gobble down some of their breakfast, pack up and leave without ever seeing another guest in or around the hotel.

Before leaving Milano we stop at a grocery store to pick up a few things for our stay at Campra, Switzerland. I am craving a soda and find some flavors on the shelf I have never seen before. I buy a soda, but am unable to drink it. I now send this as a message to my former boss "Starkey" at The Odom Corporation/ Coca-Cola Distributing in Anchorage: NEVER bring in any sodas that are cinnamon-flavored. I end up using it to clean the corrosion off the van's battery terminals—amazing to watch, but disgusting to think about.

That afternoon we arrive at Campra, way up in the mountains, and find the ski trails in a sun-protected valley to be just what we were hoping, and also very cold. The snow temperature is −22° C (-8° F) and those who have been to Campra will have a better understanding how the humidity can still reach high levels in these conditions. There are a lot of little open water creeks dropping from the high mountain passes. And through the middle of the ski trails there is a small river which is also still open and flowing. With such cold air and snow temp and the water's warmer temp, there is almost always a slightly humid fog lingering around.

FIS Campra

I've come to Campra to take part in some International Ski Federation (FIS) races. To keep a decent ranking on the FIS points list I must compete in at least four FIS races every year. It will be a welcome change to race in a skiing event where far fewer problems can occur, given that there is no rifle involved.

The first race is a 1.3k classic sprint. Besides the time trials and disastrous biathlon races, this is my first official ski race of the season. Before the start I test wax, post the Holmenkol recommendations on the main door to the wax room and apply the top layers of race waxes to my best Salomon classic skis and let them sit outside to cool as I grab my warm-up skis and head out for a solid warm-up. My skiing experiences and knowledge leads me to believe "the shorter the race, the longer the warm-up."

I go out for my warm-up and do some 1-minute pick-ups, thinking I am on a 2.5k loop, but it does not seem to be turning and with less and less time on my watch before my start time I am far from the stadium and starting to panic. It takes me about 20 minutes of "short cuts" to get back to the stadium and this is almost like a race in itself. In sprint races every second counts and if you miss your start the clock for your time is still going until you come across the finish line. It is common in sprint races to have many finishers within the same second during the preliminary round.

With less than 10 minutes before my start time I am still 1k from the stadium and continue to ski at race pace all the way back. Only one problem left: I have only five minutes to take my warm-up clothes off, go all the way to the other side of the stadium to grab my race skis and weave my way back though the maze of people and course markings to get into the start area. I don't know how I manage but I make it there and with 30 seconds remaining I push my way through the ski marking and hurry the guys to attach the electronic timing chips to my ankles, put my skis and poles on and then begin the race almost instantly.

Sometimes it is good not to have time to mentally think before a race as I like to call it "not letting yourself get the chance to over-think the situation." In this rush to get there on time I end up spot-on with my stride, double pole, and rhythm. I ski that 1.3k loop almost perfectly how I imagined I can ski it. I feel great all the way around and I even pass the guy who started 15 seconds ahead of me. With over a hundred men from 14 countries and more than 10 Swiss ski clubs all aiming for the top 16 places to make the eliminations, I, skiing as "the U.S. Ski Team" post the 12th fastest time of the day.

It feels really good to see my name posted on the big board selected to start again in the elimination rounds. When the time comes I do another warm-up (this time staying close to the stadium) and prepare to go round two. I am all set, standing on the line with three other guys looking down the ski trail with four separate lanes ready to lay it all out, fighting for the top two places to go on to the next round. Bang! The gun goes off and we are all hammering down the track side by side.

About 10 strides into the race the velcro on my left pole strap comes loose (first time this has ever happened). I must not have folded it down all the way, probably because I was nervous. Luckily at 130 meters there is a sharp turn followed by a slight downhill where I can tighten it quickly. After rounding the corner gripping my left pole with a "death grip," I am in 3rd and fall a little behind the first two guys as they are in a tuck while I mess around with my pole strap.

The moment it is tight and secure I dive into a huge double-pole stride, leaping forward and slamming my poles down with as much force I can create. It works like a charm, and I am right on the tails of the first two guys. From there we ski in a very tight pack up the short steep hills, scrambling around trying every move to get an inch ahead of each other.

Meanwhile the guy who had been in 4th makes a dash inside on one of the uphill corners, almost sending himself down the steep, ungroomed area, but he manages to keep one ski on the trail and stay in the race. The rest of the race is tight and we all finish within 1-2 seconds of each other. Unfortunately, I do not make the cut and am done for the day. I do receive my best FIS sprint points ever, thanks to my preliminary race.

The following day's race is a 15k Skate or also known as freestyle. The course consists of three laps on a hard 5k loop. The start list has been created based on FIS distance-race points and there are only two guys younger than me that have better points. As I've already mentioned it's been evident that in America I am starting to be considered one of the older skiers, but here in Europe, I am still one of the youngest.

Because of the course and its intense climbs I decide to use ski poles (Infinity Elites) that are 2 cm shorter than my normal skating height. The temperature has warmed up significantly and after my ski wax testing I post Holmenkol Matrix Red with the mid-powder as an added fluro. That combo turns my Salomon race skis into rockets. Even though the air temp had risen, the snow temps are still relatively cold and it is important to have a durable wax to battle the friction and sharp crystal structure of that cold snow.

My first lap goes well—solid skiing, good rhythm, and no lactic acid. I even catch the guy who started 30 seconds in front of me, a member of the Swiss National Team. He is a jerk to pass; first taking the inside of a corner when I call it out to pass on that side, then after skiing the long way around, and just before a slight downhill my ski tip collides into his. On the next climb even though he is slightly behind, he stomps his ski on mine. I take a few quick strides to get away from him and he keeps kicking my pole. What a jerk, luckily my pole doesn't break and I am able to ski away from him. His behavior is completely outside the normal courtesy of racing.

Over the second and third loops I ski well, but as I usually don't ski my best in December/ early-January, I have a hard time racing all-out. From all my years of racing I see a pattern, and that is my performance always peaks from mid-February to the end of March. Even though I don't feel I had my best race, I am satisfied with my performance.

Turning Mountains into Speed Bumps

Moments before the start of this 15k, I almost broke down in tears. It was one of the most important races I have ever competed in, and I finished a decent 12th. With the pressure of the race over I am finally able to reflect. A year ago, I was not feeling well mentally, not performing well physically, injured with a bum knee, and knowing surgery was near with the unknowns of rehabilitation looming.

There are still unresolved issues between me and my former University Team trainer and athletic department. Not being able to run for two years (and running being my biggest stress reliever and overall volume hours in my yearly training logs) unable to even walk for all of April, May, and part of June, along with all the energy and stress included with moving to Europe (right when I could walk without crutches or a cane), learning a language, and trying to compete in biathlon when my country's organization is resistant. My emotions nearly spill over me like a tsunami as I stood on that start line.

As 2008 draws to a close I can say I am content, partially due to the sprint race acting as confirmation that I persevered, overcoming all road blocks, both physical and mental, which I then turned into speed bumps and sailed over. It's not easy going though life, and nobody says it is, but even though this ski trip and living in Europe has been a very memorable time of my life, it has also been difficult and challenging.

CHAPTER SIX
Work, Travel, Race

Father Arrives

2009 has arrived and with it comes some good news. My rifle has finally arrived at Marc Sheppard's shop and my father is flying into Frankfurt to personally deliver it to me. At last I will have my own rifle again.

On January 5th I load up the van and depart O-town, accompanied by Ramsey, with the frosty headlights pointing toward Frankfurt Germany. After driving seven hours headed north, mostly in a blizzard, we arrive at the Holmenkol Factory. There I hand in the money I have made from selling the first order of products and pick up another order of product (about 10,000 euros/ $14,000 USD worth). By that time it is dark and we haven't had time to stop and eat, so we drive around the block to the ALDI supermarket and pick-up some bread, jam and some other random items that we wolf down while sitting in the parking lot. As we eat we watch the snow blowing across the windshield and prepare to drive a few more hours north to reach Frankfurt.

The autobahn is no fun to drive on in this weather and, to make it even more challenging, the van isn't performing well. The day before we left the driver side headlight burned out, and for a few months now the passenger side windshield wiper has not been working. After competing in the traffic, at autobahn speeds ranging between 75-80 mph, with low visibility because of the van's problems combined with the weather, we are really pleased and relieved to arrive at the Europa Hotel in Frankfurt.

My father will meet us here and he has already booked accommodation. It feels a bit strange to be staying in a skyscraper after living in such small villages located in the mountains. Both Ramsey and I agree that the van looks even more out of place than we feel, parked on the street between a Mercedes and a BMW.

Ramsey has accompanied me on this trip because he needs to get himself and his three large bags, weighing about 80 lbs each, two small bags, huge ski bag (10 pairs of skis), rifle case, and two full ammo cases to the airport to meet his coach who is flying in to join him before going on directly to the World Cup. It is very convenient that my father is flying into the same airport just one day before Ramsey's trainer.

My father arrived in Frankfurt on an Air France flight. He took extra precautions to make sure there would be no problems getting my rifle through customs and into Europe with his checked baggage. All the bags had arrived but one—the bag with my rifle, which seems to be lost in Paris!

The following morning we drop Ramsey off at the airport and check to see if the missing bag has arrived. The bag has not arrived and so it seems my anticipation of holding the rifle in my hand will have to be extended for a little longer.

Altenberg to Service the Brits

Leaving the airport, we head east to the town of Altenberg, located in the corner where Germany meets the Czech Republic and Poland. Following the 'magical work' I had performed, at the second IBU cup in Obertilliach, with the Brits' skis and wax, they have requested me to be their wax tech for the future IBU Cups and the next race is in Altenberg. Upon arriving we find the British have arranged accommodations for both my father and I, which is a nice change from my usual experiences.

We are given the fanciest 3-star hotel I have stayed at the entire time I've been in Europe, with all our meals provided. Compared to the past week's living arrangements, where I'd been living in a one-room apartment, sleeping on a couch and sharing it with three other guys, this is like royalty.

The Altenberg event is the fourth IBU Cup event for the year and as the first race arrives I have all the British athletes' skis waxed up the best I know how. In the few days leading up to the event, while the athletes were training, I spent my time testing different wax companies' products and different ski base grinds. From these tests, on the specific snow the athletes will be racing on, I identified the best grinds and wax for the race.

The night before the first race Walter Pichler, the British coach, had each of the athletes wax a pair of their own skis to his wax recommendations and gave me a second pair from each for me to wax. After trying them, out of the four men and three women, all but two selected the skis I prepared.

This convinces Walter that I know what I'm doing. As with other Cup events, this Cup consists of two races held on successive days. At the end of the competition, six of the seven athletes place within the top 20%, qualifying them into the World Cup. It is impossible to tell just how much influence my wax work had on the results, but I am certain it has been a factor and this fills me with a sense of satisfaction.

If I cannot race myself because of the IBU restrictions, then at least I can help these guys get into the World Cup. Underneath that, however, is a feeling of loss, a knowing that I could have possibly done as well as most of them and qualified myself. I yearn for the opportunity to prove this and know it is blocked by a structured system. In one sense it seems like I am wasting my time here. On the other hand I'm learning a lot more about both skiing and biathlon from behind the scenes and get to watch many of the world's next generation elite perform in-person.

At one stage during the race I was standing on the course, in a very popular spot, where I could see all the racers go up a long hill, into the woods for 100m then emerge out of the woods onto a long downhill. One exciting confirmation of the impact of my wax serviceman work occurred when I witnessed one of the Brits being overtaken on the uphill portion by two French guys and a Russian.

After they emerged from the woods one by one my athlete was about 20-meters behind all of them at the top of the downhill. But on the downhill leg it became very evident to all who stood around me (French trainer and wax tech included) that my athlete's skis were gliding above and beyond anything that could be attained by their athletes. Nearing the bottom of the hill, my athlete had a 30-meter lead on the other three who had worked so hard to pass him earlier. There was no doubt that my wax expertise had helped the British in this case, quite considerably.

After the event Walter is approached by several people with comments on the evident speed of the skis that his athletes have used compared to the rest of the competition. The team departs immediately to Ruhpolding, Germany to compete in the next World Cup. Walter wants to bring me along, but I have to remind him that I didn't come to Europe to wax skis, but to compete in events as an athlete. If only I could be going with him as a competitor, but this is not my lot at this stage.

Wax Tech on Demand

The only British athlete who missed out on the cut is a woman named Olwen. She was the 2008 Great Britain Cross Country Skiing National Champion and, like me, she is attempting to stretch her athletic skills by taking on the shooting aspect to compete in Biathlon. As she is not going with the rest of her team to Ruhpolding she joins my father and I in the van as we head to Liberec, Czech Republic.

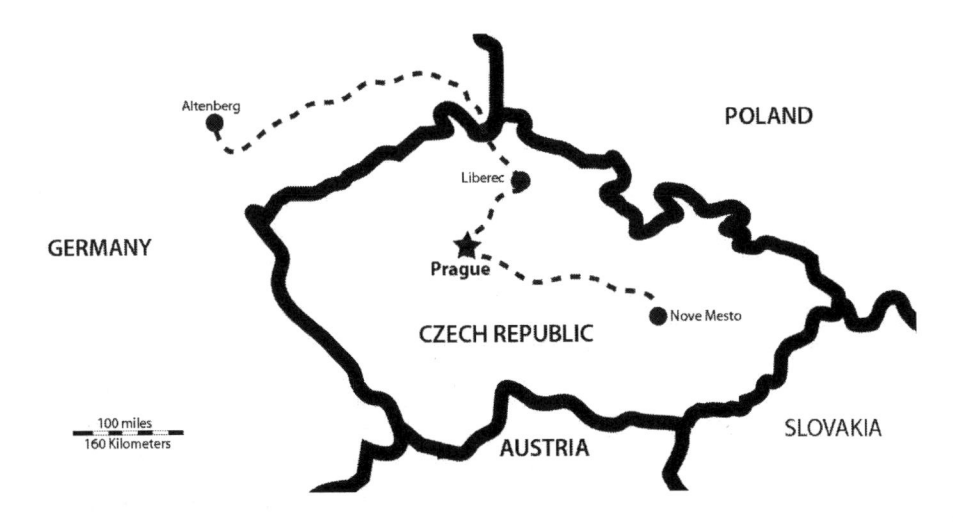

After arriving in Liberec (pronounced Li-ber-ets) we stroll around the upcoming race course for the Cross Country Skiing World Championships that will be held there in a month. Apart from the thrill of racing on a course set aside for the Worlds, I want to scope it out because there is an FIS race scheduled to begin at the end of the week which I am registered in. The Liberec course has a remarkable resemblance to 'Soldier Hollow,' the site of the 2002 Olympic course for cross country and biathlon, in Utah.

With time on our hands before the race, we pack up and head to Nove Mesto, deeper into the Czech Republic, where the 5th IBU Cup race is being held. Olwen is competing in the race and as I only have her skis to wax, I am able to spend lots of time selling some of the product I have brought with me from Holmenkol. When Leandro discovers that I am here he calls all of his South American amigos, and so the teams from Argentina, Chile, and Brazil pay me to prepare all of their skis for the races. Word of mouth spreads and I end up waxing skis for New Zealand and Greenland as well.

I spend a lot of hours skiing the trails in Nove Mesto, testing waxes and grinds. It is so far the hardest location I have experienced to determine a definite wax. The snow is mostly man-made and dirty. What works well for one loop doesn't work quite as well on the second loop. I find that the grind is more important for overall long-term consistent performance than any particular wax. My entire time in Nove Mesto, I spend all daylight hours either on the race course or in the wax room waxing skis like a maniac.

A Preview of the World Champs

After the races I load the van to prepare for the 3-4 hour drive on the autobahn back to Liberec. Leandro comes to me moments before I depart with some updated news about the races in Liberec that I will be competing in. He has just been informed that it will be a skiathlon, which is a mass start race with a 7.5k classic race then a 7.5k skate race, switching skis and poles halfway through the event with the race clock continuing to count. I tell Leandro that he will make a good travel agent someday, acknowledging his news about events and organizational travel skills. With that news

I will be able to prepare my race skis with an educated guess for the events' conditions.

I am tired! That is the best way I can describe my state of mind. Even though I've been skiing here and there on some of the best ski tracks in the world, the long hours I've spent in the past two weeks in wax rooms working has exhausted me. I've picked up a head cold and it has restricted my throat a little bit from taking the normal amount of oxygen and my nose has been plugged most of the time with snot. This is only the second time I've been sick in two years. I could barely stay awake last night as we drove from Nove Mesto to Liberec. Fortunately, my father is along to share the driving. After crawling out of bed this morning and driving to the ski tracks I find the race office and pick up my assigned race number/bib.

There is an old saying that could be applied to me right now. It is about how the mechanic works all the time on everyone else's cars, but the mechanic's own car is always broken down. I've waxed hundreds of skis and applied more fluoro powder in past weeks to many skis, but my own have been neglected. Also I don't know anyone else here that can help me test skis and waxes prior to the race.

Luckily I waxed my classic skis in Nove Mesto based on a wild guess of what the day's conditions would be and much to my luck it is perfect. But my skate skis are not prepared and I do not have enough time to do my best job or apply any fluoro layers so I end up going without.

The snow is somewhat wet and icy, so I apply klister to my classic skis and then a skier's nightmare occurs. It begins to snow dry snow. With little time to spare I grab the grip wax I always keep in my box for times like this when all hell breaks loose. It is made by the wax company START, and is called "Black Magic." In most conditions when using klister if you do not cover it with a thin layer of grip wax it will ice up and can sometimes cake up so badly that the tip and tail of the ski are above the snow completely.

At the time of mass start I cannot understand a single word the announcer is speaking. Even the countdown spoken in the Czech language sounds nothing like English or German. I basically wait for the moment when everyone else starts to move to know when it is time to go. Even though this race is only a common FIS race there are hundreds of fans who have showed up to watch and cheer along all parts of the course.

The significance of this race is that it is considered the pre-world champs as next month the Cross Country World Championships will be held on this exact course. Basically, we are the guinea pigs sent out to find any issues along the course and ensure the timing equipment works properly along the checkpoints. The snow is good, very firm and lots of it.

When the race begins I start out in a good position for the first 50-meters but during the first long uphill I get boxed in, finding it hard to gain an open space to even keep skiing in a straight line. On this first hill I don't ski that well, which is partially due to my weakness of fighting forward and skiing well in tight conditions, the weird feeling of classic skiing in stiff solid Salomon skate boots, and lack of a quality warm-up.

I must have been passed by the better part of the field by the time I reach the top, but what goes up must come down, and as my skis glide down the other side I pass a dozen people only because of my skis. From there on I keep moving up in the field. The course consists of three loops of a 2.5 km classic course and then another three of the same distance on a skate loop. On the third lap of the classic leg I end up catching and passing a pack of guys, which puts me in about 24th place at the exchange.

I ski into my lane and quickly switch into skating gear. As I round the bend in the stadium listening to the roar of the crowd, I quickly have to adapt my muscle groups from classic to skating. My legs have a good deal of lactic acid and I am thinking this skating part is going to be tough. But after the stadium bend and onto the straight trail leading up the long hill the skater in me begins to come alive. I feel good right away and sense that this feeling will continue to increase as the race goes on.

On the first hill I catch and pass two guys then over the top and down the back side I pass two more just because my skis are gliding better than theirs. A good feeling comes over me as I realize my skis are performing extra-well. On the skate course there are three hills and one of them is really similar to Soldier Hollow's 'Herman's Hill.'

After one skate loop I am feeling good with technique and strong with each stride. I find that by gliding longer I can slow down my heart rate and the lack of friction makes it easier to do that. I am racing on Holmenkol's Matrix Black/Red HF glide wax with nothing else and it seems to be doing an excellent job. Through my second and third lap I catch and pass more guys one by one.

As I ski down the home stretch in a V2 I am gaining on the 15th place racer. I nearly catch but have to settle for 16th place. After crossing the finish line I hunch over my poles and cough up some pretty nasty mucus along with blowing a long white-and-yellow snot-rocket out of each nostril. I think I am on the back end of this head cold, and by thinking in this optimistic way about it, I am sure it will be gone soon.

Something had caught my ear while racing that I could not understand out on the course. But when I finished I realized that three people on different parts of the course were calling out my name and cheering for me in English while I was racing. After the race I discover that they were Knut Nystad (former head coach of Denver University and brother of Trond Nystad, former head coach of the U.S. Ski Team), one of the coaches of the Hungarian Team with one of my Hungarian friends István Muskatal. Knut is here in Liberec testing skis and waxes for the World Champs, working for the Norwegian National Ski Team.

10k Classic

The following day I race in another FIS race, a 10k Classic. Being a Jedi wax master, I decide to use my race skis with regular hard grip wax instead of klister. I know my classic style and I would rather muscle the race and be on the slippery side. The weather is changing and it is snowing slightly as each racer is let out one by one. I know I will be safe from any icing up by using grip wax. It works out pretty well and I end up finishing well and am only 2.5 minutes behind Lukas Bauer (2007-08 Overall Cross Country World Cup Champion) who is the winner of the event.

Despite my sickness and work exhaustion from the prior two weeks, I am very pleased inside to have had the opportunity to compete again as the U.S. Ski Team in this International event. I, being the only representative of the United States in attendance against all the other skiers from six different nations, I am proud to have given my best effort on this course and am excited to see the real U.S. Ski Team compete here soon.

Only a few hours after the race we pack up the van once more and drive to Prague (spelled Praha in Czech). Praha is a really old city and especially beautiful at night. Leandro had driven Olwen to Praha earlier that day so we connect up with them. In the evening we walk around, ride on the subway system and eat at a pretty cool Irish Pub. Olwen is from northern Scotland and tells us all about the culture in that part of the world. Afterwards we walk over a bridge that was built around the year 1200, with biblical statues all over it that were sculpted in the 1500's.

Andy in the 10k Classic

British Championships

After meeting with the two Directors of USBA in December I had sent a further petition to the association, seeking approval to take one of the available spots at the IBU Cup events. Now I receive official word that my petitions to compete have been denied. All that is left for me now is to compete in as many events, outside of the IBU, as I can to get any more biathlon racing experience.

I had planned to compete in some FIS races in Slovakia over the coming weekend but have received an invitation to compete in the Great Britain Biathlon National Championships which are being held in Obertilliach. The British Biathlon Nationals is the largest National Biathlon Championships in the World for any one country and will serve as good experience for me. The British are pleased to welcome me to compete as their guest.

How strange it is that a foreign nation such as Great Britain, is so happy to welcome me and yet my own association seems to have its mind set on crushing my chances of competing. I feel terribly disappointed that USBA is not considering any of my results so far as being good enough to support my entry into IBU Cup events, but this also feeds the fire inside of me. I know that six of the British team have qualified for the World Cup and if I can beat some of those guys in their own championships then it will show my current level and ability.

Since many are individual start events, we are really out there, alone, racing the elements. This means there is not much difference between major and minor races when you are out on the course ripping down the hills and hammering the climbs. It doesn't matter what event I'm in, the point is that I keep going through the motions and feeling how the races go, so that I can take what I need from these experiences for improvement.

The British Nationals begin on 24th January and take place over more than a week. The first part of the event is the biathlon, with the second part being the cross-country skiing championships. The British typically have held their championships in Ruhpolding Germany, but now they switch every few years between there and O-town. The British have teams in training year around for these championships. They do have a training center up in Scotland, but I don't know if they have ever hosted their nationals there. The venues in Germany and Austria are so much better and professionally groomed with lots of snow that it makes sense to hold them there.

Given the reputation I've developed with the British as a wax expert, my services are in high demand. On the night before the first race I end up waxing 15 pairs of skis starting with base wax, finishing with top-end Fluoro. I am so exhausted from waxing skis that I only have time to wax one pair of my own. On the up-side, a benefit of only having one set of race skis is that I can really focus on my pre-race warm-up and preparation. When I have to choose between better skis or a better warm-up I will take the better warm-up nearly every time.

10k Sprint

The first race is a 10k biathlon and I start out on the first of three loops slightly scrambling to gain solid technique and, in the process, waste a lot of energy. I am able to calm down as I approach the shooting range for my prone stage. I shoot pretty well, and in less than 40 seconds on and off the mat. This is only the third time I've ever shot with my new rifle. For not having any rifle for over a month, to even hold and dry fire, I was okay hitting three of the five so I'm feeling pretty buoyant as I rock out two penalty loops. While I am doing that I hear the familiar voice of Joe, my trainer, cheering for me. I had written him an email three days before to let him know I would be racing here. This is the first race he has ever seen me compete in.

Back out on the course, knocking out my second loop, I feel quite a bit of lactic acid building up, but I keep truckin' around the course. I come into the range ready for my standing shooting stage and nail the first three, but catch a splitter (a half-in, half-out shot that doesn't trigger the sensor) to the upper right on my 4th and a solid miss on my 5th. After another two 150m penalty loops I am back on the course and this last lap feels like I have rocks for legs. Joe comes out on his skis to cheer me on around the course and it really helps having him support me in such a painful state, with a river of drool and snot stringing from my face.

After finishing and recovering enough to breathe right, see straight, and ski a warm-down the results are posted and I have placed 4th overall. What is interesting is that the three guys ahead of me and the three guys who finished behind me are all currently qualified in the World Cup and are headed to Korea in a few weeks for the Biathlon World Championships. Comparing them to the U.S. biathletes, there are U.S. guys who continue to compete in IBU cups trying to achieve the top 20 percent to qualify into the World Cup and if I can finish in the dead center of these 6 biathletes, I am at the level I have been training to improve into. This result, from my perspective, makes a mockery of the USBA's refusal to allow me to compete in the IBU events.

My father serves as a course marshal during the men's and women's race. This, combined with all my past weeks of waxing work for the national team as well as my performance in the first race, results in many people approaching us and thanking us for coming. There is more positive energy at these biathlon races than I have seen at most other biathlon races, especially those in America.

Later in the day I am approached by the director of British winter sports who introduces me to a 4-star general, who speaks to me about the possibility of adding me onto the British National Team. The general says he will contact his people back in England to get the options and info for getting me dual-citizenship.

One option that sounds good is if I could be sworn in as a British Officer because of my prior military service, my current inactive reserve status, and the amount of college credits I have achieved. Before I make any decisions I will be sure to read all the fine print. But to have them interested to that level and wanting me on their elite race squad, to possibly represent Great Britain in the future, is a high honor. As a British Army Officer, I would be assigned to a reserve unit with overlapping direct orders assigned to the National Team. That is what all the current members of the National team have done and that way they get a full time paycheck along with having all their racing expenses taken care of by the national governing body of the sport.

Another interesting thing that occurs is that Walter Pichler, the British national team coach, expresses an interest in me joining his racing squad, when only two weeks ago he only knew me to be a wax serviceman. It's like a 2-for-1 deal. If he acquires me in the future, he acquires a professional wax tech and an athlete for the World Cups and World Champs. Although doing both well is very difficult and quality of performance and concentration suffers.

12.5k Mass Start

The second day's race is a 12.5k biathlon mass start, where all the competitors start together rather than setting off at 30-second intervals. The best way to describe this amazing event would be to call it a 'cat and mouse game.' With four shooting stages and five ski loops, I have my best skis waxed up and spend extra time zeroing my rifle. In many cases, in biathlon, it's hard to have a good day of shooting and skiing at the same time but I feel that today I am going to ski well, so I hope that my shooting skills hold up as well.

As I stand in the front row of the mass start line, moments before the cannon goes off to start us, a guy behind me yells out, "A tooth brush? Is that an American thing to do to a rifle?" I reply by saying that I am sponsored by Oral-B and indicate this is my way of advertising. This got a big laugh. In the second biathlon race of the season I had taped a tooth brush to the stock of my rifle because the real bracket broke. Even though I now have a new rifle action, I'm still using the same stock; hence I'm still sporting the 'toothbrush' look in place of the lower hook on the butt plate.

There is no time for any more frivolity because the cannon goes off. I manage to sprint off the line, ski into the lead and enter the range with a lead of about 15 seconds. I will need it because my range times (on and off the mat) are still not at the level of the best Brits.

In the first shooting stage, I hit three and miss two and am the second guy to get off the mat. Simon Alanson, who was the guy who won the previous day's race and had been the first guy behind me skiing, is the first one to finish shooting. He also misses two and so we round out two penalty loops together and start again for our second loop. There are four guys who shot clean and we pass all of them within the first kilometer of skiing. Mark Raymond (Ramsey) is the last guy I have to pass before I take the lead again with Simon directly behind.

My skis are excellent and performing the best I could expect, I ski all of the flat and gradual sections without using my poles. All the time lost in the shooting range has been made up for and again I come into the range in the lead, but again I am going to need it because I miss three of the five shots and so have to do three penalty loops.

Marc Walker, a trainer of the best UK Army Team and former member of the National Team for 10 years, shoots clean on the second stage and passes the penalty loop area, looking at me and waving as he proceeds to glide down the hill through the tunnel and out of the stadium. Talk about antagonizing! It takes me almost the entire loop to catch him, but I do and I pass him. I am really feeling great on the ski trails even on the third loop. The only problem is that I am starting to lap some of the slower skiers and it is really congested on the steep up hills.

The third shooting stage is standing and I have a hard time keeping my muscles still. I hit two of the five, a bit disappointing, but anxious to keep my position in the top five I hammer out the penalty loops and skiing lap, still feeling strong and gliding long. The entire kilometer leading up to the range I have to ski without my poles, because the fingers on my left hand have gone numb and I need some feeling in them to sense the stock of my rifle for this stage of shooting. Surprisingly, I am able to maintain my speed keeping my distance ahead of Simon, the guy following him named Rob, and I also catch up to Marc just as we enter the range.

Again Marc shoots clean and I peg two of the five taking way too long on and off the mat. I still have a shot for the podium but it all depends on my final lap of skiing. Marc is too far ahead to catch, but Simon is within reasonable distance. I come out of the penalty loops with Rob right on my tails. As the final loop unfolds I sense I am skiing even better than the previous laps. I give my absolute best effort and hop-skate up all the hills gaining on Simon and Marc. I can hear Rob drift further and further behind me as the people cheer for him later and later in the distance.

Coming into the last 100 meters I am still about ten seconds behind Simon and end up finishing seven seconds behind him to finish in 3rd with a total of 11 misses. Marc had four misses in total, Simon had ten misses, and Rob had eight misses. Overall I am happy with the result primarily because I am feeling so good skiing again. Besides my own inner feeling of satisfaction, externally the guys are pleased to have invited me to provide a friendly challenge.

This was possible because of my prior skiing experience and all that I've learned about biathlon up to this point.

Left to right: Andy, Marc, Simon, and Rob.

20k Individual –The Blizzard

The night before the next race, the 20k, I wake up in the middle of the night with a terrible pain in my foot. I have had this problem before and it is brought on by a lot of impact with a combination of overuse. It is called 'plantar fasciitis' and in the morning I almost choose not to compete due to concerns about creating more damage and making the pain last much longer. However I decide to tough it out and compete anyway. I ski the whole race at level-3 (on a scale of 1-5, 5 being the max), caring for my foot, and keeping my heart rate in better control with hopes of shooting better. It works well.

The conditions are in my favor, being a complete white-out blizzard to the point where we can barely see the targets, causing everyone to miss at least five shots. In the 20k there are no penalty loops, but for each shot missed there is a minute added to your finish time and with 20 shots total it is smart to back off the skiing anyway. When there is consistent snowfall the ski trails become slower due to the increase in resistance of the skis. I feel this biathlon race is one of those races, which can increase skiing abilities. Lugging the rifle around on my back for five long loops in slow conditions is not easy and part of my motivation during the race comes from the aspect of how beneficial it is as a skier. I ski okay and shoot okay, hitting 13 of the 20 for 5th overall. I am eight seconds ahead of my good friend Ramsey from Australia who had just competed at a World Cup Biathlon event in Antholz, Italy three days before finishing in the top 20%.

Andy crossing the finish line of the 20k.

10k Pursuit Cross-Country

After placing within the top five in every event of the many biathlon races in the British National Championships, the day arrives when the pure cross-country ski races for the Brits are scheduled. Unfortunately, the top biathletes are not competing because they are headed to Korea for the Biathlon World Championships and the top British cross-country skiers are away competing in the

World Cup. I am still here, though, and I stand on the line of the mass start with the other athletes, ready to take on 5k of classic followed by 5k of skating.

Knowing that the 'big dogs' are not racing, my goal is to win by more than two minutes. If I am successful I will complete what American skiers call "pulling a Babikov," named after Ivan Babikov, meaning that, as a foreigner, you compete in a National Championships and win by one, two, or even more than three minutes.

In the classic leg I ski well even though I don't feel comfortable on classic gear in skate boots. I manage to extend my lead to about 1.5 minutes at the halfway point where the exchange point is to dump the classic gear off and put on my skating gear.

During the skating leg, my muscles start to really feel fatigued and so I slow down my tempo and decide to just cruise, gliding long on the flats and hop-skating the hills. Throughout that last loop I am cheered on by most of the spectators by first name. The announcer, who is heard over most of the course, has been keeping time in-between me and the second-place racer, so I also know how much of a cushion I have. As I ski the last 100m to the finish line I am hardly out of breath, I finish and quickly put on my warm-ups to start my warm-down. It is over three and a half minutes before second place comes into the finish with third on his heels. I have now successfully "pulled a Babikov."

The following day is the sprint competition and from my ski performances in the biathlon competitions and now the pursuit, the race committee will not allow me to compete, for reasons that I can perfectly understand. I enjoy the chance to watch and cheer, feeling well satisfied with my week's effort.

Czech Republic

As I've mentioned, with my chances of competing in IBU events over, I'm focusing my efforts on gaining as much biathlon experience as possible and my next target is a Czech Cup event that is taking place in Jachymov over Feb 7th and 8th. Just before leaving O-town with my father, to make the trip to Jachymov, I receive a letter from the German authorities stating that I must prove within three weeks that I have employment which no other Germans can perform. The time has finally arrived where I need a more formal work contract with Holmenkol and hope that it is satisfactory to the authorities. I contact Holmenkol about the more specific details needed in my contract and put off my personal visitation for now since it will take me in the opposite direction of the next races.

On the way to Jachymov, we stop in Regensburg for the night. All the British night events, waxing skis, and racing efforts have left me with an incredible need for recovery sleep. It is only 4:00 pm but I am so exhausted that I go to bed and do not wake until 8:00 am the next morning. In the morning my father and I arrive in a once-lively town called Ostrov. In the Ostrov area, there are ski tracks and the biathlon center in Jachymov, pronounced "*Yak-ah-mof*", the neighboring town, is up on the hillside.

The history of the area is rather fascinating. There are many ski trails and far below the surface of these trails are rooms and tunnels. Under the ground floor of the main Biathlon Center building and waxing area there are 10 levels that go down that were once used as a factory for handling uranium and plutonium.

The entire town of Jachymov looks like a ghost town and

possesses one of the largest mines to extract uranium and plutonium in the World. Despite the presence of such a deadly energy source, the buildings that appear to be occupied are heated by coal. This is one of the most unhealthy and toxic areas to reside in. We stay within a few kilometers of Jachymov and even in Ostrov the air stinks from the burning of soft coal and the water has a bad taste to it.

The first race in Jachymov is a 12.5k with four shooting stages, following the order of prone, prone, standing, standing. The sun comes out for this day and it changes the crystal structure of the snow just enough to create unexpected havoc among the racers. I was expecting similar conditions so prior to arriving at the venue I had selected the most aggressively structured skis with a warm wax with a combination of molybdenum and graphite. When my start time comes I cruise the first loop with a smooth, crisp technique.

Coming in to shoot the first time I miss my first two shots but nail the following three. With only two penalty loops to do I hammer the entire second lap and come into my second shooting stage with a much higher heart rate. I nail four of the five and it sure feels good to only have one penalty loop before heading out on the much harder section of the course that is set for the 3rd lap.

I notice my skis are slowing down due to the amount of tree crap I have skied over in the first two laps. The first two laps were on a section of thickly-forested trail. The dirt, sap, and air junk collects on the bases of the skis and slows them down significantly, but since I continue to pass other biathletes along the course I can tell it is happening to everyone. The snow is quite wet on

Andy taking a sharp corner during the race.

many of the downhill legs and I remember an old trick I learned from Adam Verrier (1994 Olympian and UAA volunteer coach) about the best way to master these sections: buckling your knees and riding the inside edges of both skis works a lot better than one or two flat skis gliding.

Unlike a mass start, in an interval start race (where each competitor starts at a different time) unless you have trailside support with stop-watches there's have no definite way of knowing where you're currently placed, but because I'm gaining on those near me, I enter the third stage feeling good and sensing that I'm in the front part of the field. The 3rd shooting stage is standing and I hit only two of the five shots, which is about my normal standing shooting stage right now.

The last two laps and final shooting stage pass well and I cross the finish line feeling somewhat tired, but satisfied. I didn't ski as well as I usually do, but I feel fine about it considering there weren't any crazy mishaps that I had to overcome in the process. When the results are posted, much to my surprise I win! —Finishing 1:17 ahead of 2nd, even with my eight penalties! The second place guy missed four and 3rd place missed only two.

I arrived to this Czech Cup not expecting to win.

To put it in perspective, though, none of the competitors in this race were good enough to make the IBU Cup races by Czech standards. The event is used as a stepping-stone for developing biathletes attempting to make the leap to the IBU Cup level. Even so, the margin of my victory, coming on top of the British success, adds to my confidence that I have improved and I feel there is much improvement I can still achieve.

The following day sees the 10k Sprint as it is known, which consists of three ski loops and two shooting stages. With my confidence level rising after the previous race, I feel good going into this race. Even though my bib number reads 92, I nearly miss my start. I cannot understand a single Czech word anyone says when they are calling the numbers up to the start line for each person to start in order every 30 seconds.

When I notice it is my turn to start I am standing halfway across the field with my warm-ups on, my skis and rifle still on the rack, and I have less than 30 seconds before my race clock will begin, with or without me. I have to really scramble and hurry to get to the start line on time. As I tighten my last pole strap, the clock shows my start time and I take off.

After the previous day, and with no new competitors arriving overnight, I am feeling very confident and ski the entire race comfortable with the mindset that I have this race in the bag. The conditions are a bit icier than the previous day and so instead of skating over some sections that I would normally, I play it safe by straight double polling. I come in to shoot very relaxed and focused, unfortunately missed two shots in each shooting stage. As I ski my last 3.3k loop toward the finish I keep my heart rate at an even Level 3-4 pace and I am comfortable.

I skied easier and more relaxed than I have in any biathlon race before and am satisfied with my skiing since it is in good control, but disappointed with my shooting knowing that I held expectations to hit more because I held a slower skiing pace. Plainly, I over concentrated and forced each shot, a common mistake. I needed to relax on the range also and let the shots come as they line up. Even though I missed four out of ten I still have an 18 second lead over second place, who only missed one, and 3rd place who only missed two. Among the normal awards I am given a pineapple. The other racers joke as they claim it is a locally grown Jachymov pineapple.

We decide to stay in Jachymov for one more day and I set out to explore the ski trails around the area. I am on my classic skis and decide to check out the outer loops beyond the main groomed trail system. Much like many other times when I have gone exploring on long runs (with the boys back in Soldotna, Alaska) this proves to be an interesting and unusual experience. I nearly get lost and find some crazy stuff. I follow random single track trails that go in and out of fields, forests, and up and down hillsides. I come across more abandoned, rundown buildings that are located in the most obscure places.

I see half a dozen little groups of 2-, 3-story stone buildings with windows missing, some boarded-up, posting hazardous symbols. Some of them are located in the middle of woods with no signs or roads to even drive a vehicle to. It's like they had been abandoned since the end of WWII when the workers just walked away. I suspect they are more uranium and plutonium manufacturing sites. They would make great hide-outs and I'll keep them in mind if I ever have such a need.

The area is kind of creepy with all the unknown facts about how toxic it might be. On the flip side, the skiing is really good, with plenty of snow, and great fun exploring the unknown trails on the border between the Czech Republic and Germany.

Dealing with the Visa

I am notified by the Wunderle family that the German government has issued me another letter scribed that I must present to them a work visa within two weeks or I will be deported. On the same day Holmenkol has notified me that my work visa paperwork is nearly complete so my father and I set off to Germany, to the Holmenkol headquarters. Christian, the CEO, continues to be of great support. He is very happy with the work I have been doing and arranges to have me taken on as a full-time employee of the company.

There is no guarantee that the German authorities will find this acceptable but it is the best chance I have at the moment. After all the forms are complete Christian and I discuss plans for the future including some marketing ideas I have for the United States and Canada.

After staying in Heimerdingen (the city where Holmenkol is located) for two nights, we continue our drive south-west arriving in Bubenbach and staying with the Wunderle family. I am able to get out and ski on the trails, which are in excellent condition. It had snowed the day before and the trails have been freshly groomed this morning. The next morning my father and I continue on to Freiburg, which is near the border of France, and turn in my work contract and the other documents required for my work visa to be approved.

CHAPTER SEVEN
Skiing World Championships

The cross country skiing world championships are held between Olympic years and this preview of the 2010 Olympics is in Liberec, Czech Republic, at the course where I had raced a month or so earlier. To make sure it is clear, these are not the biathlon championships, but cross country, and I am not competing, but the New Zealand team has commissioned my services as their wax technician. On arrival at the accreditation center I hand the officials my passport and tell them I am checking in.

The man responds by saying; *"You are listed twice, once for New Zealand, and once for USA."* I tell them to check me in for New Zealand. They take my picture and hand me the credentials. The following day I return to the accreditation center, hand them my passport, and tell them I am checking in for the USA. The guy hands me credentials as an athlete on the U.S. Ski Team.

Months ago, I had written to the director of Nordic skiing offering extra help at the championships and their response was *"Maybe, we'll let you know if we need you,"* and I never heard anything more. They had obviously registered me anyway so I give my father the U.S. credentials so he can access the waxing areas and to help out doing things.

It is a good thing I did because on the day of the sprints, moments before the start of the men's individual preliminary races, my father is walking near the parking lot entrance when he notices U.S. athlete Andrew Newell in a predicament. Andrew has been in the parking lot warming up and has forgotten his credentials on the other side of the gate. The guards are refusing to allow him into the athlete area, where he definitely needs to be to get through his gear check and to the starting pen.

My father walks over with his/my badge from the U.S. Ski Team and vouches for him to be allowed in. Andrew Newell is one of the best sprinters in the world and within a few short minutes of my father's act of kindness and workings of the universe, Andrew starts his race and posts the second fastest time overall at the 2009 Skiing World Championships.

My father watching the races at the World Champs

All the events are amazing and exciting to be a part of. I recognize most of the skiers from training on the glaciers in Ramsau and the Dachstein in Austria. Only now, they are skiing at their best. The World Championships in the year prior to the Olympics is considered an Olympic preview. Within the first three days of competition thousands of fans arrive forming lines of spectators that border the trails as well as filling the stadium.

Behind the ski courses and media cameras I am able to observe many different personalized race preparations, something I've been curious about for years. From seeing the Europeans on the Glacier and talking with most of them in the tram during their critical training time, and now witnessing them in high performance action, I learn quickly the answer to a question commonly asked by American skiers: What makes European skiers better than Americans? —They love to ski and enjoy skiing well. They don't care about what other people are doing, or change their plan or mentality because of a competitor's actions or statements. The best seemed to follow their own specific routines out of that same love for the sport that Ole Einar has.

A funny thing occurs today when I am out on the course cheering along with about 100 Czech fans in one area. As James Southam (Alaskan Grown Skier) races by I ramble off a bunch of English words of encouragement. Suddenly all the Czech people become silent and are staring at me. A voice comes out of the large group in broken English, *"Where you come from?"* I respond *"America."* After that they are all friendly and I speak to a few of them. Then an Australian skier skis by and I teach the Czech citizens how to cheer for the Australians: *"Aussie! Aussie! Aussie!...Oooi! Oooi! Oooi!!!"* is the call that goes up.

It snows continuously for the first four days of the events, which makes it difficult for the trail groomers and racers. Testing waxes and skiing around in those snowy conditions on those first days is not an easy task. It is impressive to see Kris Freeman of the U.S. Ski Team place 4th in the 15k classic trudging through deep, slow conditions. Another highlight of the World Championships for the U.S. Team is Kikkan Randall's silver medal in the Sprint. It has been many years since any Americans have finished anywhere near that well in any World Championships. Pete Vordenberg, the head coach, and I talk for a bit and he looks pleased. I also meet up with Charlie, who's been competing in the biathlon world cups all season and share a few laughs. He gives his best effort competing in the cross country sprint race and finishes within the better half of the field. My computer breaks down and on the same day my father meets a skier who can fix it. Roberto Carcelen is from Peru and he and his coach are affiliated with Microsoft residing in Seattle. We strike a deal, I wax Roberto's skis for a few races and they repair my computer.

Being a wax technician provides me with a rather unusual perspective of the whole event. I wake early, catch the first bus to the venue, wax skis, test waxes and ski grinds, provide individual support during and after competitions, all on a daily basis. It has been great but exhausting and I am left feeling satisfied.

One afternoon, during the World Championships, I happen to be back at the Liberec University, where all the athletes are staying. I'm in the food hall and just about to finish my meal in the nearly empty hall when a girl sits down at the table next to mine. She looks familiar and, after thinking for a few seconds, I remember that her name was Sylwia Jaśkowiec, from Poland. She skated the second fastest leg in the women's 4X5k relay the previous day.

I strike up a conversation with her: "Hello, congratulations on your race success this week."

"Tank you, I hod da bes skis," she replies in passable English.

"Besides the skis, it was obvious you are a very good skier. It was amazing to see you begin your leg behind and work your way to the front."

She smiles while blushing and simply says *"Tank you, it was good day"* and points to the chair next to her for me to join her.

We talk for a while, and for someone at that level, you would never know it by what she says or how she acts. She is such a lovely, open person, so natural and without any sense of superiority. I like her immediately. She informs me about a popular, large, public ski race in Poland the following week called the 'Bieg Piastow,' and the thought of attending it has a certain appeal.

Sylwia at the 2009 World Championships

Bieg Piastow

At the end of the Skiing World Championships I move into a local house that is owned by the Soukal family. I became great friends with the Soukals after a series of random events and contacts. It all started with Facebook. One of my Mexican friends had a network connected to Croatia and a girl from the National Biathlon Team of Croatia, Ana-Marija, ended up as one of my friends.

She was the one I was looking for months ago when I took my first train trip to Croatia and tried to buy a van there. Months later we met while skiing on the Dachstein Glacier in October. Charlie and I became friends with her and other members of her team. Her trainer is Karel Soukal and he always gave Charlie and me 'hard looks' as if he was signaling *"Stay away from my girls, they are here for training!"* Standing along the ski trails on the glacier, Karel could have been mistaken for Santa Claus, beard and all!

Three months later, when we were at the range in O-town getting ready for a competition, Karel noticed my rifle stock was made by his good friend, Marc Sheppard, and he spoke to me for the first time. He then offered me his home to stay in to live and train whenever I was in the Czech Republic.

So now, all these months later, my father and I stay at the Soukal's fully-equipped apartment under their home so I can train in Jablonec. Gabi Soukalova, Karel's youngest daughter (Czech female's last names end in "-ova"), has just returned from biathlon races in Ufa, Russia. Before Russia, she was in Canada for the World Junior Championships where she won a gold medal.

I get to know Gabi and find her to be a fantastic art student with an incredible sense of humor. She wants to compete in the Bieg Piastow 30k Marathon also and knows the route to the venue and has no ride. This convenient situation convinces me that I am destined to go and so she climbs into the van with my father and I to navigate our way to Poland, where the race venue is.

The Soukals live less than 45-minutes from the ski venue in Jakuszyce, Poland. The venue is the first establishment after crossing the Polish border.

After arriving we do our pre-race preps and head down to the start, about 1km away from the finish, which is near the parking area. There are people of all levels everywhere and there is noise and confusion as with any major public competition or event. As Gabi and I strip down to our race suits, we put both of our warm-ups into a bag that I tie up and tuck under a tree because at this marathon they aren't transferring bags from the start to the finish. Gabi's good friend's mother is the race director and she gets bib #4.

I had emailed the FIS contact person for the race and they submitted my entry. Unfortunately, the seed rankings go off of

Worldloppet points first, then Euro Marathon points second, and FIS points third. As I have only FIS points I am placed in the second wave, only three numbers away from being in the 3rd wave.

To understand the significance of this appreciate that there are about 2,000 people in this race. Each wave consists of about 200 people to reduce trail congestion. So instead of being right at the front, with clear trail ahead, I'm starting behind a huge wave of skiers. There is a two minute break between waves, so the front pack starts two minutes ahead of me. This totally changes my race strategy without leaving any time for second-guessing.

Most marathon racing is all about pack racing and hanging with the pack, drafting, gaining, and recovering. Now, as I watch the few hundred top skiers take off, I think it is going to take a hell of a lot of skiing my butt off (getting around and passing a lot of people) to even get near the top skiers. I search my mind to find a positive mental aspect to ride on!

Aaaahhhh, I have it...I recite a personal motto: *"I cannot control my competitors, but more importantly, they cannot control me."* I follow-up by making a prerace promise: *"I will make my body give up (physical) before my mind does (mental)."* I will ski relaxed knowing I have a huge disadvantage starting without the top dogs, and try to catch the front pack. Then if I can finish my race in 1 minute and 59 seconds or less after the winner of that first wave I will actually win the overall. If I can catch and finish with the leaders, I will win by two minutes without them even knowing it. It's kind of sneaky, but hey, the officials placed me there. These hold-backs are also suffered, and occasionally found to have a pleasing time-gap surprise, in the U.S. Birkie.

The officials also place me in the back of the 2nd wave, but I am able to sneak up to the front line, even though they are not allowing anyone to start outside of the classic-cut tracks. At Worldloppet races there are so many people competing so I am up against a huge quantity of people concentrated on a narrow trail.

Unlike in the American Birkebeiner, they do not allow each wave to move forward to the actual start line, so we start about 50 meters behind the front-runners. As I wait on the start line, the cool wind is blowing in my face, I cannot understand a single word the announcer is rambling on about since it is all spoken in Polish and then in Czech. Finally, we start. I double-pole as hard as I dash into the front group of the second wave. After a few strides I take the lead and hammer the first kilometer.

It only takes 1k to catch some folks in the first wave and for the majority of the first 5k I am skiing mostly on the very outside edges of the trail, passing people. I am hammering extra hard and mostly either double-poling or using an old-school technique called marathon skating. In the days before full-on skating began people would keep one ski in the track and push off to the side with the other ski. In my case there is no room on the main part of the trail, so I use the tiny amount of space between the classic track and the woods to get by. It is quite frustrating and harmful in some ways because my poles are kicked a few times, and I run into a few people's poles and step on quite a number of skis.

By the 7k mark my lungs and arms are more taxed than any other parts of my body but I have passed a significant number of skiers. It is around this point that the course begins to show its toughness and the serious climbs begin. I keep a high tempo and my pace is quite high for this length of race, but I manage to limit V-1 to only one section. When I reach the 10k mark, I think the uphill will never quit, but it keeps going and actually gets steeper—ugh! By the time I reach the top I have passed another 30 people and feel like I am going to keel over and have a heart attack. Luckily there is a long gradual downhill following that I'm very thankful for.

Another positive aspect dawned on me after cruising that downhill in the tracks. I notice that they are nicely glazed over. It takes a lot of skiers to ski in tracks to get them glazed and they glide much better then, so in a way they are paving the way for me. Also I think about how packs usually ski. Some sections they go fast, some slow, and knowing that I have kept a solid swift pace all around, I may have gained on the leaders if their pace is slower on some sections.

I am refreshed at the 12k mark to get a feed of warm tea to slurp down—there is snot and drool already dripping off of my chin and I need to rehydrate. At this point I look forward and see there is a great empty gap in front of me. Only on the long, straight sections can I catch sight of a few skiers, and I begin to wonder if I have caught the tail-end of the front pack already. Either way, they are still a good minute ahead and I am not even half-way through the race.

It takes me a solid 5k to catch that pack of four guys. I pass them on an uphill as I am in a rhythmic V-2, while they are all V-1ing. Two of them shout in Polish or Czech. Whatever it is, I hope they aren't asking me anything, because I can't understand a single word.

Over the next three kilometers I think I figure out what it is they're talking about. They are using me as a pacer to draft off. If they are capable of skiing at this pace I decide to take advantage of this and so I back off to let one of them lead. It feels nice to ski in a pack (for the first time in 20k) and I am able to get a draft from the headwind we are skiing straight into. This part of the course reminds me of the McNeil Canyon ski trails in Homer, Alaska. I feel really comfortable out here and am pleased that my body is maintaining good muscular strength (technique) and fitness/energy (frequency/tempo). As we pass the 23k marker I look back to see that two of the four guys in the pack have dropped off the pace and I feel I have taken enough of a break with these guys.

I still have no idea if these guys are the lead pack, but I am not going to assume they are, so I push off on my own. Over the next kilometer I drop those two guys easily by hammering a few hard V-2's over a steep uphill and over the gradual hill following.

It is not long before I spot another pack of guys far into the distance. Again, like so many times before, I think to myself *"Could be the lead pack?"* They are a ways ahead and I have doubts if I can reel them in, but I think about how my skis are gliding really well and commit to giving it my all to catch them. I really surprise myself, because within three kilometers I have caught and passed them and still have a lot of energy to keep the pace. When I see the 27k marker I still am not sure if anyone is still ahead, but then I see there are ski tracks marking the trail ahead so I have a suspicion there is.

Within that kilometer I spot them about 800 meters ahead, and again, I think to myself *"Is that the lead pack?"* My goal from here to the finish is to keep skiing as hard as I can. When I glide past the 29k marker in my largest, most powerful stride I am about 100 meters behind the now noticeable pack of three guys still ahead. My chance of catching them while they are sprinting for the finish area is slim but it does not matter at this point, I've skied a solid race. The course then flows around a big corner on the back side of the finish area leading to the final 100m finish stretch. On the corner I try to see over the crowd to see how many guys have finished already and I can't see any! So maybe this **IS** the lead pack after all!

As I round the final corner, and enter the final 100-meter stretch of the race, I see the cameras all focused on the three guys ahead. I realize *"Yes! This is the lead pack from the first wave!"* I hammer in a solid last 100 meters and the crowd goes wild as those three guys finish. I trail their finish by only 9 seconds. As I cross the line I raise my right hand and index finger up in the air as high as I can yelling *"I...WON THIS RACE!!! YYYEEEEAAAAHHHH!!!"* I have overcome the odds and won my first Worldloppet Ski Marathon.

The media is all over those three guys, especially the guy who finished a boot-length in front. For the first minute after I finish nobody pays any attention to me and my father yells from across the track, *"Did they account for the two minute handicap/ bonus?"* I reply *"Not yet."* It's during this noisy moment that I remember my personal quote that I recited at the beginning, *"I cannot control my competitors, but most importantly, they cannot control me."* It holds true for everyone.

Once I catch my breath and take off my skis, I ask around to find an official who speaks English. I explain that I have won the race while pointing to my bib number and then my watch with two fingers, signifying two minutes, explaining that I started two minutes behind these guys. He walks to the announcer, who at this time is going ballistic with the fantastic photo finish that had just occurred, and informs him about the important discovery of the actual time and story of the guy who looks like he finished 4th.

He then announces the updating news in Polish over the loudspeaker. The faces on the three guys change instantly. The guy, who is currently sucking up the glory with about 10 cameras in his face, looks at me like someone just stole his puppy. *"Tough luck bro, I skied my butt off out there and had to overcome a lot more than you to win today,"* I think to myself. I am nearly pushed backwards with all the cameras suddenly shoved in my face.

There are reporters, including the main announcer for the event, who walk up to me, rambling off all this Polish and my first response to all of them is *"Can you ask me that in English, please, I am an American."* That makes them step back in a bit of shock. One of the questions they ask is how I came to be in this race. I give credit to Sylwia Jaśkowiec, from their National Ski Team for encouraging me to enter.

After the questions are over and cameras go away, the race director thanks me for winning. Apparently there has been a long tradition of only Germans, and Czechs winning this race and they are happy for me to change that. To add to the positive day Gabi wins the women's race by nearly six minutes! We are laughing at the awards ceremony when we are brought together to stand on the top of the podium. Someone asks real loud, *"Do you two know each other?"* They find it even more interesting that we are living in the same house and have carpooled here.

After the race, I'd skied down to get our warm-ups back from under the tree in my bag—it was nowhere to be seen. It takes the race committee two hours to locate it—and Gabi's and my expensive jackets, pants, and gloves. Whew, we were worried. And I got quite cold not having anything besides my over-coat to wear during the time outside for the awards and media.

A week after the Bieg Piastow Worldloppet I return to the same trails to compete in a FIS 10k Classic that includes some of the national team members from both Czech Republic and Poland who have returned from the World Cup. It goes like an average classic race for me. Even though my classic skiing is getting better, I still struggle out there. In the past I would only have one real good classic race out of about every eight, now it seems I have one in every four, so there is marked improvement.

It is very warm, nearly raining, so it is for sure klister for the grip wax of the day. I ski solid, nothing fantastic, but feel okay, come across the line well out of breath and know I did all right since I passed quite a few people and was not passed by anyone. My skis felt great and I am very pleased with their performance. In the results I end up 6th overall, which I am happy with since I didn't have a real good race. It was the best I could do that day.

Race prep with klister.

WILD SHOT

Andy mid-race.

The top 6 finishers, Andy in 6th.

After the race my father and I venture into town to walk around the street markets and vendors. I like Poland and feel comfortable in such an environment. The village of Szklarska Poreba is a nice-looking, pleasant, friendly village. I get the idea that Poland could have been named by someone from the south-east U.S. because it could easily be translated as *Po'land*, meaning "poor land" in our southern dialect. No disrespect intended. Everything we've seen is beautiful and there are some very nice things for sale among the locals, but the costs are really low, hence the change pops into my head.

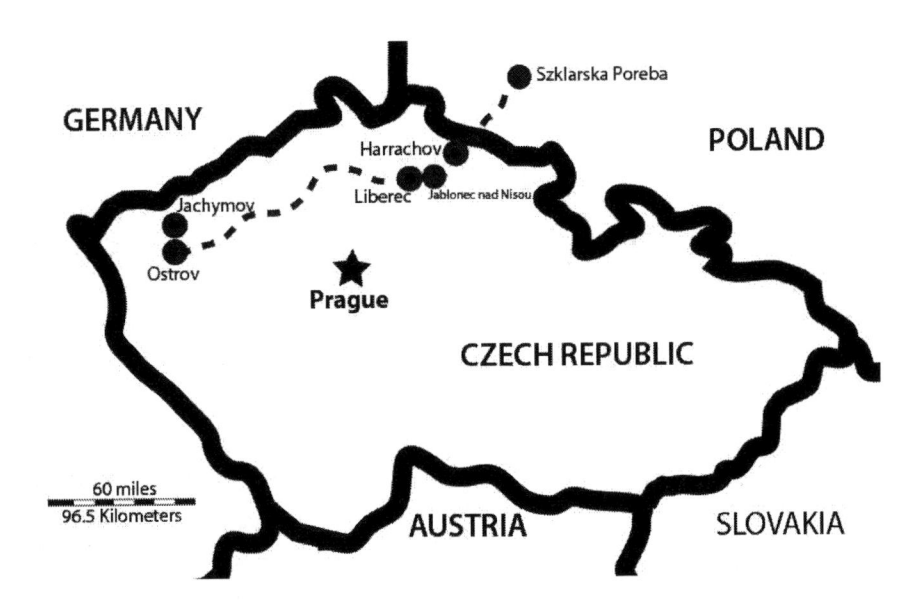

Czech Biathlon Championships

We stay in the area because the Czech Biathlon National Championships are held in the little village of Harrachov, about 30 kilometers from the Soukal's house. As my father and I drive to the venue the windshield wipers are working the entire time clearing the constant rain that lands on our windshield. There are only a few things I hate and one of them is skiing in the rain. It takes a lot for me to overcome my negative attitude and get my race face on for this event and I am not feeling any better during my warm-up.

Once I am let out of the starting gate starting the 10k sprint, I throw down a few strides and my mood changes into competition mode. My skiing pace and rhythm are at my top level and my skis again are like rockets, as I cruise the first lap and pass five guys. My first shooting is good, considering how much I dislike laying on the wet mat feeling the water soak into my suit from head to toe. I am pleased with only missing two and gladly hit the penalty loop and then hammer out another 3.3k loop, gracefully passing more people. I am confident that I'm doing well.

I come flying into the range for my final shooting stage (standing). Unexpectedly, as I take my rifle off my back, my arm band (used for prone) catches my full magazine, flinging it into the deep snow toward the targets. Then, as I am bending down to grab it, my empty clip comes out and falls into a deep footprint in front of the mat and toward the target. …This is not good. The race clock is always ticking, so I quickly grab the full clip, jam it into my mag-well and take my five shots. Experience will hopefully help me master crap like this, but now, just before my standing stage, I really am not thinking right and only hit my last shot.

After a bum shooting stage I feel very disappointed as I dig my other mag out of the snow. I must find it because I am afraid they will disqualify me if I do not finish with two mags. I throw it to my father to have ready at the finish line just in case. After doing four solid penalty loops, still with the mindset of a possible chance of doing well against the national team guys, I ski the last 3.3k loop hard and well. In the results I end up 7th. Later, as I get back into the van, I feel okay, considering how I was feeling when arriving. I still dislike skiing in the rain!

On the drive back to the Soukal's house, in a little town we have to pass through, an elderly man walking along the road must have noticed the German plates and big letters "TSV Schliersee" (a professional handball team in Schliersee, Germany) sticker on the hood. We figure this because he raises his arm high in the air and shakes his bare fist, cane in hand, at us with a mean look. There still seems to be a lot of bitterness, even after all these years, toward Germans and their abuse of the Czechs during WWII and we just got a taste of it.

The local ski/biathlon trails in Jablonec are like a secret training location. There is no parking lot, and the long, steep, slippery hill you need to walk up to get to the trails is intimidating enough. But at the top of the hill is a world-class ski trail network and biathlon venue; and they're glad to follow this route to experience the thrill. I've been invited to train with the biathlon club that Mrs. Soukalova coaches. Gabriela, Karel's wife/Gabi's mother, was one of the best skiers in the world during the 1980's, winning a silver medal at the 1984 Olympics as a Cross Country Skier.

I like training with the team, who are mostly juniors, as they are a fun, friendly group that hold a competitive training philosophy. The trails are always kept well-groomed and some days I see the Czech National Ski Team and Biathlon Team training there as well. It feels nice to be invited and to participate with a team again. The area and the trail scenery with the amount of pine trees and rolling hills remind me of the Noquemanon trail located in Marquette, Michigan.

My father and I finally venture out of the Czech Republic on March 16th, after being there more than a month. The sun shone for a total of 20-minutes the whole time and we are looking forward to seeing different lands. I have a lot of work that I need to take care of at Holmenkol. I have to turn in the unsold wax items and provide payment for all items that I had taken money for. My yearly total of sales is over 12 thousand euros, on which I receive a 20% commission. It takes two full days to complete everything. I discover that the end of March is a very busy time for the office staff, marketing personnel, scientists, and warehouse staff.

My father and I stay four nights near Heimerdingen, where Holmenkol is located, and each morning I get up early and commence the day with a delightful run. There is no snow and it is warm enough to really enjoy the fresh, crisp, bright morning air and listen to the birds chirp as I run through wooded areas and farm fields. What makes the fields interesting is that they are on hillier terrain than in America. As the sun rises I think about this layout and realize why they do it. When the land is sloped and terraced like grandstands there is more surface area for planting. And the sun's exposure can also be maximized. Smart thinkers, these German farmers!

I really enjoy running here and take note of the many paved pathways between the crops—they'd be excellent for roller skiing.

The joyous morning runs may have been induced because of the combination of seeing the sun screaming down its warm rays for the first time in a month. It feels so good to have no knee pain while running, and to stretch out in effortless stride with a good rhythm once again.

The time arrives for my father to catch his flight back to the U.S. and so upon our departure from Stuttgart, we say our goodbyes. It has been helpful and fun having him with me but it feels like it is time for him to go and for me to continue on my journey alone. He heads to Frankfurt via train and I continue south-east to O-town. The long day of driving is exhausting and also a bit boring since I am on the road alone once again.

I find that O-town still has an abundance of snow. Even the ski trails have a solid two meters/ six feet of packed crisp, clean snow. They will be skiing here for another two months! After being in the sunless Czech Republic for so long, I have been looking forward to the endless days of sunshine in O-town. With farming fields in-between all the little towns in the area it makes for excellent crust skiing.

The crust skiing rave can only be experienced in the spring time and in the early parts of the day. I will never forget the spring crust skiing in Marquette and Joe Haggenmiller (now the ski coach at Michigan Tech University) tapping on my window to wake me up and go crust skiing out near Big Bay and County Road 550. Yes, it's that fun! You can ski everywhere including thick forests at high speeds dodging trees and with nearly effortless movements.

It is nice to be back in familiar territory and able to somewhat speak to the locals. At the Biathlon Center the only team that is here for the first two weeks after my arrival is the Turkish National Biathlon Team (more like development team, as they are all juniors). Of all 15 members only two speak English and they are the trainers. One is a good friend of mine who was formerly on the Slovenian Team, and the other, a Turkish trainer with a PhD in Exercise Science.

To illustrate the range of approaches that people take to the sport, my trainer, Joe, is one of the more casual. Maybe we could say unpredictable, probably due to him always having to be three places at once. I emailed him my schedule so he could plan when to work with me. As with many other times this fall and winter he fails to show up or communicate. Leandro was disappointed this fall and winter when he was expecting to work with Joe who always arrived late (at the end of training sessions) or not at all. At the British Champs he came to my first race (10 minutes after I started) and said he would come to the rest of the events to help, but I never saw him again.

Now, as I return, he shows up on my third day of training. I have an outline of things organized to talk about the season—good, bad, things to improve on, etc. We plan to meet the next day, but, again, he fails to show up. He had written all of my training plans for the summer, fall, and winter and I thought he would like feedback on how they went.

I do get a bit frustrated, especially when Joe continually does not show up on time, but I am not as frustrated as Leandro. My Brazilian friend is a very good organizer and quite structured and Joe's easy-going style is a struggle for him. In my case, I do not really need a coach, especially during the racing season when I don't want to be making any major changes anyway. I asked for his help when I felt I needed it. But that's the type of club he runs and that was our unwritten agreement. At this point in the season, I am ready for a break, so now I only need him to help me zero my rifle.

Austrian Championships – Season Finale

On April 2 I compete in the Austrian National Biathlon Championships. It was to be arguably my best performance yet. The race, a 15k mass start, is at 5pm, to allow some of the younger athletes, who are still in school, to compete. The day before it had been very sunny and hot and I was really looking forward to another day of wearing sun block. But this morning my smile turns into a stunned expression as I open the curtains to see heavy rain dumping. It rains hard the entire morning and as I drive to the Biathlon Center, only a kilometer away, I am thinking there is a good chance the event will be cancelled. After speaking with Hansjorg, the Obertilliach info manager and race organizer, I am assured that the race is going ahead. This rain is worse than in Harrachov and the trails are completely slush.

I wear my Holmenkol alpine overcoat and pants to zero my rifle and warm-up because it was my only waterproof clothing. *"Bite the bullet, Andy, and get out there and race,"* I continue reminding myself to stay motivated prior to the start. I will never forget standing ready at the mass start, waiting for the start signal gun, and all the while feeling the rain soaking my uniform and running down my neck and back. I usually take a shower after a race, but it's a new experience to have one on the starting line. Joe had shown up unexpectedly and helped me zero my rifle and suggested that I hold back on the first lap and ride the pack. I take his advice and halfway through the first lap am in seventh place.

Right after the half-way marker an incident occurs that I still feel bad about. The top five guys are surging and I am behind the sixth guy who is not keeping pace. I try to pass him on his right side but he is not giving me much room to pass and my left pole plants directly onto the top of his right boot, stabbing his foot.

I lift the pressure off of my pole immediately, but the motion has stopped his rhythm enough to flip him onto his back. His rifle hits the snow first (luckily not breaking) and he slides on his back until his momentum stops. As I ski away, I yell *"I'm really sorry!"* A kilometer later the race leader slips on the sharpest corner of the loop and wipes out. Coming into the range as a pack of five, we rush to our assigned shooting mats.

Skiing through such sloppy wet snow is really hard and even after only the first of five loops I am already completely soaked. On one hand, given my saturated state, placing my elbow into a puddle of water doesn't bother me as much as I had imagined as I lay prone ready to take my first shots. There is more noise coming from the fans than I have heard all year and I am still getting use to it.

It sounds like someone is banging a set of crash cymbals over my head as I try to concentrate on each shot. It isn't easy and I only manage to hit three of the five, also taking about 15 seconds longer (in total) to shoot than the pack. As I ski two penalty loops I notice that everyone else had missed at least two shots also, and many trainers line the sides of the penalty loop area yelling out corrections to make to our sights for the next shooting stage.

Luckily Joe is there and instructs me to take two clicks left. Much like those other guys, my shots may have looked perfect from my sight, but they were off because I zeroed on a different target which was only 30 meters away. Even if you zero-in at the correct 50 meters, if you're competing at a different target and the ground is slightly lower or there are lumps in the snow under the mat, it can throw off your left resting elbow, your main anchor-point for the prone position.

As I ski over the second 3k loop I really haul and pass two Austrian guys. A kilometer later I pass a guy from the German National Team. One kilometer before the range I pass one more Austrian guy and as I come into the range I am right on the heels of the race leader! I know I skied well over that loop, but my heart rate is singing at full song and I struggle to barely hit two of the five on that shooting stage. After skiing three penalties I have to re-pass a few of the guys I had caught because they shot clean and had already hit the trail while I was skiing my butt off in the penalty loop area.

I ski the third loop more conservatively and even though I come into the range in 4th I am more comfortable and ready to shoot standing. I complete my standing stage in less than 40 seconds (on and off the mat), which was my goal for the year and hit three of the five. I am happy with that as standing has been harder for me. I repeat the same pace over the next lap and hit just the same.

But on my second standing stage (last of the race) it takes me about 50 seconds to hit three of five and the guys in both 4th and 5th place shoot next to me and finish about 20-seconds faster after hitting four of five, leaving me there still shooting while they take off. In this race I shot better than in any mass start or pursuit style four stage all year even in these crappy conditions, so that was a mark of improvement! Even so, the competition is shooting more accurately and faster than I am.

From the moment my 20th and final shot is taken and my rifle is slammed onto my back I am in full-on ski mode. *"Screw this rain, it's just warm snow,"* I think to myself as I whip out two penalty loops, reel in those two snipers and keep pushing harder and harder until I reach the finish line to become the 3rd place overall finisher at the 2009 Austrian Biathlon National Championships!

A short while later I stand, proudly, listening to the announcer at the awards ceremony as he says (in German, of course) *"1st Place Alexander Nuss Austria, 2nd Place Tobias Reiter Germany, 3rd Place Andy Liebner USA."*

Standing there, I remember the very first week I arrived in Obertilliach, one sunny day in July when the Austrian National Team was training here. I distinctly remember watching them and thinking how professional they looked as I observed both their roller-ski/running and shooting training sessions. Looking back at that time I would never have believed that in nine months I would be on the podium after racing against them.

Two days later there is a 10k sprint, which is a forerunner to the pursuit the following day. The 10k sprint is extremely important because it determines your starting position in the pursuit. In this race I learn a valuable lesson. I am so pumped by my performance the previous race that I push too hard, get too excited and shoot terribly. I ski really hard, come in to shoot with an extremely high heart rate, don't concentrate properly, and miss two prone and three standing, a total of five misses out of ten shots. On this day with great weather conditions and this level of field it completely took me out of placings and I am left to rue my inexperience. I knew better than to ski all-out, but did it anyway.

I am much more relaxed in the final race of the season, knowing that my poor result the previous day has effectively eliminated me from any real chance of finishing among the placings. Perhaps because of this I shoot better than I have done previously. I get 14 out of 20, while the winner shoots only 17 of 20. I also shoot a clean five in both a prone and a standing stage. I don't even know where I finished on the results list and at this point I don't care. The season is over and it is time to do other things, take a break, go places, see people and reflect on the season so I can then re-focus on next year's training program.

This ski season has brought many new learning experiences, such as awareness of foreign laws, very adaptive and flexible scheduling, and the never-ending eye-opening dramas of different cultures. This April marks the first in two years I have not undergone surgery. Two years ago I underwent gum surgery, and last April was my infamous knee surgery. This April I can eat solid foods and walk pain-free!

Throughout this season I sent emails to family and friends outlining my experiences as I traveled foreign lands pursuing answers to my own questions about the world's best skiers and biathletes. Some of them asked if the denial of support from the USBA bothers me. Other inquiries revolved around how I have learned to always stay positive, even when it appears there are many things against me. My answer: *I hold something within me that no one can ever take away:* **self-respect and self-belief.**

CHAPTER EIGHT
Greece Here I Come!

I load the van in O-town, pick-up some documents from my good friend Hansjörg at the community info office, and drive away with the van clock reading 8:30 am. Ancona, Italy is the final destination for the day. On the way I have to detour and stop in Bled, Slovenija. Bled has become one of my favorite towns in the world for its beauty and small town comfort. It is often described as a fairytale village; the bright blue lake makes it picturesque. There is already much greenery and new plant life in Bled this early in spring.

The reason for stopping there is to meet Klemen Bauer and Peter Dokl, of the Slovenijan Biathlon National Team. Klemen has offered to hold my winter ski stuff while I am away. I was invited to train with the Slovenijan team for an unlimited length of days, so I plan on being back again to reclaim my winter gear.

The guys have just been to Ljubljana to get some last ski sessions in for the year at the ski venue in Pokluka, about 20 kilometers away. It's a three hour drive from O-town to Bled and I arrive just at the time the guys arrive back from skiing so we decide to go out for pizza. The place they take me to does not look at all appealing from the outside, but they lead me around the back and up two flights of stairs to a sunny porch patio. It turns out to be a pretty cool place. Only the locals know about great restaurants like this and within minutes our drinks and pizzas are on the table.

It is really nice catching up with these guys and sharing a few laughs about the past few months. Upon leaving we notice a van with many logos pull into the parking lot. The largest logo is the ever-popular German National Alpine Ski Team. Into the pizza place walk some of the team members who also apparently know about the local secret.

Leaving Bled, I travel southwest through the famous shape of the Italian boot. For anyone who wonders how long it takes to drive from the top of the boot to the bottom of the foot, I can't tell you. I only drive to the middle of the calf, which takes eight solid hours. The first two hours, coming from the most north-eastern part of Italy, I face high winds through very steep hillsides and drive over many tall bridges, and through many tunnels. I don't care how long it is going to take; my mind is fixed on mental freedoms to relax and time outside of skiing.

This is my transformation period; time to find myself as a person and not just as a skier or athlete. A chance to get away from it all, to find and explore areas of the world that I have always found fascinating, mysterious, and historically significant to life and athletics. To what am I being led? I do not know, but I am on my way and that is all that matters. Memories are to be made and another chapter in my life will be opened, written, and closed within a few short weeks.

I had been in a snowy environment since September, when there was already fresh snow on the Dachstein glacier. It is the longest continual on-snow season I have ever experienced. For an endurance athlete to continue to improve, he cannot afford to slack off for even a week, and I have kept pushing myself relentlessly for that entire time. Now that I am finally away from the snow I realize how desperately I need this break. I yearn for the chance to go far away, to go wherever the wind blows me, not tied down to any schedule or events. The world of exploring awaits me and I have no expectations other than bliss and peace of mind.

The remainder of the drive south through Italia is similar to Nebraska, only instead of thousands of corn fields there are grape vineyards, grape vineyards, and more grape vineyards. I know Italy is famous for wine making, but this is impressive! The sun set before I arrived in Ancona so I pull off to the side of the road about 17K shy of the city and park next to the beach. Already I feel like I am on vacation. The warm wind, the smell of warm blacktop mixed with the sweet salty sea air is confirmation that I have traveled far in one day. From the snowy Austrian mountains to the warm sunny beaches of Italy. I love Europe!

It feels good unrolling my sleeping bag onto the back seat that I have dismantled and laid out horizontally, supported by two spare tires. I fall asleep listening to cars whiz by on the nearby road.

I have stopped at Ancona because it is the location from which I can take the ferry to Greece. In the morning it is not easy to find my way through the city but I make it onto the Greek ferry 'SUPER FAST VI'. For the next 24 hours this ship which seems larger than the Titanic will be my home.

I planned to sleep in the van, which is parked in the cargo area, while the ferry is en-route, but when I venture down there to sleep, a worker kicks me out. I have barely a minute to grab something to cover myself with on the deck. I end up having to sleep outside with a polyester blanket. It is freakin' cold and windy out there. I wake up at least every 30 minutes, eventually rising for the day at 4:30 am but, at this point, I simply don't care. I am going to get to Greece no matter what!

My first destination is the island of Crete. Back in O-town, I had discussions with a girl from the Greek Biathlon team who told me some of the best places to go and, in particular, spoke about Crete. While this trip is first and foremost a holiday I'll also be doing some work while I am in Greece. Holmenkol and its CEO, Christian, have been really great to me, saving me from deportation by the German authorities and now I am a salary employee. Apart from ski products, Holmenkol also manufactures a line of boating and biking goods and it is my plan to try and establish a network for them in Greece, and the starting place is Crete, with its many boating businesses.

To get to Crete from where the ferry unladed me I first have to travel four hours to Athens and take a ferry from there directly to Crete. By the time I reach the ferry terminal my joyous exuberance has been all but ground away. Athens is a hot, dusty city where people drive like maniacs. I'm so much in need of mental and physical rest, but driving around Athens is certainly not restful. However, finally I make it onto the ferry 'El Venizelos'.

Moments before the ferry departs I sit in a grass-woven seat next to a little table gazing outside witnessing the final moments of the day's remaining light shining upon the ancient stone pillars standing on the Athenian hillside. The sudden glimpse of this ancient symbol conjures up thoughts of what little I know about Greece. Athens is the home of the Olympics, and whether it is strictly true or not, in my mind, those ancient Games symbolize the gods testing young men to see if they were worthy athletes.

Then the strangest thought passes through my mind. I know I have been on a journey to try to reach my full potential, in that singular moment, I can almost imagine that I am being tested by some unseen god, or gods, to see whether I am worthy of playing my role. I am not one to get into esoteric aspects of life, being pretty well rooted in the here and now and very goal-focused, but here, looking at this ancient place, I can almost sense that my quest is part of something much larger than skiing, and that I do not understand anything of what is really going on in my life.

The ferry arrives on Crete as the sun is coming up and I drive out of the belly of the ship at 6:00 am. I feel exhausted and hungry having slept only for eight hours in the past 48 and most of that wasn't really sleep. Without stopping the van I drive aimlessly before parking at a beach about 20K east of Chania.

After sleeping for a few hours I wake up feeling nauseous and despondent. I have been looking forward so much to this trip and had felt great joy at the anticipation of being here but that has all been swept away. The only thing that occupies my mind is thoughts of how I could have been so stupid to come. I suddenly feel lost and alone in this unfamiliar land, unable to communicate with anyone. My physical presence on this island feels as if a great vice is closing its jaws around me trapping me in its grasp. I have nowhere to go.

For months I have been able to escape the darkness that occasionally consumes me. I have been able to turn negativity into positive emotions and use it as motivation for my races, but here, when the pressure of training and racing is gone, my mind has nothing to hold onto. I feel like I'm spiraling downward into a terrible pit of fear. I can almost imagine the Greek gods laughing at me, at my arrogance for thinking I could withstand any test, as they toss me into the dark underworld where my deepest fears lie. In that moment I want to be somewhere I know somebody, anyone, just as long as I am not alone.

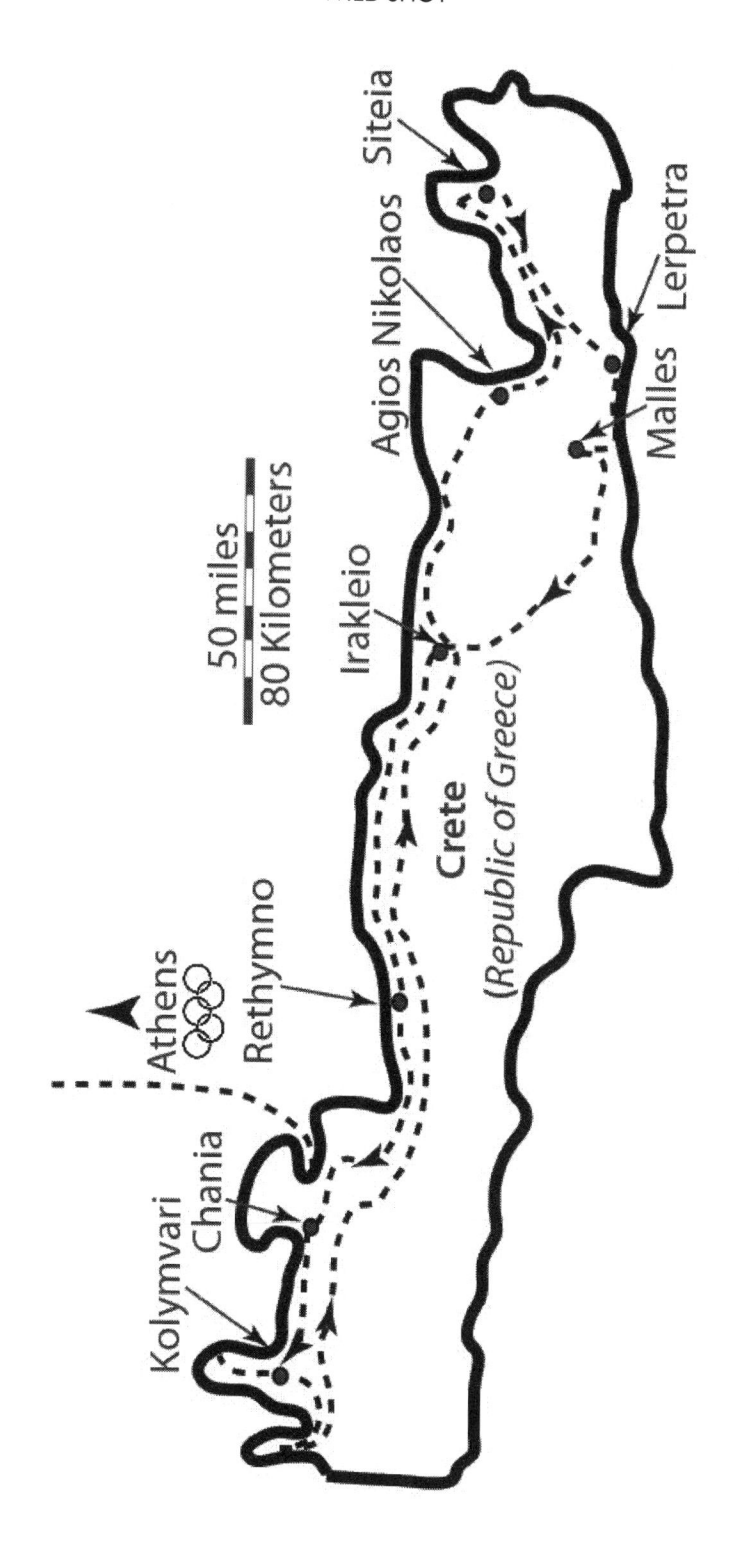

Kolymvari
Chania
Athens
Rethymno
Irakleio
Agios Nikolaos
Siteia
Malles
Ierpetra
Crete
(Republic of Greece)

50 miles
80 Kilometers

In the past, at times like this, I have always found it best to move and so I decide to try that strategy again. I need to find an Internet source so I can print out the documents I'll need for the work aspect of my trip. At this moment I just want to get that work done and get off this island as quickly as I can. I drive along the north coast, desperately seeking the Internet, as if my very existence depends upon it, but there is none to be found and my fear of being trapped here closes around me even more powerfully.

When finally I locate an Internet connection I check my inbox and see the very email I am waiting for. When I open it, however, the message reads "sorry, will get it to you next week." This is not what I need and I spin even further out of control. I feel as if keeling over in a ditch would be a better option than continuing on.

Fleeing town, I find myself at a tiny harbor containing one broken down car, two boats in the water and one little fiberglass boat full of holes and flipped upside down in a parking space as if it drove there. It is hot, humid, and I do not want to be here. I try to sleep, try to read, but nothing will take my mind off the fear that consumes me from being in this place. I just want to get out but no matter how hard I try, no other place comes to mind. I want to be here, but I don't want to be here at the same time.

In desperation I decide to completely rearrange my stuff in the van and as I am doing it, two women walk into the harbor parking area, with a little dog running in front of them. I say Hi. They are in their fifties and are originally from Great Britain, although they say they are now considered locals. It is so good to hear their voices and be able to speak in English and the terror that has consumed me slides away, as if I've been given a reprieve from death-row. They also know the local businesses and give me some ideas on where I should go as well as pointing out the best running spots on the island.

By the time they continue on their way my energy has shifted completely and I finish rearranging the van with a dramatically different outlook on this trip, feeling better—relieved, welcomed, joyous—and motivated to stay, train, and work.

Over the next few days I find myself melding into the flow of life on Crete. I spend my time running and riding my bike along rocky coastlines and exploring the mystery and magic of the area.

At night I listen to the ocean and sleep peacefully, on the beach or in the van. The sense of terror that had descended upon me that first day has vanished.

On the fourth day I finally begin the business part of the trip. Travelling along the northern coast headed east I stop at businesses along the way. I have brought some catalogs of the aquatic and biking products that Holmenkol has to offer and prepared an introductory letter, translated into Greek. All in all I feel pleased with the way the day progresses and believe there is an opportunity here. I make a mental note to begin looking for someone who I can train to become the local distribution representative.

By mid-afternoon it is time for some exercise and I turn onto an old farming road that follows along a steep hillside where I park and make camp for the night. The road dead-ends about 1k off the main road and I am camped near it, in a green and rocky valley surrounded by steep hillsides in three directions.

Andy about to run.

I immediately go for a run and discover my route strewn with metal fences that traverse the hill-side. I keep running into them as I climb up steep ridges trying to get to the top of one of the three noticeable peaks. One of my passions is running on ridges, even though I'm scared of heights. There is a sense of freedom, accomplishment, and satisfaction in it. It takes some back tracking and road mileage, but I find an open gate near 30 bee hives and run through them like a gauntlet.

As I make my own route up I run, leap, duck, and climb over

the obstacles as fast as I can move. The obstacles are real, but in my imagination they are barriers that the Greek gods are placing in front of me. I imagine that they are testing my strength, speed, and agility the whole way. I scale most of the obstacles without using my hands before eventually making it to the top!

There I stand on the highest peak for as far as the eye can see, arms spread up and out, legs bleeding in several places due to the sharp prickly bushes and jagged rocks I encountered along the route. I feel like king of the mountain. It is a glorious moment. *I have passed the test and the Greek gods have let me stand atop their podium. I have been welcomed as an Olympic Champion!*

The next few days sort of mesh together as I follow the same daily routine: run in the morning then spend a few hours navigating through the major cities on the northern coast as I head east. It's interesting how crammed together these cities are and how difficult it can be to locate all the boating stores, bike shops, and hardware stores. Each evening I drive halfway to the next city until I find some nice hideout, where I run again and sleep in peace.

Friday, April 17 is the first day of the Easter weekend in Greece. Easter had been the weekend before in most of Europe, but the Orthodox Church celebrates it a week later. It is kind of neat, therefore, that I end up that day in the village of Malles, the birthplace of Zeus, the king of the Greek gods. On this day I decide to venture to the south part of the island. Once I am on the coast, I feel a calling to stay along the ridge of the steep landscape between the little villages that rest the mountain side.

I drive into the hills and stop in a parking area that is part of a hairpin turn next to a little stream. In the evening I head out for a bike ride through some of the villages to explore the surrounding areas. Malles is near the southern coast on the east side of the island. I find the roads to be relatively new looking, maybe 2-3 years old and black top—excellent for biking, with very little traffic, many up and downhills, along with twisty turny cuts into the steep hillsides, all possessing an incredible view. The view from my van is of island landscape below and the Mediterranean Sea towards Egypt.

Near the end of my ride I am coasting down a hill where some houses and cars are parked, when suddenly a little boy (about 3-4 years old) darts out from behind one of the parked cars. I have only a fraction of a second to react. The boy stops and stands broadly across the road, facing me center view. My first thought is pure panic. *"I am going to run him over, killing him, and it will be my fault."* Reacting instinctively, I swerve the bike to the right and give both brakes the death grip. As I fly over the handlebars the bike takes out the kid, knocking him flat.

The second my body stops sliding, I jump up to care for the little boy who must have seen the grim reaper for a second. He is okay, has a slight abrasion to his head and may have other bruises show-up later, but he begins to cry right away. That is a good sign. His mother comes right out of the nearest building, a house with no front door and a dirt floor.

She had been looking out the window and witnessed the whole event. She scoops her son right up and gives him a little spanking, rambling off a bunch of Greek words to the boy. It sounds like he has been warned many times before to look before crossing the road. She nods to me with a notion that it's okay so I pick up the bike, including a piece that has broken off of it, and ride away, dripping blood from three limbs and dirty all over.... Kids!

Malles

I have now stayed in Malles for three nights, which is the first time I have remained anywhere that long on this trip. There is something about this place that calls me. I found it by accident and yet feel as if, in some way I do not understand, it is the most important aspect of my trip.

As I am walking through Malles I notice a large monument that stands tall and proud. It is a statue of a man who has his foot placed on a helmet. On the helmet there is a swastika. Apparently, this town was one of few that defended themselves from the WWII German invasion and they are mighty proud. I then understand why so many of the people who drive around the corner where I am parked give me glaring looks and honk their horns as they pass. The van's marking suggests I am German.

The statue that stands proud in Malles.

A close up of their emblem of pride.

I have strange and conflicting feelings surging through me this afternoon. I can almost feel a sense of something greater, something mythical moving through me. Perhaps that is a natural result of being in such an ancient place with a deep and colorful mythical history, especially here, at the birthplace of Zeus. I cannot deny the appeal of the notion that I have come here to present myself to the hard-core gods of athletics. I have come here to be judged, to find my place within my sport. I have come to discover either a real athlete inside me or a man who is trying to act like an athlete and should be doing something else.

A few days ago, when I ran up the mountain, I felt that I had passed their test, and that feeling was as real as any 'normal' feeling one might experience. Yet there is a lingering doubt, a fear that percolates within me. I remember a quote that I try to grasp, but not yet ready to give in to. It states: *"Our deepest fear is NOT that we are inadequate. Our deepest fear is that we are powerful beyond measure. It is our light, not our darkness, that most frightens us. Playing small does not prove anything. There is nothing enlightening about shrinking your abilities."* –anonymous.

From my parking spot on the corner of that little road, way up in the mountains, I can see ancient ruins that still exist. The adventurer in me says I should get the most out of the trip and walk down there to check it out first-hand. After all it is no more than a 20-minute walk from my van. Yet there is an inner instinct keeping me from going there. It is like something is telling me that it is okay to see it from my perch, but the feeling says: *"You don't want to go there, it will hurt you, something bad happened there."* I don't know anything about the ruins but my normal nature is to explore everything and see anything that is there to be seen, so this reluctance to go is out of character. There are no fences or signs restricting me from going, yet my inner feeling advises me not to.

As I stare at the ruins a twinge of panic rises within me and I push myself away from it, afraid of relapsing to the state I was in when I first arrived on the island.

The next morning I wake up with the realization that I have regained my perspective on life. The balance has been restored and all the pressures are released. The remaining ideas of exploration on Crete instantly seem not necessary. My European trip is feeling extra long and for the first time in five years I sense the strong feeling of homesickness. I go out for a fast run and, when I return to the van, I pack up immediately and as I drive away nagging doubt lingers just beneath the surface.

Have I really finished here, or am I running from something deeper within me that is too threatening and challenging? I have planned to run the mountain ridge in the south center of the island. Part of me feels that there is something waiting for me to discover. Perhaps this is the ultimate athletic test of the Greek gods. But I turn my back on it and drive half the day relocating to a very busy parking lot next to the waterfront in Chania.

Before leaving Crete, in Chania, I meet a guy who is perfect for the representative position for Holmenkol and the business part of my trip reaches a successful conclusion. I stay a few more nights in Chania and take in the local culture. There are locals and tourists everywhere and I enjoy meeting them and diving off the main pier collecting items off of the sea's floor. For once I felt like one of those local kids who have nothing better to do but entertain the tourists with conversation stories and back flips into the cold water. All that is left to do now is to get back on the ferry and move on. Yet, as I sit aboard the ship, looking back on the island of Crete, I cannot help but feel that I have left something unfinished behind, and that, one day, I will have to return to this place and complete my exploration here.

At the time I visited Crete I had no awareness of the story of Greek mythology and, in particular, of Zeus. The connection I felt there was all part of my imagination and yet it felt so real. If I allowed myself to, I feel I could have dropped through a doorway into a deeper level of insight but the cost of doing that was to confront the fears lurking within me and I could not do that. Sometime later, however, a man who is involved in mythology gave me his interpretation of the story of Zeus and how it relates to my own quest.

I share it with you at this stage, but I stress that I did not know this at the time I was there, or even during the rest of my stay in Europe.

Zeus was the son of Cronos. Cronos was the son of Gaia, the mother of Earth, and her husband Uranus. Cronos took the rulership of the gods by castrating his father but in doing so he also took on a prophecy that he was to be overthrown by one of his own children. He was driven by the fear of this prophecy and, in order to prevent this from happening, he swallowed his children as soon as they were born. This dismayed his wife, Rhea, and so when Zeus was born, she tricked the boy's father by replacing the baby with a stone, which Cronos swallowed.

Rhea then gave Zeus to his grandmother, Gaia, who took him away to the country where she personally oversaw his development. When he was ready, Zeus returned and took a job working for his father, in the guise of a servant. When the moment arrived he slit open his father's stomach and liberated his siblings.

Of course, mythology has to be read in a symbolic manner rather than a literal one. The story of the battle between Zeus and Cronos that followed this act has been made popular in the recent movie, "The Battle of the Titans." My friend suggests that Cronos represents the energy behind large, authoritative structures, and their need for stability and control. Looked at in this way, the German empire under Hitler was a reflection of Cronos as they sought to create a perfectly ordered world based on a super-race. It is therefore rather interesting that the people of the little town of

Malles, the hometown of Zeus, would stand up against tyranny just as their famous founder had.

More relevant to me, however, is that this is the one constant that has followed me throughout my journey. I am constantly bumping up against authoritative structures that seem to want to suppress my desires and my freedom. They are not doing this out of malice, but out of a desire to create a safe and controlled environment. Nevertheless, the result is the same. In many ways, my own journey seems to be a struggle to overcome the barriers placed in my way by these structures (of Cronos) much as Zeus had to do.

The other thing that my friend pointed out to me, after I related my experiences to him, is that I seem to have a fear, bordering on terror, of being penned in and stuck in one place. This is the fear that really surfaced when I arrived on Crete. I felt trapped on that island, and it was almost a life-threatening feeling. This fear is consistent with the terror one would feel of being, symbolically, swallowed.

You can probably tell by now that I am not a mystical beast, but I am an athlete and I am on a quest. Any serious athlete will tell you that success is as much about what is going on inside of you as it is about your level of fitness and technical expertise. An athlete's journey is at heart a quest into the unchartered depth of his own being, a journey to draw out untapped depths of passion, power, courage and perseverance. In times gone by the quest was a mythical journey and so perhaps, in some way, an athlete's struggle has become the equivalent of a modern myth, a means through which we tap into a reality within that takes us beyond normal perception and allows us to exceed the commonly perceived limits of the body.

Now let us return to my own personal quest through the pitfalls and barriers of the sporting world.

Transition

On the way back from Greece I stop in Slovenija at Klemen Bauer's house to pick up the gear I left there. Klemen owns part of his parents subdivided house and he invites me to stay at there.

For the first time in nearly three weeks I sleep indoors, in a real bed. Klemen and I go out running, hiking, and biking together during the few days I stay and I realize how much I miss being able to train with someone else. Much as I love to be alone and the freedom it gives me, there is something wonderful about training with a kindred spirit. While we are out training we see several other members of the Slovenijan team.

At the end of May I am planning to make a trip to Australia. There are several reasons driving this decision. First and foremost, as part of the conditions of my German visa I need to leave Europe for three months so that I am able to return and continue to stay here for another period of time. This will bring me up to the end of October when I plan to return to the States. I could go back to Alaska, and while I am planning a brief trip home, I'm not ready to go back on any permanent basis yet.

The second reason for choosing Australia is that it will be winter down there and it will give me an opportunity to continue my training on real snow, something I've never done in July before. And, I have to say, it will be good to be somewhere where they speak English. The final reason is that there are opportunities to expand the Holmenkol brand 'down under' and, as they have been so good to me, I want to take every opportunity to repay the favor.

Andy and Klemen hiking in Slovenija.

With a two-week trip planned back to Alaska, that leaves me just over two weeks left in Europe and I have several things that I need to do in that time.

Since meeting Sylwia Jaśkowiec at the Skiing World Championships, we kept a regular communication by email and skype and it is a relationship that I find stimulating and rather amazing. She is opening my eyes to a spiritual dimension I had not realized was within me. The most powerful thing that she says to me seems kind of simple, but it is something that I will always remember and I feel is the most important part of our connection: *"Everything has a beginning and an end."* Her view of life and her energy towards power and drive to work hard, I love.

She thrives on my consistent efforts to help her with her attitude with the goal of getting the most out of believing in yourself, always looking for the positive to help overcome barriers, especially in sport. So, as you can see, we have a great deal in common and I want to take the opportunity to visit her before I leave Europe. Yet I would not say this is a romantic relationship, even though there are elements of that. We are both so focused on our journeys that we don't have much time or interest for more.

Two days of driving is enough to take me across Slovenija, through eastern Austria, Slovakia, and into southwestern Poland. Sylwia has invited me to visit and so that's where I'm headed. During the months of April and May she attends a University that specializes in athletics. After entering Poland I continue northeast to the city of Katowice (pronounced *'Cat-o-vitza'*).

It takes some keen navigating and a few stops to ask for directions to find my destination, but I make it eventually. I approach the guards at the gate of the University armed with a smile and her name on a piece of paper. They do not speak any English and so I hold up the paper and they make a few phone calls before allowing me onto the campus. I am excited to find the building and walk up the four flights of stairs to her dorm room. As I knock on the door I hear a voice that sounds pleasant so I open it and see a welcoming and happy look on Sylwia's face. She knew I was coming, but hadn't known the exact day. She introduces me to her friends and invites me to many of her classes.

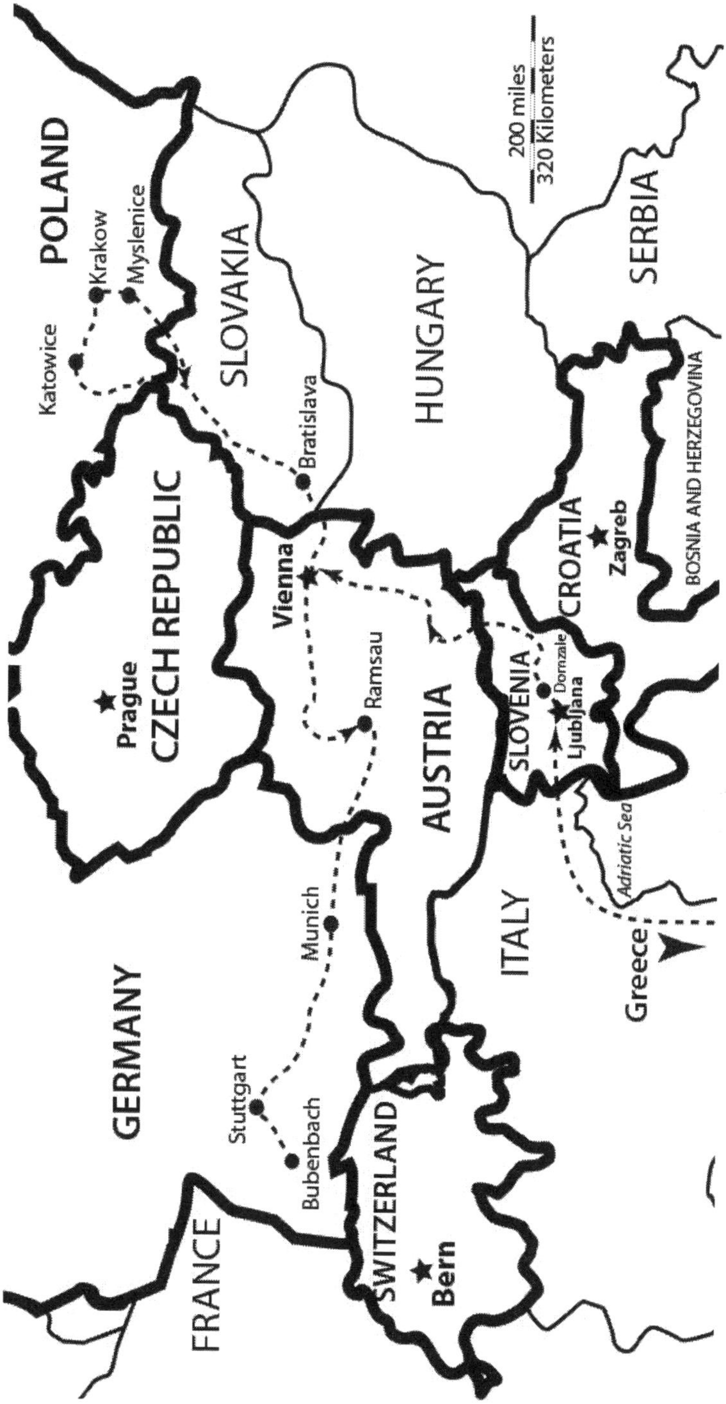
POLAND
Katowice
Krakow
Myslenice
SLOVAKIA
Bratislava
HUNGARY
200 miles
320 Kilometers
SERBIA
CZECH REPUBLIC
Prague
Vienna
Ramsau
AUSTRIA
SLOVENIA
Domzale
Ljubljana
CROATIA
Zagreb
BOSNIA AND HERZEGOVINA
Adriatic Sea
ITALY
Greece
GERMANY
Munich
Stuttgart
Bubenbach
FRANCE
SWITZERLAND
Bern

Sylwia has received approval from her professors to let me attend, observe, and participate in their activities. The three years I spent in college, I've been in the Physical Education (PE), Management of Health and Fitness, and Nutrition areas of study. Since she is a PE major, all of the classes are held either outdoors or in the gym. It is really a lot of fun. The education system for the University level in Poland is much different than in the United States. Different in that the only people on campus are in the same two month school block and all seem to be athletes. Everywhere I look are people my age running around in athletic gear hurrying to and from classes.

It's very interesting how they teach some of the basic steps to sport. Some of it is identical, but I've taken mental notes of other ways of teaching. They even had me out on the playground working with elementary age kids during scheduled constructive PE time one day.

The Katowice University sports equipment and fields on campus is very nice and I am able to get in many excellent training sessions while I visit. I even run a few track workouts on the new red rubberized track. Every time I run track workouts I've seen different groups of students learning about the various track and field events. Some of these sports, such as javelin, I've never really seen taught and I've been able to watch the instructor break down each step and proper phase. Luckily all of this is visible, so it is not necessary to understand the words they are saying, because it's all in Polish, of course. Sylwia always translates the important info into English and giggles a bit when she has trouble finding the right words.

We also participate in a large University study that is going on during the week. It is a physical fitness test that the University needs. Completing the activities takes an hour and a half and is very interesting. We complete many activities that I have never seen or even heard of before. Some I'm really not sure make any sense, but they have a good way of testing. They cover everything from isometric strength, physical endurance, balance in place, balance in movement, rhythmic strength, arm speed, hand coordination, foot speed, and stretching distances. All of which are completed in a gym with over a hundred other students going from station to station completing the tests as the instructors observe and document the results. Sylwia and I secretly compete against each other and keep score, one point for out doing the other. Interestingly, we tie and both score into the highest bracket of athletic ability on the study scale. I now have a broader range of activities to test people if I ever end up being a PE teacher or coach someday.

I learn a lot during the week and acquire many new training ideas. At the end of the week Sylwia and I drive into the famous aged city of Krakow where we walk through castles and churches that are several hundred years old. The land and castles are great to see and I felt lucky to have her showing me the best sites, translating everything on the spot.

From there we go to her house and meet her family. The moment we walk in we are instantly surrounded by loving hugs and warm handshakes. She grew up in this house along with her brother and three sisters and they are all there with their families when we arrive. Only Sylwia, her brother Dominik, and one sister speak English and her mother is nearly in tears trying and wanting to speak to me. Dominik attributes 100% of his English speech to watching American movies.

The next morning Sylwia takes me out for a "bike around the area." She lives in an area surrounded by thick forested hillsides as far as the eye can see. I never thought of Poland as a place like this!

I consider myself an average or maybe above average mountain biker, but following her on a mountain bike, down those hills, through those trails, makes me feel like I have training wheels on. She does end up smashing her helmet beyond repair on the ride, but still!

The following day we say our goodbyes and, while she heads back to another intense week of school, I head down the road. It has been a really fun week and a nice feeling to be welcomed by her and her family. Sylwia and I have plans to meet again when our training plans parallel. She is already qualified for the Olympics and is really looking forward to the Vancouver Games.

On the way back from Poland I sleep in a parking lot somewhere in the middle of Slovakia before driving the majority of the next day to the little town of Altenmarkt, tucked away in the Austrian Alps. It is a beautiful sunny Sunday and I spend the remainder of the day sitting outside reading a book while parked up on a hillside along a road with a glorious view. The reason for stopping here is that it is the location of a large ski factory from which I have arranged to pick up my new *SALOMON* skis.

After collecting my new skis I make the four-hour trek to Heimerdingen, which is where Holmenkol is based. There I meet with Christian, the CEO, and am involved with several other smaller meetings before getting back on the road and driving another two hours to Bubenbach where my friend Raphael Wunderle lives.

I spend a week at the Wunderle's and it feels so strange to be settled in one place, and enjoy a relaxing easy pace of life after weeks of hectic running around. It is a very quiet area and I enjoy training in the surrounding countryside and helping Raphael's parents with lots of jobs on the farm.

The second Monday in May arrives and there is only one more day before I fly to Alaska for a brief trip, then returning to Germany only en-route to Australia. Leaving the Wunderle's early I make the trip back to Holmenkol for another series of meetings. I've been thinking a lot about my position in Holmenkol and have come up with some fairly ambitious ideas on how they can improve and the role I can play in those plans. I've asked Christian, the CEO, if I can present my ideas to him and am a bit nervous about how it will pan out.

The meeting with Christian starts well. He had not known about my trip to Greece and, as I had hoped, he is surprised and impressed with the establishment of a market network in that country. With the positive energy from the Greece surprise still in the air I float an idea for a new job position of *International Distributor Relations* and outline the responsibilities and goals of the position. I feel a little sensitive because, strictly speaking, liaising with international distributors is his role, but he likes the idea, likes the approach and is positive about my enthusiasm.

He also realizes that I've effectively been performing the role in any case as I have direct involvement with the U.S., Australia, New Zealand, Argentina, Chile, Greece and Turkey. As a result of the discussion he decides to extend my work contract for a few months, which means I'll continue to get a steady pay check and health benefits. I'll be in Australia for most of this time but I'll make sure I set up a proper network when I am down there.

At the close of the day's meeting Christian gives me a lift to the Stuttgart airport and we continue our discussion. It really makes me feel good to be able to communicate on a personal level with such a senior executive. I love the business side of life and know there are plenty of opportunities for me in life after skiing.

Alaska – The Last Frontier

The flight to Alaska does not leave till the following morning so I spend the night grabbing what sleep I can at the airport. The flight is reasonably uneventful and, as the plane touches down in Anchorage, it feels both strange and yet comfortable to be in my home state and country. It is quite a shock to see all the road signs in English, the wide roads and the huge four-wheel-drive pick-ups. As we drive to my mother's place so many familiar things come into view. After unpacking I go for a run to clear my head and stretch my legs and it is during this run that I come to the realization that I am suddenly terribly homesick.

The two weeks I spend in Alaska are incredibly busy and many times I think of simply forgetting about my travels and remaining here in the comfort of the known. In-between catching up with people I compete in a 5K running race, running a personal best of 15:48.

Andy working on the roof.

I still own a home that I have been renting out for the last year and there is a bit of outdoor maintenance work to be done on it. My mother's friend, Larry, and I move my 8'x16' shed across the yard, build a deck with steps, repair a leaky roof using a knife and lots of tar, and remove a 7'x4' solid concrete slab with a cable, rope, and car.

During the weekend I drive to my hometown, Soldotna. I visit a few people, one of which is Justin Freestone, a high school classmate who has muscular dystrophy. He has lived far beyond what the doctors had expected and is someone I look up to for his strength and endurance in life. We watch a movie together and then I hit the road headed back to Anchorage. On the road back, I stop at a trail called Devil's Pass. I have never been on this ten mile mountain trail to the pass. It is a beautiful run and crosses more and more avalanche chutes the higher in altitude I run. There is a 2-3 mile stretch that shows recent heavy bear traffic. Running in the wild alone I luckily do not see any bears. I end up running a few miles past the pass sign to make the total run about 24 miles.

A couple of days before I am scheduled to leave, I enter an eight mile trail run called Turnagain Arm Trail Run. This race is emotionally challenging for me to enter. My former ski coach is the race director and I have not faced him for over a year due to bad blood that was created when I left the team. Facing him is awkward but we are professional about it and keep our manners. The day is hot and I make sure to have the proper elements from the periodic table in my system along with lots of water. At the start line I dump half of a liter of water over my head just to get a cool fresh feeling again. My former coach starts us off with the race watch and we take off down the trail.

For the first mile I run in the front pack and it feels great to be feeling 100% and competing with my Alaskan running buddies again. This race is the first of the mountain running series and my first running race (besides the 5K a week before) in 2.5 years. After that first mile, which is uphill the entire way, I blow past everyone and pick up the pace to create as big of a gap as possible. The only runner who dares to keep up is Mark Iverson. I lead with Mark following closely behind for the next two miles as we cruise over rolling terrain and leap over muddy creeks. I love this type of running course and feel really comfortable gliding swiftly along the trail.

At the three mile point I ask Mark if he would like to lead for a while and he takes up the offer. Right away Mark picks up the pace as the trail hits a steep uphill that I am not ready for. He gaps me a little bit and I think to myself *"If he keeps this pace up he will have the race for sure."* Two miles later, however, I reel him in on a long downhill and we run together for another two miles, until I feel the pace is going just too slow.

Because the trail is so narrow I have to ask him politely for him to move over. He complies and I resume the lead. I thought he would have followed me, but he seems to drop behind pretty fast. From there I still feel that I have a lot left in the tank, so I keep pushing it more and more. A few minutes later I am running far in the lead and am more relaxed than ever. I know that as long as I don't break my leg I will win for sure. Nobody has ever beaten me on a downhill run in my life, and the last mile is all downhill.

Finishing in good physical condition, clocking the third best time in the race history, gives me good confirmation that all the miles I ran in Greece, Slovenija, Poland, and Germany over the past few weeks was right on. I must credit the old-fashioned hard-core will to succeed. My former coach is at the finish and we shake hands.

Afterwards I hear, *"I know why you won. It's because it was ******* (my former coach) race and you wanted to rub it in his face."* I disagree, responding with *"I'm a competitor and that it's the duty of all competitors to give 100% from start to finish!"*

The final two days in Alaska are amazingly busy but I have a growing sense that I have come home too soon and I know I have to go again. As I am leaving I feel that I'm leaving a lot behind but the world waits for me and there are things I must do, so I turn my back on the familiar once more and step off again on another leg of the journey.

CHAPTER NINE
Skiing Down Under

It's May 30th and I sit in a little seat on a large Condor jetliner, feeling the walls and floor shake, and listening to the engines rev while taking off. *"A new adventure is just beginning,"* I think to myself. The direct flight from Alaska to Frankfurt takes nine hours and passes over the North Pole, before landing ten time zones ahead. Once in Frankfurt, Germany, there is a 12-hour layover (12 HOURS!), before my connecting flight to Stuttgart departs. Thankfully, I sleep plenty even though it is the middle of the day because it is the middle of the night in Alaska.

My connecting flight arrives in Stuttgart at 11:30 pm Sunday. Christian had told me to call him personally on his mobile when I arrive and he will pick me up, but I decide not to call him until 10:00 the following morning. I am still wide awake as it is early afternoon in Alaska, so I wander down the road to the McDonalds to read and catch up on business paperwork all through the night.

As I stand waiting and expecting to see him drive up in the company's SUV, I see a black Alpha Romero coming. After months in Europe I've decided that is my dream car, to own someday. Much to my surprise, it stops and the window rolls down. It's Christian! This is his personal car!

After we arrive at the factory we grab my pre-packed parcels and add more stuff from the shelves in the warehouse to better prepare for my next trip. We return to the airport and I attempt to check my bags in, but I'm instructed that I have to wait another four hours. I go sit and sleep for four hours.

When I once again hand them my tickets and rifle papers they look more closely at them and begin to freak out. They advise me that I should have checked in with them hours ago because it is not permitted to carry weapons around in the airport without police supervision. Immediately they make a phone call and two German policemen arrive to stand guard over my rifle for the entire two hour process that it takes to check my bags in. They tell me when flying with weapons to always notify the airlines and—each connection along with final destination—at least 24 hours before traveling.

I have already gotten authorization from Melbourne airport, which is my final destination. The connections are not aware and I stand in Stuttgart on the phone checking in with each stop and incur many problems. Apparently, even though my flight plan schedule stops in such places as London and Singapore for less than two hours, and I'll never see my luggage, I'm still required to have a permit to transit those airports. It is such a problem that my ticket has to be re-routed to Bangkok instead of Singapore to get to Sydney.

The extra cost is 25 Euros for each connecting flight just for the rifle. Those extra charges plus the overweight charge for my other bag and the flight change fee cost me quite a bit and this is just the beginning of the trip. At first, the airline (British Air) will not take my ski bag because it is over their maximum limit for weight. I happen to have a backpack and a shoulder bag so I pack my side bag with the really heavy stuff and it now weighs in at 33 kilos.

The moment I have my boarding pass I turn the large heavily-filled cart in the direction of the oversized luggage intake and push with all my might as the two German police walk beside me, one on each side like I am a criminal being escorted. People move out of the way, giving me odd looks the entire time. Once my bags are riding down that black conveyer belt I feel relieved and the two police wave goodbye and say good luck.

The Stuttgart airport officials don't let me off the hook yet, however. As I pass though the security check they take my side bag with both hands and heave as they attempt to lift it off the belt on the exit side and back to the front to run it through again. Then the security officer turns and informs me that *"Dirt, sand, and soils are not allowed to be carried on airplanes."* The 200 catalogs and 1000 stickers along with other heavy items are so dense that my shoulder bag is the heaviest small bag I have ever lifted. But once they look inside they let me go.

My four day travel plan is: Anchorage -> Frankfurt -> Stuttgart -> London -> Bangkok -> Sydney -> Melbourne. After spending that much time in airplanes and airports you start thinking in one of two ways. Either you are anxious and annoyed that it's taking so long, or (like me) you forget what life is like apart from security checks, sleeping on public benches, and going without showers. My mind has become numb and I have no idea if it is day or night by the time I arrive in Bangkok, Thailand.

Andy in Thailand.

Bangkok airport is only two years old and many people are walking around with masks on to protect themselves from the infamous swine flu that has plagued the planet. I don't have room in my 70-lbs of carry-on luggage for such things and I figure that with so many people wearing masks, the majority are protecting the minority because they are filtering their own emissions.

I decide to buy a 12-ounce coke in a can for my friend Steffi, in Austria. She has coke cans from all over the world and I know she doesn't have one from Thailand. Even though I have purchased the coke duty-free and it is sealed in a plastic bag they will not let me board the plane with it. Australian law prohibits any food, drink, or wood. So I chug the coke then and there! Standing next to me is a guy in the same situation who just bought a bottle of wine and is drinking that. He doesn't drink the whole thing, but I am laughing at the thought of him doing so.

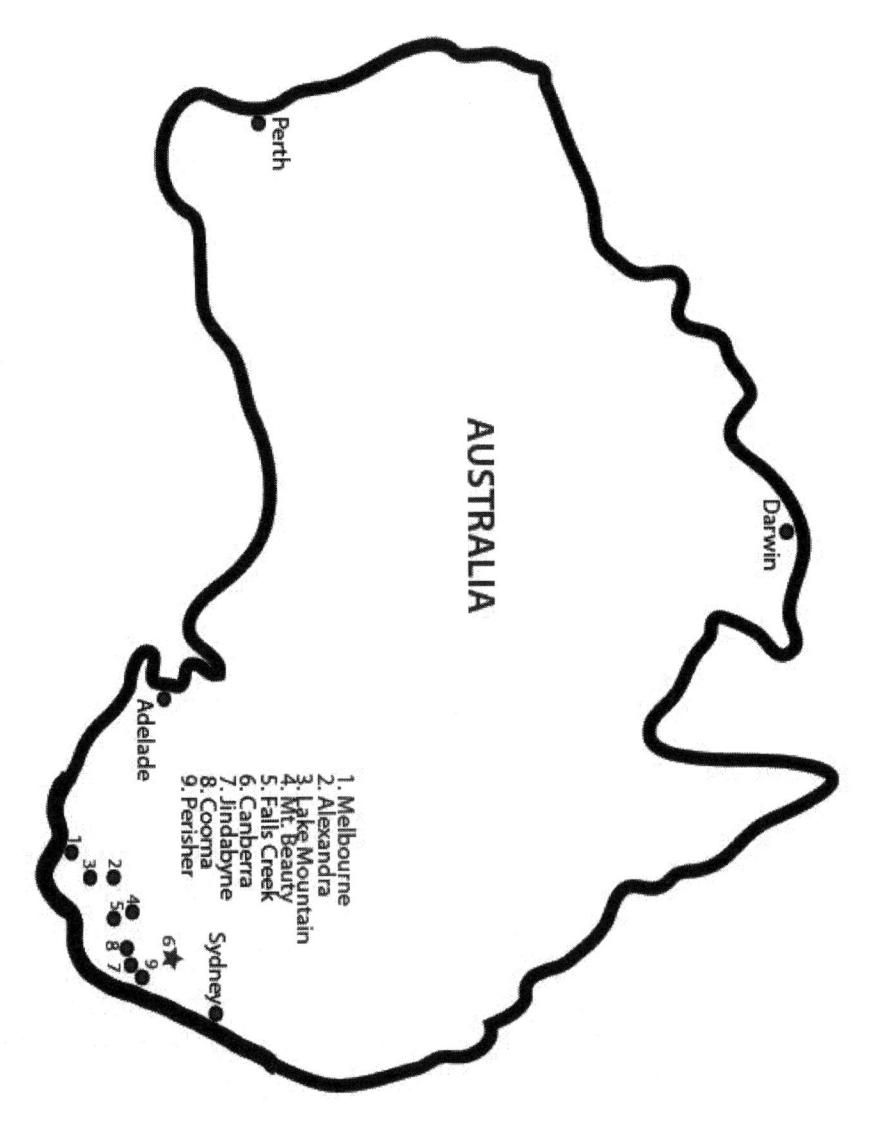

1. Melbourne
2. Alexandra
3. Lake Mountain
4. Mt. Beauty
5. Falls Creek
6. Canberra
7. Jindabyne
8. Cooma
9. Perisher

After another nine hour flight I am in Sydney. Customs will not let me check my rifle through to my connecting flight because my permit is for the state of Victoria and Sydney is located in the state of New South Wales. It takes them two hours to tell me this so I miss the final leg of my trip to Melbourne. ...And my rifle is confiscated by the Sydney customs officials.

I am not too stressed by the Sydney customs officers holding my rifle because at that point the officer leads me to believe that, once a certain document arrives from Victoria, then it will be shipped directly to Melbourne, so it seems to be no big deal. Also, in the back of my mind is that I will be coming to Sydney within the next week or so anyway as part of a side-trip to visit retail shops on behalf of Holmenkol. I've arranged for Matt de Freitas (we met in O-town in the winter) to be my guide and driver, and have funds to pay him. In addition I am not planning on using the rifle within the first two weeks because there isn't any snow yet on the ski trails to even ski, so I am not in a hurry.

Catching my final flight I have one less bag to check, which turns out to be a good thing because the airlines won't allow me to carry such heavy bags onboard. They give me a cheap, thin type of bag, and I even out the weight to make sure all the bags are just below the limits.

After arriving in Melbourne I call Matt to come pick me up. Meanwhile I am able to open a bank account at a well-known Australian Bank to get business rolling. After Matt appears he asks if he can carry a bag to the car-park. I point to the side bag, which I have repacked like it had been earlier. He thinks he is getting off easy when I am carrying both my backpack and large ski bag, but when he lifts it, he let out an *"Ooofff!! This is one **heavy** little bag!"* After loading Matt's car, I go around to sit in the passenger's side. I wait by the handle and Matt comes to the same door with an odd look on his face. Then we both realize that I have forgotten that Aussies, like the British, drive on the opposite side of the road so the driver's side is on the right side of the car, opposite to what I am used to.

I had departed Anchorage at noon May 30 and now it was noon June 3, although it is only mid-afternoon of the 2nd back in Alaska since Melbourne is about 19 hours ahead. I am tired and only want to take a shower, a nap, and eat some food. Unfortunately the shower, nap, and food are delayed by a few hours because Matt has to get back to the University before going to his house. I wait a few long hours for him to finish his daily study in a lecture hall. Later I finally feel that I have made it through this series of travel-marathons and my life in Australia can begin.

The first few days in Melbourne are spent living in a house built in the early 1900's with Matt and his four roommates. The place is freezing cold and in the mornings you can see your breath. I usually throw on some clothes quickly and run out the door and down the street to warm-up before re-entering the house/freezer again. There is a really nice dirt single-track a few blocks away that parallels the Yarra River in Melbourne that I run along. The water is muddy and the trail sometimes runs right down to the bank.

After acclimatizing it is time to set out on the business side of the trip. Matt drives me from Melbourne to Sydney, through a mountain pass. After driving around Europe, where everything is so close together, it is a shock driving in Australia. It is not much smaller than the U.S. but with less than 10% of the people. Amazing! Matt and I spend nearly a week on the road visiting almost every retail ski shop from Melbourne to Sydney. From a business side the trip is very successful and I make some good connections and deals. The rifle situation is not so good, however.

It had been my plan to pick up the rifle from Sydney airport when we are in Sydney, but after spending hours on the phone it is clear that they are not going to allow me to do that. They insist on flying the rifle to Melbourne for me to collect it there. They want to charge me money to ship the rifle to Melbourne but I argue against this, pointing out that the system is at fault. In the end I am not required to pay for it and they ship it to Melbourne.

I have spent hours running around collecting all the paperwork necessary to have my rifle released and am confident that I will be able to collect the rifle without any further hassles. But when I arrive at the airport they refuse to give me the magazines (bullet clips). I can't believe the garbage I am being put through here. I have asked all the questions I could think of, followed all the rules, done everything that is known within their regulations, and now this.

There is nothing on any of the forms to even include a magazine. It's either a weapon or ammo. Mags/ clips are accessories. It is not easy but I manage to get them to package them up and have them ready to ship them out when I have the right people contact them and fax more papers to them. I am so sick of dealing with rifle issues. I decided right then that I will never return to Australia with any type of weapon.

By this time I am boiling inside. There isn't even any space on the form for magazines, so why should I be punished for not including them when I couldn't even know that it needs to be documented? Their rules seem silly and as an American, having no weapon restrictions such as these, the rules here make no sense. It is all I can do to keep my cool.

Once I have my rifle I leave Melbourne and travel about three hours into the mountains where the de Frietas' parents live. Mrs. de Frietas (Jen) welcomes me into her home and I set up my base there for the next week or so. On some mornings I get up at six and walk down the dark cold street to catch a bus designed for employees that work at the Lake Mountain Resort ski area. Alan Eason, another friend of mine from Europe is the manager of the ski school.

The ride is about an hour. It is entertaining because of the scenery and remnants of the intense fire that consumed the area last February. The woods are black and green. If you're a real tree buff you'd know that Australia has forests full of trees that require fires to reproduce. Some release seeds upon the sensing of burning and others release little buds right from the sides of the stock. Most of the trees look black and are covered in bright neon green fuzz.

To put real skis on in June is exciting. The conditions are good and there are over 300 skiers on the trails during my first two days. It feels weird skiing in Australia and zipping around completely different types of scenery. Something I never expected that caught my attention right away is the amount of eucalyptus and snow gum tree leaves that have fallen onto the track.

Skiing over eucalyptus leaves, when stepped on just right, nearly stops the ski due to the oil glands within the leaves. I am able to get some good training hours in, which is why I am here above all else. The sun is very bright and the snow seems to be constantly transforming, causing it to be more dense and wet as each day progresses.

By the fourth day of skiing at Lake Mountain I come to a huge wall within me. I find myself sitting on the top floor at the lodge just starring out the window. I cannot hide the truth to myself anymore. This is just not working. Since being in Australia I have found it increasingly difficult to be motivated for training. Thoughts of returning to Europe or America continually float through my mind.

I feel like I've only been giving my training a half-ass effort and the worst thing is that I feel like I have not future interest in training or competitions. An interesting statement pops into my head during this mind-breaking moment. It is a statement that I told to myself over and over again as my Coast Guard career was ending: *"Never work in an environment that continuously makes you unhappy."*

The feeling here is different from the one that consumed me in Greece. Over there I was not trying to train, but here, where the people speak English, and I am focused, or supposed to be, in training, it raises more serious questions about my future. I feel like the athlete in me is giving up. My mythical experiences in Greece are recollected as a far off distant dream and I wonder about the truth in it.

The phrase "falling down" comes to mind, triggering a thought as I remember one of my favorite quotes that stops the dark energy restraining me from my workout that day. It is: *"Every life has its setbacks. Falling down is no disgrace; it is getting up that makes the champion. Get up one more time than you fall and you will always succeed."* by Paul H. Dunn. This is enough to motivate me and I ski one more workout at this venue. I know this negative mental energy is not going to go away, but if I keep trying to move forward I can hope it will too get left behind by my pace.

There is little doubt that feeling so physically far away from all the places and securities of familiarity in this world is causing this discomfort. Every time I think I am past the worst, another problem emerges. It has now been brought to my attention that I must have a storage box built to a detailed specification, according to Aussie law. Last year alone the Aussie police did 17,000 random weapon checks and put hundreds of people in jail, just because of inadequate storage boxes.

They actually have a maximum penalty of two years in jail for failure to comply, and even though surely it is rare to get the maximum penalty it is enough to scare me into getting this sorted out. Just when I think I'm through all the red tape, more comes up. —And everything seems to be going like this!

I end up spending about six hours building a storage box using thick hardwood. I like building things with wood, but they don't always come out looking pretty, especially when I'm in a hurry. The project serves as a great opportunity to change the mental channel in my mind and for brief moments I forget about being an athlete. In the end my locking rifle case for travel is much more secure than this new box will ever be, but it is less expensive to buy the materials to build a box than to pay for bail so now I have an Australian-specified rifle security containment box!

Rifle in its new box.

It turns out that finding accommodation in the ski regions of Australia in the winter is far more difficult than I imagined. It took Ramsey months to find a little room in a cold basement. While it is fine staying with the de Freitas it is not a long-term option and I need to be closer to the snow. They hit on the idea of loaning me their old trailer (called a *caravan* in Australia) and towing it to a caravan park near the snow-fields. We have located a caravan park in a place called Mt. Beauty and now I am sitting in their car with them towing the trailer behind.

Mt. Beauty sits between the only biathlon range in Australia and another large set of ski trails where the Aussie National Ski Team is based. During the entire three hour drive I feel like telling Mr. de Freitas (Greg) to turn around and go home. I would much rather go back to the airport and fly somewhere I feel better mentally. But I hold my tongue.

Thoughts run wild in my mind, ricocheting off my brain like stray bullets in a gun fight. *"What have I got myself into?" "It's too late to turn around now."* And on they go. I've tried everything I can to shift my mental state. This is something I've prided myself on being able to do but this time the negativity is getting the better of me and I feel myself close to sliding into a deep, dark place.

After arriving in Mt. Beauty we find the *Mt. Beauty Holiday Centre* and pull the trailer into camping spot number 102. It takes nearly two hours to set everything up. The awning is quite difficult and has many pieces. Greg has to wrack his brain to remember how it all goes together. I am very thankful they are lending me the trailer and for everything they have helped me with to make this possible. After the trailer is set up we go to lunch and then hit the grocery store. It's about 2k to the only grocery store in Mt. Beauty and so I stock up on all the heaviest food. From now on I have to carry everything on foot.

As I said, I'm really appreciative for the caravan, but it is not a thing of beauty. The roof leaks, the screens and fabric walls inside are ripped. The plywood ceiling and upholstery are covered in mold and some of the zippers on the awning are broken. But there is a newly built rifle box bolted to the floor under the seat! This caravan is where I hope to make a fresh start and the place I will call home for the rest of my stay in Australia. I will make the best of it!

Falls Creek, near Mt. Beauty, is the actual skiing area where the National Team trains and is known to have the best skiing in Australia. On my first day here it is not so good. I hitchhike up the road (45-min drive) to get to the trails. I find that the ski trails go along open areas that resemble the moon. Have I accidently skied though a portal which put me on the moon? I turn around and look back at the lake and some trees to confirm that I am still on planet Earth.

It is so warm up here that poles are nearly worthless, as they punch straight through to the ground. It begins to rain pretty hard after I have been skiing only an hour and am only halfway through my workout. As you know, I hate skiing in the rain so I call it a day and hitchhike back down the mountain. The skiing is just not very good yet and I decide to not go back up until it snows again. Dry-land training is much more appealing.

Upper portion of Falls Creek ski area, or "ski area on the moon."

The majority of the Falls Creek ski trails congregate on one major hillside that winds up, around, and over the region. There is a large lake that is dammed at the top and a portion of the ski trail is groomed straight along the rim of the dam to connect to the rolling hills on the opposite side of the lake. The trails are wider than most and groomed well. What is most different is the brightness of the sun and the types of trees and bushes that line the trail. I'd never seen anything like them before.

The next morning I head out for a long run to explore these new surroundings. A lot can happen during a four hour run while covering territory that is entirely new to my eyes. I feel the old sense of freedom returning as I bound down the quiet and simple streets of Mt. Beauty ready to take on the mountain it rests beside. I follow typical signs of trails right from the edge of town that lead to a creek-side trail heading in the right direction. Soon after the trail disappears I notice a game trail across the stream. Hop, hop, hop, I cross the stream on stones that are well placed for crossing.

The first minutes of running on that single-track trail are horrendous. This outback bushwhacking is hard and painful. A lot of the plants have barbs on them and they come at you at different heights—similar to wild blackberries in the Pacific NW and Devil's

Club in Alaska. My legs are getting thrashed and sometimes one foot will catch a snag just right and pull it across the other leg feeling like sliding barbwire. Lots of blood right from the start! There has to be better outback running trails than this and I am determined to find them.

There are also many spider webs and snake holes that I discover by running into and stepping over them very intimately. There is a certain feeling one gets when catching a spider web across the face. Being winter here now is a good time of year to be pushing through these forests. But I have a lurking fear of waking a snake out of its hole and when they do come up in winter they are known to almost always strike because they are mad. Australia is known to have the most deadly spiders and snakes in the world. After 20 minutes of bushwhacking I find an old forest road that winds up and around through the mountain next to the one I wanted to run.

I see many kangaroos, wallabies, deer, massively large trees, thick bushes, and birds, birds, more birds. There are so many colorful and loud birds it is unbelievable. The noises they make remind me of jungle movies. Only this is real! They squawk, cackle, chirp, and make just about any noise imaginable. One type sounds like a dying cat, while another sounds like a monkey, and I often turn my head thinking I will see a monkey and chuckle because it is only a bird.

There are so many amazing things to discover while on foot and the outback seems nearly endless. Besides the cuts and bleeding legs, I really enjoy the four hour run and am looking forward to another long run, exploring the outback.

"Today was beautiful, tomorrow will be perfect." That's the town saying—and they're right! It was beautiful yesterday and today is perfect. Imagine waking up with the sun beaming into your living room. You walk out your front door, stretch your arms wide and breathe in the fresh, warm morning air. Then go out for a run and do 4x4-minute intervals followed by 4x1-min. intervals, all at Level 4 pace (80% of max). Do it on a loop with rolling hills for over an hour. Spend half the day working. Then more physical training consisting of core strength, including my favorite push-up/sit-up ladders, all the while dry-firing five rounds between each set. I have finally found a comfortable living arrangement in combination with a convenient training route.

Since new snow has yet to arrive, Ramsey is not going up to Mt. Hotham (the only Biathlon range in Australia) any time soon. In that time I continue to create my own marksmanship training routine, aiming to sharpen my accuracy when I have a high heart rate. If I can handle my rifle for as many hours a day as I train physically, I should be well within my goals for improvement. Of course, I am only dry-firing because they haven't given me back my magazines yet. Practice, practice, practice!

Maybe it's a good thing I do not have any ammo, because these birds continue to make racket in the trees above my caravan. Having my rifle in hand, clicking the trigger, and listening to those birds for a few days has got me thinking. I hope my ears will adapt so they will just be background noise.

Mt. Beauty is a nice town and on days when the sun shines it is almost perfect. Even so, I cannot maintain my momentum. I want to enjoy my stay here, but in reality I am having difficulty staying positive and motivated. I do not understand why I feel so bad and why everything seems to be against me. The mental difficulties of sport are never expressed on NBC's "Up Close and Personal" interviews with athletes. And I'm not at a high enough level of skiing that anyone would notice my disappearance from the sport if I decide to quit. I can't believe that I am thinking of quitting, and feel that if I were in O-town right now the thought of quitting would never even come into mind.

Sitting in my caravan I write about all the good things I can possibly think of and try to tune out the negativity that haunts me every other second. But it is not working. I can't stop thinking about every minute here being one less minute I have to be in Australia before I can return to Europe.

While I am focusing on training, desperately attempting to maintain my motivation, I am also pursuing business connections. There is a Worldloppet race over here and I make an arrangement to meet the race director and one of his staff members to discuss details. At one point of the meeting I notice a stack of ski hats from various ski marathons. Alan, the director, picks them up and sorts through them and, as he does, one catches my eye. It is from the Bieg Piastow Worldloppet in Poland that I had won in February. Right away I say, *"Hey, I know that hat. I was there and won that race!"*

Alan and his staff member both turn to me with a puzzled look. The next thing Alan said, *"You're an athlete too!?"* Not to make myself look like Mr. Done-Everything, but it's reactions like that, that help me keep moving forward during tough times and help me realize why I've chosen to take these odd jobs around the world so I can continue training and racing.

Alan is on the Worldloppet committee and will be traveling to Szklarska Poreba (the Polish race site) in a few months for a meeting and was sent a bunch of stuff including those hats and some race flyers. After glancing through some of the race flyers, I notice one for the Marathon in Obertilliach that has my Austrian trainer Joe on the cover. It sure feels like a small world sometimes. …And I *do* feel like I belong but some inner aspect of me is dragging me down.

In the early days of July good snow arrives on the back of a thunderstorm that nearly shakes my caravan apart. But I feel no enjoyment in this snow. The daily grind of having to stand out on the road and hitchhike 45 minutes to ski is wearing me down. What I would give to have old "Camp Alaska" here with me now.

The idea of coming to Australia to get some extra kilometers on the ski trails was a good idea. But the reality that I had begun last ski season in mid-September and skied all winter through to the first week in April, to now ski again in June and July has my passion for skiing pretty low. Things are working, but when it comes down to it, I need to listen to my mind and feelings and do what is best for me to live and train correctly with a healthy positive mindset.

Even though there are setbacks here and my living situation is not ideal, I've been able to stay consistent with the important factor of being here: training. Along with the many hours I'm logging, the consistency of all the special technique drills, specific strength, and endurance training has been really good. Outside of preparing orders for Holmenkol through the retail shops that I met the first week of my arrival, there is nothing else to do here but get outside and train. Other work I've done from time to time with Holmenkol has been with club teams, individual athletes is holding wax clinics, which I do after my training up at Falls Creek. I've never been able to log so many hours before with my rifle, dry-firing.

I've been creative with a lot of the shooting drills, by mixing strength routines, sprint drills, and aerobics in with getting in and out of shooting position every few minutes to stimulate shooting with a high heart rate. I still miss the great shooting facilities of O-town and the presence of Bjørndalen along with the many different national teams training. I think about what it is like there often, and how life would be different if I were there now. I often stand or lay in shooting position, close my eyes and convince my mind that I am actually there. I've always said "The most valuable freedom is one that no one can take from you, <u>your freedom to think</u>."

Andy holding his rifle next to the caravan during a dry-firing session.

After a good two hour ski one day I feel frisky enough to walk into Mt. Beauty in search of something that I feel a calling to buy and read. Of the few stores located in Mt. Beauty one is a book store and it has an unorganized pile of books cluttered in a large clearance-sale bin on the sidewalk. I spend less than a minute picking and tossing books around when I come to one that speaks to me. *"In Search Of..."* by an Aussie named Alistair Smith. There is something mysterious about it as I hold it, gazing at the preface. I buy the book!

Refreshing Move

Rescue comes in the form of Ben Sim, the best skier in Australia, whose nickname is Simbo. He invites me to come and stay and train with him for two weeks. It's a life-line, an escape from the daily grind in Mt. Beauty that I have come to love and dread at the same time. I'm hoping that living and training with Simbo will revitalize my enthusiasm.

We will be staying in a flat on a ranch owned by the parents of Simbo's girlfriend, also an elite skier. It is about 20 minutes out of the town of Jindabyne, near the Perisher ski resort. The first morning in the house I look out the window to see a herd of kangaroos munching on grass and hopping about. A layer of frost completes the scene. An hour-forty run that morning is brisk due to the chilly breeze blowing across the valley. A few weeks in Mt. Beauty may only seem like a short time, but now that I am away, in the company of friends, it's like a breath of fresh air. Oh, how nice a solid roof is, along with a real bed, and such things as a sink, toilet, couch, and cooking supplies!

Unfortunately, I am not able to enjoy training with Simbo as much as I would have liked because he has to take part in a week-long testing program for the Australian athletes who are either qualified or likely to qualify for the Olympics. I take the opportunity to check out the Nordic ski trails at Perisher and they quickly become my favorite in Australia.

There are only three real cross country ski centers in Australia. The furthest south location is called Lake Mountain, (near Alexandra where I lived at the beginning of this trip). Second is in Falls Creek (near Mt. Beauty) and the third (the most north) is Perisher. It's interesting watching and listening to the skiing community talk about the two other ski centers and the stereotyped people of Victoria.

Andy at the ranch in Jindabyne.

They call them "Mexicans." The main reasons: Victoria is south of the border from New South Wales, plus Victoria does not have the yearly auto inspection. So Victorians often drive older, junkier autos whereas all autos registered in New South Wales are frequently tested and require higher standards to be fit for the road, which makes them in much better condition.

In the mornings Simbo drops me off at a well-known roundabout, right on the edge of town. From there he drives another 15 km to get on a transport carrier called the "Ski Tube." It costs $50 for one day or $150 for a season to use the Ski Tube. I'm only here for a short time so I hitchhike every day to and from the trails. It costs over $100 for an auto pass to drive to the ski area because it is in a national park. It's only about 20 km from town, all uphill. Hitchhiking from the roundabout is usually easy. There are always other people standing in line hitching and we get picked up quickly.

The Perisher trails are real nice though it is a challenging course that requires a lot of agility for corners and short steep climbs. There are big loops that inter-connect for convenience to take short cuts if desired. The snow is excellent and there is plenty of it. In the morning it feels really cold and the snow (unless it snowed overnight) is transformed from the day before and hard packed, sometimes ice. The best skiing of the day is usually between 9:00 am and 12:00 am due to the great impact of the sun and how it softens and transforms the crystal structure of the snow.

At Perisher the main parking lot is shared with the major alpine hill on the other side. I am disappointed that the skiers I have come to train with, including Simbo, are tied up with testing. As I ski around alone exploring the trails, I think that I should be excited to be here, but inside I still feel sick of skiing. This experiment of being on snow early, with hopes to peak earlier in the northern hemisphere season, is becoming a total bust. I have become less and less motivated to put forth the effort mentally and physically.

It is July 17 and I choose not to ski today. I go for a quick run with some 2-4 minute threshold pick-ups and feel terrible. I really only want to gain the free, rhythmic feeling of a good pace but just cannot get it going. Later, I drive into town and sit in the only place I can use wireless Internet for nearly free. Every day I think over and over about ditching Australia. I've tried everything I mentally know of to get through it, even taking this trip to Jindabyne to stay with friends, which I thought would be the answer. But the feelings remain strong.

I open up my feelings about it to Simbo as we drive back to the ranch tonight. He is very helpful in helping make the final decision. Even though he says that he is sad to see that I am unhappy here and is sorry that he is busy with the testing most of the time of my visit, he totally understands. Simbo shared a similar experience he had while training a double-season in Russia some years ago.

Every person has their breaking point. I've met mine only a handful of times in life so far. This day I hit it straight on. What is my problem? I don't even have one! I eat a normal diet and don't drink alcohol, why am I so depressed? No more mental debates and daily thoughts of thinking I should catch the next plane back to Europe. It's over. I feel better now that I know I'm leaving.

"A 10K Skate," He Says

It is July 18 and I am mentally counting down the days until I can flee this land and return to the north. At the breakfast table, Simbo asks, "Are you going to race today?" I look at him with a blank early morning expression and ask, "What type of race and how long?"

"A 10k skate," he says. I think about it for about one minute and say, "Okay, sure" with no spark. Note to self: *If I have to think that* long to make a decision whether I want to race, I should not race. My heart just isn't in it. I have been more unmotivated over these weeks in Australia than ever before. I keep thinking I will feel better soon but it is just not happening. Raphael Wunderle (my former teammate and roommate) always used to say, *"If you don't like it, then change something."* Enough said— I'm outta here!

All yesterday evening, I thought about where I would go for the month of August now that I plan to leave Australia. After hour upon hour of thoughts, I realize that I feel warm inside, excited, happy, and energized. I am going back to O-town! I know it may create problems with the German visa authorities, but it is my skiing home and I need to get back there.

The race does not start well, even though I try to prepare and am temporarily psyched. It starts poorly because I am still putting on my skis and have yet to put on my poles when they yell, *"3-2-1 GO!"* It being a mass-start race, and the trail narrowing to 1.5 lanes within the first 100 meters, I am behind from the beginning. I scramble as hard as I can, having to double-pole through the middle of the 40 starters. Simbo is not in the race due to a commitment to do a TV interview. The first kilometer goes up a long gradual hill and at the top I have just caught the lead pack of three skiers who had already separated themselves with a bit of a gap from the rest.

"Yes! I caught them. Now I'll hang with them until my heart-rate decreases and then I can make a move," I think. But on that first downhill I discover that my skis are not the best for the day. I had left all my skis in Mt. Beauty and am using a pair of Simbo's that he pulled out of his shed with an unknown wax on. I hadn't planned on racing during this side-trip to Jindabyne/ Perisher.

By the bottom of that first long downhill, I have already lost 10 seconds. Oh-oh... That's a lot of time to lose on one downhill. After another long downhill the gap between them and it grows to over 30 seconds just due to the skis not gliding well. The middle section of the race is mostly flats and graduals, the wind is blowing a stiff breeze, and there are many snowdrifts that sometimes break at the ankle. I am able to keep my distance equal with the three of them during most of that time.

I keep pushing, pushing, and working hard. There are a few

minutes where the competitive athlete in me rises to the surface and I feel a refreshing moment of having the right attitude. The three of them have spread out to nearly equal distances about five meters apart. Near the halfway point I have made up a little bit of distance on the uphills and kept nearly the same distances on the flats.

The final three kilometers are mostly downhill and even after the first one, I have lost all sight of them. The rest of the race I ski alone. Even though I've been faced with the worst motivational issues, I still feel good and sense some racing instincts. I finish the race skiing as hard as I started, congratulated the first three guys, and put my warm-ups back on to head out on a cool down. I feel it was all a bit of a shock to my system, which increases my spirit's desire to return to Europe for the better quality training (mentally and physical).

During the cool-down I stop and stand to think and enjoy the view from a high point. It is a sunny day, the wind is blowing, but the visibility is good and Perisher is among the tallest mountains in Australia. I can see for miles and on that spot I know that this will be my final day of skiing in Australia. The inner conflict within me screams at me, *"The snow conditions and ski trails here are excellent, what's wrong with you? There are thousands of skiers around the world who would love to be skiing on real snow right now and you can't even complete one session without being negative. What kind of a skier are you?"*

With the decision made to get out of Australia as soon as possible, I have to conclude my work for Holmenkol and that means finding someone to be the rep for Australia. I have accompanied Simbo's father to the New South Wales High School Skiing State Championships and it is there that I meet the perfect guy. He shows up at a wax clinic I am about to give, asking about the Alpine rep position. He is the Aussie national coach for snowboarding and it doesn't take long to find that he is the exact person I have been searching for. I hand him a stack of catalogs and stickers, take his contact info down and he walks out with a smile on his face. Maybe now, that I've decided to leave, the universe will begin to work in my favor.

I spend a day hitchhiking back to Mt. Beauty, and am fortunate to get a lift from a wonderful elderly businessman named Larry Adler, an inspiring man, filled with the spirit of youth even as he enters his 80s. He is the owner of a retail store chain and I had been dealing with them with Holmenkol wax. It was one of those synchronistic moments when I feel as if some force in the universe is working with me. Ever since I decided to leave Australia I've felt this sense of support and Larry arriving really confirms it.

He was only going to drive me a short distance but after we speak for awhile he says he is going to drive me to the town of Khancoban. As we head down the main road we pass a sign that reads "Khanocoban, 76 km." I argue with him, telling him he does not need to drive me that far. He has already told me he was planning on skiing and this will take him well out of his way, but he insists and so I get the chance to share some valuable time with this inspiring and wise man.

He is 82 years young and a very successful businessman who started as a pharmacist and now has six retail ski stores and an import business, but he is the easiest guy to talk to. I take the opportunity to ask him many questions about business fundamentals and I learn a lot.

When we get to Khancoban, which is a three-shop town that you would miss if you were not paying attention, I try to give him some money but he refuses. We find out that the postman will take me to a place that will enable me to easily get a ride to Mt. Beauty. The postman will not arrive for an hour so Larry and I eat lunch in the café before making our farewells. As he is about to go he says something that I will never forget: *"Keep smiling, Andy, because if you're not, then something is wrong."*

When I finally arrive in Mt. Beauty, a warm feeling of having "made it" comes over me. It is starting to get dark by this time and walking down the driveway I notice the site next to my caravan has been marked off with police tape indicating a crime scene. The lot is now empty but there are fresh tire tracks and pin flags marking something. I don't even want to know what has occurred next to my caravan as long as my trailer wasn't affected, which it wasn't. Putting the key into the keyhole of the caravan feels good. I have made it, and in only one day. The trip to Jindabyne was very productive. I sold over $5,000 worth of wax and tools, hired two reps (1 Alpine, 1 Nordic), and put on two successful wax clinics. The mini-trip is complete and I suddenly gain the urge to go out into the settling dusk for a run.

I wake up the next morning feeling excited. The remaining challenge for me is to get rid of the caravan and get all my stuff packed up. Internally I am feeling better and as the day grows nearer to return to Europe I am entering a better mental place. I have made the most of this experience in Australia and I am grateful for the people I've met and friends I've made.

My flight leaving Australia is scheduled to leave in 48 hours and I still have a lot to do. The weekly rent payment in the caravan park is due. The total rent will cost $600 just to cover the time it will sit empty until the de Freitas family will be coming to pick it up. Instead of paying the bill right then I have a sudden idea and walk over to a yurt that a guy named Leigh lives in. He is also renting within the park and I have made friends with him while I have been here.

The de Freitas family said they wouldn't mind if I sold the caravan, because they are going to throw it away anyway. So I sell the caravan to Leigh, call up the de Freitas's and tell them about the extra skis and poles I am hoping to find a good home for to lighten my checked bags on my return trip. They agree on the deal. I keep the cash. Leigh gets the caravan. The de Freitas's get the value of the caravan from my skis and poles. Everyone wins! That's how it works out. I will never stop being creative!

Getting from Mt. Beauty to the airport on time with a huge ski bag and rifle becomes easier after talking further with Leigh about the route. Coincidently, he has to pick up a friend at the bus depot in Albury that afternoon. So I throw my bags into the back of his "Ute," as they call them (short for *utility vehicle*). Basically these vehicles are new El Caminos made only for Australia. After an hour drive to Albury, I hop onto a bus for two hours before arriving at a train station.

Then I hop on a train for an hour to Southern Cross Station, which is the main train station and bus depot in Melbourne. From there I catch the "SkyBus" to the airport. The Skybus is the only bus I need help to get off of. With two carry-on bags and my long ski bag and heavy wooden rifle case it becomes very awkward to move in tight, crowded quarters. It is so nice to be traveling using reliable public transport. No more hitchhiking in the middle of nowhere in crappy weather in Australia for me!

At the airport I expect the check-in process to be lengthy and difficult. Arriving at 7:00 pm I am already tired from the full day of traveling. The feeling of accomplishment is strong because I traveled a long way in one day, and with all that gear. I have booked this flight through British Airways and they have put me on a Qantas flight for my return to London. I wouldn't have had a problem with that if Qantas didn't have different rules for checked bag weight limits. Qantas only allows a total of 23 kilos for all checked bags combined and only allows 7 kilos per carry-on. For every excess kilo they charge $50 AUD. That's $40 USD per pound in extra charges! Flying on Qantas with large bags—never again!

I have given away my personal waxes and sold my wax bench along with some other gear to some of the developing skiers to lighten my ski bags. I had planned it perfectly within the British Air limits, which allow twice as much weight. My rifle and case weigh 20 kilos and my ski bag weighs 23 Kilos with the bare necessities. And I am facing $2000 in baggage fees.

The manager is called over. I *love* talking to managers. We discuss the issue and go around and around in hopeless conversation with it. He is not willing to do anything out of the ordinary, standing behind the counter, drinking coffee, restating the rules. The conversation ends when he walks away, barking to the ticket agent to *"Cancel this check-in!"*

She is a nice lady and has tried to accommodate my needs. I tell her that I will think about the baggage and meanwhile she directs me to the floor below where customs is required to inspect my rifle to check it out of the country. When I arrived in Australia it took 2.5 weeks to get it out of customs and now they are talking about holding it again. You'd think they'd like to see me taking it out of the country.

After a tricky move going down a level with these awkward bags perched on a cart on an escalator, I make a brief appearance in the customs office to begin the process of filling out a dozen forms and documents. I soon get a moment to think about solving the puzzle of how I will be able to check my two bags with minimum expense. I begin by throwing away some items like older socks and underwear. Some gifts I give away to random people standing nearby. I also shift some items between my bags and then an idea a good friend, Michael McGauley, once jokingly mentioned comes to mind to save the day.

I waddle back into the building looking much fatter. I am wearing 3 pairs of socks, 3 pairs of pants, 2 shirts, 4 jackets (with all pockets crammed with items like racing suits, etc.), hat, gloves and a lovely ski boot necklace. Right away as the ticket operators see me waddling towards them they crack a smile. *"Problem solved!"* I state. After re-weighing my bags I am still 9 kilos over. —$450 extra.

I pull my bags off and arrange for my ski bag to be checked now. I have to wait longer to check my rifle because of the paperwork still being processed and the time it is taking is dragging on even though they put a rush on it. The nice ticket agent gives me my boarding passes. She says I am going to have to pay at the check-in of my second bag for the extra fees. I have to walk clear across to the other side of the platform to check this other bag (a 5-min walk).

I am roasting in all of those layers, but it is worth it to make it easier to get between the upstairs where the ticket counter is and downstairs where the customs room/ weapons office is. Neither agency will allow me to leave my bags with them, so I am forced to haul everything everywhere I go. Going to the bathroom is always a headache, because the long bags often don't make it around the entrance corner and I am forced to leave them there blocking it, unattended, and at risk of being stolen or confiscated by authorities.

It is nearly 11:00 pm when my rifle papers are finalized and they organize a police escort to go from the customs room, upstairs to the ticket booth, get the ticket, then walk another five minutes across the platform to check the bag. It is near closing time and very busy so they forget to charge me the extra $450 baggage fee and I hope I am home-free as I watch the rifle case roll down the conveyor.

With only 20 minutes to go before my flight is scheduled to board I am still standing in line waiting to get through security. Wearing all of these layers, I am going to need a lot more time to get through. At the checks, besides the usual computer, shoes, belt, hats separated, I wipe the sweat off my head as I peel off three jackets. Then I pile it all back on and head toward my gate. By the time I arrive I feel as if I'm in an African desert and thought that if there was a polar bear dive going on, I'd love to take the plunge.

At midnight I board the plane and am glad to have made it through this mess. I dread being called up to the ticket counter prior to boarding, but my name is not mentioned. In that short time of waiting to get on the plane I take off many layers and cram most everything into my two carry-ons, now that I've gone through security where they weigh them. I feel very thankful that I have gotten away without the baggage weight fees. *I'm in the clear. Yes!*

Of course, my challenges aren't over yet. My seat is in the middle. To my right is a very fussy lady who has the window. To my left is a super fat guy who hogs the arm rest and his body odor is noticeable immediately. Soon after the flight takes off the guy next to me falls asleep with his head propped back. I wouldn't mind his snoring so much if his breath wasn't terrible. The stench drifts over me like a toxic vapor. I turn on the air above, his air adjustment first, to direct the fart-mouth breath the other way, and then my own, full blast right in my face. That flight takes nine *lllooooooonnnnggggg* hours.

We land in Hong Kong and, as I see bits and pieces through the window, I notice that Hong Kong and many other outlying cities are built in between steep, tree-covered, very green-colored mountains. Lots of tall buildings crammed up against green slopes. We only have an hour in Hong Kong and it's nice to walk around and loosen up. Five minutes before boarding, I hear an Asian voice over the loudspeaker *"Mr. Andrew Liebner, please come to ticket counter."* I thought, *"Oh no, here it comes. It's either the baggage fee or some sort of rifle problem."*

It's the rifle. The agent is on the phone with the security on the ground crew. They need all the details of the contents. I write down all the details in very large plain print. I give them all the right answers and that's all they need. It really doesn't make sense to need special permits and licenses for transiting airports, but then again I've said all that before. Then, to my surprise, they offer me a seat change. How they read my mind, I will never know, but I am so happy.

My new seat is on the isle of the middle section. There are five seats to a middle section and only one other guy on the other isle. Also, as a bonus it is the first row past first class, so I have a lot of foot room. Directly behind me are bathrooms. I can tilt my chair back. It's the best seating I've had. Another break!

Now I can catch some badly needed sleep. When I awake I am drawn to pull out the book I've been reading that I bought in Mt. Beauty. I've been keeping this book a secret, not mentioning it to any friends in Australia, or in any notes I wrote home, other than to mention when I first found it. The truth is, however, that it has hooked me like no other book I've ever read. By hooked, I mean that I think about it day and night.

I can't wait to read the next few pages. Some of it is disturbing and causes me to cringe and it actually made me feel worse at times while I was back in Australia, but I also felt I needed to keep reading. Sitting on the plane I think to myself, *"This book, with its weird dark-but-sunny cloud picture on the front is going to change my life."* Even the title, "In Search Of...", reflects exactly the open-ended answer I am searching for at this time in my life.

They say that when the student is ready the master appears and I have a strange feeling that, through this book, I am meeting my mentor, someone who will help me on the next stage of my journey. That makes no sense, because I'll likely never meet this guy, but I can't help shake the feeling that it is true.

What makes it even more challenging is the nature of the book. The author is a corporate executive in a large Australian energy company, but he has gone on a really deep inner journey and has written about it. The scary thing and what caused me to feel worse at times, is that he does not deal with his darkness in the same way I do.

With me, as you might realize by now, when I encounter negative aspects of my mentality I fight and fight it. In my early years, sometimes it won, but I've become stronger and have learned to defeat it. So when I win a daily battle with my mental struggles it is a big deal to me. Because I was on that day, in that case, in that issue, at that moment, a real champion and I felt good about it. I have come to think that I can conquer whatever negative attitudes arise within me and turn them into positives.

But this Alistair Smith does not do that – he seems to draw his darkness to him, almost like a lover, and embraces it. You would think that I'd have no interest in such a book and yet I am fascinated by it and sometimes, when I was reading in Mt. Beauty, I was overcome with some of the dark energy that was evident in his struggles.

So what is going on? Have I really been that successful in conquering my own darkness? I felt it in Greece and was left with the sense that I fled rather than facing it. Now again, in Australia, my negativity has arisen and sure, I can find all sorts of excuses for it, but I have not been able to overcome it and now here I am, on a plane, fleeing it again. I don't like where this is leading me, but I can't deny the reality that is being put in my face.

I read the book for a while then set it aside. I cannot go into this now. I'm heading back to Europe and things will seem a lot clearer when I get there.

CHAPTER TEN
European Surprises

It feels good finally to be back in Germany. Clearing my rifle through customs was simple compared to Australia. I only have to show them my receipt of purchase and the letter of invitation to a few national biathlon events from the British National Team director.

After stopping at Holmenkol, debriefing with Christian about the Australian market I load up the van with a variety of products to sell over the next few months.

As I go to leave, my van will not start. There was plenty of electrical current and it never would rev, not even once. I think it is either the relay switch or the starter itself. The warehouse guys slap their hands on the van and push me down the road. I pop the clutch into second gear; turn the key and the engine starts. The fuel is low and I have a 30 minute drive to my hostel. The van makes it, and I decided to first stop at the food store before it closes. The store is close to my hostel and immediately after parking I try to restart the van, but again the engine would not turn over. This isn't good! I shake off the negative thoughts and buy some food. I'd been starving for 14 hours by this time and the time difference (10 hours) was making me very sleepy.

After settling my stomach growling I realize that there is a fuel station on the other side of the parking lot and it is an actual Renault dealership with full repair shop. I walk over and they say *"Come back in the morning at 8:00 am."* This is the second time I've needed auto repairs in Germany and I can say, *"It's been too convenient."* I pack up my stuff and walk five minutes to my hostel and fall asleep immediately. I wake up at 4:45 am, lace up my running shoes and complete a great 1.5 hour run. The sun was just starting to come up and I feel very peaceful inside.

At 8:00 am I'm at my van with a mechanic looking under the hood. He came with a hammer and long piece of thick steel. My starter was hard to get at from the top and the plastic guard was covering everything from the bottom, so he wasn't able to do much, so he pushed the van and I slammed it into second gear to start it again. I drive into the shop and take off the plastic guard to then hit the starter directly on the side with a hammer. Moments later, it starts. I throw the plastic guard into the back and the mechanic gives me the little hammer to take with me. He doesn't charge me for any of it and I thanked him gratefully.

The next fuel station I stop to fill up. After fueling, I climb under the van, hit the starter straight on with the hammer *"WWHHAAKK!!"* and it starts. *Now, that's some new anti-theft device that I have!* A new starter costs 1000-1500 Euro, which I cannot afford. Driving on the other side of the road takes some time, but the conversion is much easier. On the autobahn, I find my CD player not working, so I listen to the radio. One station is playing American hits from the 80's non-stop. I rock out all the way to the Austrian border until I hear a loud *"KLUNK!"* followed by an ongoing *"VVVVRRRROOOOMMMM!!!!"* noise. I know right away the exhaust pipe broke at the manifold connection.

Now my Americanism is exposed by all who hear me drive by. Unlike many Americans, who have straight pipes or glass packs custom applied to their trucks, Europeans don't pride themselves with the level of noise their autos make. I dared not to stop to get it fixed with only three hours left on the road till O-town, and a shop not allowing me to continue due to some Austrian regulations. I turn up the music and laugh at my situation. I decide to stop at the beginning of a large tunnel near the top of a mountain pass. I pick up an Italian biker who is in need of a ride through the tunnel. The Tunnel is 10K long and bikes are not allowed, as I have learned months ago. I keep the engine running and throw his bike onto the pile of boxes filled with ski wax in the back of the van. Because of my recent consistency of hitchhiking daily, I feel for this guy and also understand that many vehicles in Europe are too small for his bicycle. He only speaks Italian, so we aren't able to communicate well. I pull out of the turn-off and step hard on the gas pedal. The guy looks straight down, and then at me pointing down at the roar of the engine with wide eyeballs. I smile, nod, and drive into the tunnel.

I make my way back to O-town and book into the same hotel I had stayed at previously. I have a warm feeling inside, as if I am close to home, and the familiar smells and sights of O-town cause joy to spring in my heart. That evening, I cannot wait to begin training and go for a run in the woods.

The following morning I complete a rollerski shooting workout at the Biathlon Center and it feels great to be back in a place where I know I can do top-quality training. Other teams training here this week are a big mix of French, Italian, Czech, and Austrian National Teams, with men's, women's and junior squads, some A teams, some B. During my first rollerski biathlon workout I do many shooting drills and shoot clean (hitting all five) in eight different stages, and with a high heart rate.

Last year it took two weeks of training here before I shot clean even once. Looking back at the experience in Australia, since I was not able to shoot any ammo, I spent hours on end dry-firing and acquired a good routine along with strengthening the right muscles to hold the rifle steady. It seems to be paying dividends.

I call Joe, my former trainer, and arrange to meet and make a schedule for the next few weeks. I discover that he has been hired by the Belgian national team and is just coming back to O-town from Ruhpolding. We meet the following day at the range.

The first week in O-town I train 6-7 hours a day outside and another hour dry-firing indoors. I run up to a mountain peak every other evening and have never been this motivated to train. Training couldn't be going any better and I'm so excited for each workout, that I am disappointed when I have to stop and go indoors because I have been out past my allotted schedule training time.

Andy in the Dolomites on the Italian-Austrian mountain border. Right, Andy on the rollerski track in O-town.

Later in the week I get a phone call from Mr. Wunderle. They are allowing me to use their home as a permanent mailing address so I can satisfy the requirement of having a German residential address in order to maintain my visa. I cannot use O-town as it is in Austria. A letter has arrived from the German government stating that I am to report to the Freiburg office with my passport, ASAP. Freiburg is a ten hour drive from O-town, but Mr. Wunderle notifies me that the office in Freiburg will not discuss it with him and that I must personally speak with them.

I call to see what I can accomplish by phone and after a few hours on the line they understand my situation and say they will allow me to stay a full three months as long as I change my address and provide documentation (e.g., a plane ticket) that I will leave Germany before November. After ending the call I am in utter disbelief at their high level of understanding and flexibility.

I knew that I had a potential problem because I had not spent the required three months outside the EU and a red flag came up in their system on my return. The unscheduled trip to Alaska for 19 days was good, but leaving Australia a month early has left me two weeks shy of the total 90 days out. I am very thankful that they have permitted this exception, otherwise I'd either have to re-activate my work visa with Holmenkol, go to Croatia for the number of days required, or pack-up and move back to Alaska, which I am not ready to do.

The flexibility shown by the German authorities does not extend across the Atlantic, unfortunately. On my arrival back in

Germany I renewed my registration with USBA. In the first week of August I receive notification that my athletic status in the sport of biathlon is still officially listed as "Retired." I had forgotten that I had officially retired in the summer of 2004, as the U.S. Anti-Doping Agency's (USADA) monthly testing times had conflicted with my work schedule. I chose to retire rather than run the risk of being banned from the sport for years. They'd like to begin testing me again, and I must inform them of my whereabouts each day, which is difficult for me as I travel so much.

All the hassles with USBA and USADA makes it difficult to keep my focus and just when I need a boost it arrives in the form of my favorite biathlon team. In the second week of August the Slovenijan national team arrives and moves into the same hotel building as I am in. I am very happy since becoming good friends with them, especially Klemen Bauer, and I highly respect their trainers. The bond is reinforced when they include me in their day-to-day training routine and they even help me to improve my shooting position and make some rifle adjustments.

Also training with them are some other foreigners, including the best biathlete from Serbia, and Jakov Fak from Croatia. Last year, at the World Championships held in Korea, Jakov earned a bronze medal. He is in excellent condition right now and continues towards success at the 2010 Olympics. During some of the interval sessions, I can barely hang on as the pack pushes harder and harder along the rollerski track. A strong group of guys to rollerski with is what I need more than anything right now and I wish I could be training with a team like this every day.

For much of my life I have preferred to train alone, often struggling to fit into the rigid structures of teams I've been a part of back in the U.S., but this Slovenijan team has a whole different energy about it. Every member of the team acts responsibly and professionally and does the right thing, not because of rules, but because they see it as appropriate and want to comply.

The coaches are very chill, very open, passive, calm, and give just as much effort as each athlete gives them. That candor resonates throughout all of them and into me. I really feel no pressure at all, but rather a great sense of progression. I am now rollerskiing on this rollerski track with the mentality that it is making me much stronger as a skier, and not going through the required motions just to apply hours in the training log to meet the requirements of some system that I must falsely believe will equal improvement no matter how I feel.

I am also shooting with a calm, quiet, mind, resulting in clear accuracy and much of this has to be put down to the Slovenijan head trainer, Uros. He is a man who emanates a quiet wisdom and depth, quite unlike some of my former coaches, who gave closed-ended instructions like "Don't do this, don't do that," etc.

Klemen once said to me, *"Uros will never hand you information on a silver platter, but, if you ask him, he will give you his time and knowledge."*

An example of this was one time he was helping me at the shooting range. *"Why do you rush when you come into the range?"* he asked me. He did not direct me to be calmer, but saw what my problem was and drew out my own deeper understanding so that I could truly integrate the lesson. Uros carries such a comfortable, quiet wisdom that his presence is contagious and it is evident that all his athletes are touched by him.

At the end of the training week the Slovenijan's arrange a men's and women's time trial rollerski biathlon race. Like most mornings in Obertilliach, it is a

Uros in his classic thumbs-up pose.

clear, sunny, and beautiful day. The Czech team also decides to race, along with the Serbian and Jakov Fak. When the start list is posted I am 9th to start with Jakov 30 seconds behind me. The course is 5x2.5k with 4 shooting stages. Instead of penalty loops they are adding 30 seconds for each miss.

The first lap goes fine, although I probably push it a bit too hard, but I haven't built up any lactate so I'm traveling right on the threshold limit. This simulation race is my first since the Austrian Champs last April and I have a hard time calming my pulse at the 185bpm it is beating while I am trying to shoot the U.S. half dollar size targets from 50 meters. Of those first five prone, I hit two (miss three), but my range time is under 40 seconds so I am okay with it. Also, I can't be too hard on myself, since the two months of biathlon training in Australia was a bust and I haven't been consistent with my physical training either outside of running. I've only been able to shoot for 1.5 weeks for the entire summer prior to this race due to rifle complications and other travel issues.

I am just coming in for the second shooting stage when Jakov passes me. I take it easier coming into the range and stand to shoot on the mat next to him and hit four of five. Back on the course, I follow Jakov for the majority of the 3rd loop. Like I said, he's in great shape and I do my best with what I've been able to get in for training. The last two shoots, I hit two and two. My mind is tired and I have a hard time keeping 100% concentration on each shot. On the track I rollerski a solid pace and finish respectfully. I don't bother looking at the results to know for sure my place, but am satisfied with my performance. Immediately after finishing, I identify what areas I need to focus on more in training. It's trial events like these that build greater motivation and inspiration to "feed the fire."

Jakov Fak training in O-town.

A Training Partner

Marc Walker, a coach with the British team, has invited me to stay with him so we can train together and so I am moving to his place in Ruhpolding. On my last night in O-town I walk through village and enjoy a show being put on by the locals. O-town is a small village but it seems as if everyone has a role to play in maintaining the community. I am sure going to miss this place.

As I leave I take a new route from Obertilliach to Ruhpolding, which looks like a short-cut on the map. It takes me over two beautiful mountain passes that reach cloud level. In the evening I pull into the driveway of Marc and Adele's house just before 6:00 pm and as I hop out of my van, they are walking out the door all dressed up. I hand Adele a box of chocolates for her birthday as I give her a hug. Marc had written me an email in the morning telling me they were leaving around 6:00 for her birthday party, but I hadn't checked my email all day. They assume I have rushed there to make it just in time, but it's sheer luck. I quickly change clothes and jump in the back of Marc's car.

A few kilometers later we stop to pick up another athlete, who turns out to be the very familiar Olwen Thorn, who plops herself into the back seat next to me and looks over in surprise, *"Andy! What are you doing here?"*

Once we arrive at the only Mexican restaurant in (I think) a 1,000 km radius, we meet up with the entire British National men's and women's teams, including Coach Pichler. We nearly pack the place and become a loud mob of noise compared to the other local shops. It is nice to catch up with them again and hear about what they did on their holidays. I am glad that they will be training in Ruhpolding this fall and am looking forward to good times.

The Great Britain team is leaving the following day for a week-long training camp in Hochfilzen, Austria. I would have gone also, but they are doing specific medical testing with each of their sessions. I was invited to train in the Czech Republic with the Soukal's and their biathlon club for a few weeks and decide to take that opportunity.

The following day I leave Ruhpolding in the morning and head towards Jablonec nad Nisou in the Czech Republic. At around noon on a beautiful Sunday I pull off to the side of the road, near the Czech border, to stretch my legs and eat some food. Just as I am ready to leave an undercover German police car pulls in front of me and two men get out. They look at my papers and ask a few questions. Everything is fine until they ask if I have any weapons and I inform them I have a biathlon rifle. The police look at it and all its papers. These guys follow everything "by the book" and will not allow me to continue until they see a waffenpass. Because I have stopped a few kilometers from the border, they are suspicious.

From there they escort me with my rifle 15 kilometers back to the station where I am placed in a room and interrogated for four hours. They document all the dates in my passport. Three different officers keep coming in at different times asking similar questions like why I don't have a waffenpass for my rifle, what my purpose is for being in Jablonec nad Nisou. During the four hour span I answer the same questions over and over again, expressing my frustration and explaining my attempts to get a waffenpass last year and how it's just not possible for an American to get one. During the time of my interrogation another officer has researched my statement about not being issued a waffenpass.

These officers explain to me that there is a hefty fine for transporting a weapon without a waffenpass and I could even be imprisoned up to two years for the offense. Later that same day I am escorted into another room with a desk and computer. I am asked to sit behind the desk and the officer in front of the computer informs me that I have the right to call a lawyer. I testify my comments for the district magistrate. I feel very uneasy and increasingly uncomfortable. I imagine that, at any moment, they are going to handcuff me and take me away. To make my apprehension even more intense I overhear the officers discussing this possibility.

Finally, they enter the room and say *"Okay, we know now that you are not a terrorist. But you will not be allowed to take your rifle with you."* They are acting like they have found "weapons of mass destruction." I can't believe their reaction over a measly .22 single shot bolt-action target rifle.

It is then I discover that the roadside officers, who took me into custody, have written a report stating that, when they arrived at my van, I was nowhere to be found, the doors were open, and the rifle was sitting fully loaded on the seat. This is a false statement, as I was standing with the door open making a sandwich on the seat when the officers approached me. My rifle was in its case underneath my clothing bags, and all ammunition was packed in a gear box on the other side of the van still wrapped in their factory sealed plastic unbroken covering, proving there was no chance it could have been loaded. These correct details are included in my own statement and the two conflicting statements are submitted to the judge. No wonder the officers at the station have been treating me with such suspicion.

As the experience prolongs I am becoming increasingly frustrated. I am really getting sick and tired of dealing with this rifle stuff. Just when training is going well these set-backs keep coming up and restricting me from proper training. Now, because of the rifle, inner fears of serving time invade my mind and I wish I had just continued as a skier and never had the interest in biathlon in the first place. The option of walking out of the door, flying back to Alaska, and forgetting all about this whole biathlon thing is something I'd like to have available, but this has gone beyond it. My physical freedom is at stake. I am absolutely sick of all these issues and feel that I don't want to keep dealing with any more of this stress revolving around a rifle. I think, *"Doing biathlon is just not worth it to be treated like this and everything else that is at risk."*

They allow me to leave in the evening, but hold my rifle and ammunition. They still expect me to provide a waffenpass (that I have been told I cannot obtain). They inform me that there is a chance that, if the local waffenpass officials authorize me a pass or transit permit, the judge might allow the release of my rifle-action and my custom stock. The police station is three hours drive from Marc's house in Ruhpolding, so I decide it is worth staying the night to wait for an answer.

I leave the building only to find that all five of the hotels in this little town are closed or full. So I drive down a road and park next to a river for the night and take a picture, of what could be one of my final evenings as a free man. I do not know what will happen. The case will be submitted to a judge. After that, will I be fined, jailed, or extradited as a criminal?

I go for a run before going to sleep. It feels good to clear my mind of all the stress I have just experienced. I call it my "freedom run." I run along a beautiful creek and I am so thankful I am out here and not sitting behind bars or in the interrogation room any longer. Dusk has descended by the time I return to the van.

As I sit there, listening to the rain sprinkle on the roof, I have the thought of announcing the end of my biathlon career. After all the things that have happened over the past month I should have recognized the signs, thrown in the towel and called it quits. I decide that if they still won't issue me a waffenpass, then I am definitely finished with this sport. This thought invokes a sense of relief in me, but then I begin to realize that I've been here before.

In Australia I had all sorts of trouble with my rifle and I felt like quitting. Here again, in the place I have felt most comfortable, I find my progress being blocked by government systems. Am I just unlucky, or is there some greater force at play? What were the odds of me having been picked up by unmarked policemen? Is some force out there trying to tell me that biathlon is not my path?

On the other hand, I'm not a quitter. Throw a barrier in my way and I'm going to do everything I can to go around it. Learning about Biathlon has been an escape and excuse at the same time for part of my reason for the initial trip to Europe and I have learned so much. It feels like such a shame to throw all that away and quit now. A very big part of it is the tension of fighting to vindicate myself and my ability that keeps me motivated and allows me to drive myself so hard, but am I really enjoying this sport? Or am I persevering just because it is what I have planned to do and what I've invested so heavily in?

I wish I had the wisdom to see beneath the surface battle I am engaged in and move beyond the confusion caused by these conflicting thoughts, but I just am not there. I simply don't have the tools to see beneath the surface to what is really happening.

The following morning on the drive into town the song *"Here I Go Again,"* by Whitesnake streams in on my radio from the local radio station. Coincidently that song's lyrics describe my entire trip and the deep meaning of this situation. In addition, it was my high school graduation class song and carries many positive associations. It sets the mood and as I report to the local government office which issues waffenpasses. I am feeling spiritually sound walking in the door.

I explain my situation to three different people as I'm sent from one person to the next. After I sit in the third guy's office (the boss) for 1.5 hours he seems to understand my dilemma. He wants to help but simply cannot not issue me a waffenpass, or even a transit permit, because I am not a citizen of Germany or of any other European Union country. In the end, he sends me back to the police station.

In the police station we call the government office in Ruhpolding to see if they will issue me a permit, since the training center is there and that's where I will be living for the rest of my stay in Europe. Ruhpolding is one of the best known Biathlon World Cup venues in the world so surely they will assist me. Again, the answers are the same; they cannot issue me anything. So the story line remains the same; *"You cannot have your rifle back unless you provide a waffenpass, but we cannot issue you a waffenpass because of your lack of European citizenship."*

I spend nine hours in the police station this second day, talking to different agencies and faxing forms back and forth. They keep telling me the papers might be coming any minute. After eight hours and 50 minutes, I get up, barge into the main room where the majority of the officers dealing with my case are. There is a folder two inches thick already with my name on it sitting on the counter. Unable to contain my emotional stress any longer, I blurt out:

"Look, I'm an American; my country has what's called the 2nd Amendment of the Constitution of the United States, the right to bear arms. You know your country will not give me the form you need to get my rifle back today, so bring my rifle to me now and I will take my stock off of it and keep the stuff in the pocket of the bag it's in, and I'll get out of here. You have wasted enough of my time.

You won't let me have my rifle back, and I need it for training, so I'll have to quit this sport, and if I do I'll never come back to Germany again. I've asked the licensing office for the documents I would need months ago to prevent this, and have spoken to two others. You are making a mistake. Customs looked at the same papers I have shown you here, and they allowed me to travel, train, and compete with this rifle. Why can't you make that same decision? You all think that I will never get this rifle out of here because of your rules? I will tell you how your rules are easy to get around. I can walk one block down the street and sell my rifle for two euros to a friend who has a waffenpass. They would then come in here and get it out and sell it back to me a moment later. Ever thought of that?"

Up until now my relationship with these guys has been relatively friendly, but that sense of cooperation ceases to exist after my little explosion. They do bring the rifle in and I am able to unbolt my stock and take off the trigger. I demand my bag and magazines. On the form that indicates what they are confiscating, it lists only my barrel and action. They grow very angry and pull the items away from my hands, leaving me with only the stock and my arm band. They throw everything into a safe in a cluttered pile. The form still reads they are only keeping the rifle (barrel and action) so I say: *"I'm not leaving until I get an inventory list of each item you are keeping. You are going to make a list and everything is going to be documented."*

I am not intimidated by these officers and inside I feel a degree of kinship as I was once a sworn in federal officer upholding the law. It is from my law experience that I learned you can't go wrong by documenting everything and these officers were being lazy. They try to convince me that they will be here if I can eventually claim my rifle and say that I can trust them. I thank them for their honesty, but mention policy to them. *"If you look in those manuals that you have been nosing through the past few days, you will also find that whenever you are holding items in a case, you must inventory each item, so do your job and write down my stuff on this form right now!"*

They list everything and as I am finally about to walk out of the station a father and son arrive in the room and asked me quickly what my name is, with hopes of seeing me race in large future events. I announce to everyone: *"I won't be competing in biathlon anymore, unless these police give my rifle back. They may be forcing me to quit the sport completely!"* I get back into the van and drive back to Ruhoplding, arriving after dark.

For the next ten days Marc and Adele are away in Hochfilzen, Austria and I am alone at their place. This gives me more time to think than is probably healthy. Every day I think about my future career and confusion continues to plague me. Sometimes I feel strong about my ability to succeed in biathlon and other times I feel like I am wasting my time in this sport and should just get on with the rest of my life and my skiing career. Of course the thought of failure plagues me and so I remain in a constant mental debate vortex about where my priorities should be. I have longed to ski under the coaching duo of Sten Fjeldheim and Jenny Ryan at Northern Michigan University (NMU) and am committed to completing my degree.

During this time I also read more of the book, *"In Search Of..."* and it has become no less mysterious to me. The book was published nine years ago and I figure there will be plenty of stuff about the author on the Internet but when I run a search I get nothing. It is like he has fallen off the face of the Earth. There is a web address in the back of the book, but it no longer exists. There is also an email address and I decide to try it, to see if I can contact him. I don't hold much hope because I presume that, if the web site no longer exists, the email address won't either.

To my surprise I receive a response to my email a few days later. The guy sounds really surprised that I found his book, telling me that he did not know there were any copies still in circulation. He also tells me he has left the corporate world and is living in Canada pursuing his own deeper journey. He seems really open and offers to answer any questions I have about his book. He also offers to send me an electronic copy of his second book, titled *"Journey Home To..."*

It is now ten days since the German authorities confiscated my rifle. Nothing has changed and there is still no move to release it. I've found a certain sense of relief and no longer experience the stressors of training as a biathlete, I've faced the obvious fact that it's just not working out and enjoy the freedom in training as a skier once again. My main fear now is of fines or incarceration requirements. My father has contacted our Alaskan U.S. Senator Mark Begich, who contacted the U.S. Embassy in Germany, requesting diplomatic pressure be applied for the release of the rifle, but that also failed. The second the U.S. Embassy realized I could be sent to prison for two years, they pulled back like a snail thrown in a desert. The U.S. Embassy sent me a simple letter indicating that I am a role model that Alaska is proud of as one of its legal citizens and included a list of attorneys. How encouraging is that?

The German authorities contacted me and informed me that they are still requiring the waffenpass and an EU transit permit before release of my training equipment (the rifle).

Maybe the universe has been trying to tell me that biathlon is not for me. Maybe this message came right at the beginning, with the first email from the USBA, telling me I was not going to be training with them. Is this what happens when you don't listen to the messages? Do they just get stronger and stronger until, one day, you have no choice but to sit up and take notice?

But to listen to this I have to come to terms with failure and I can't "be" with failure or accept a defeat which has no real reason for it. To me, a "giving up" kind of failure comes at me like an angry cat clawing in every direction, ripping everything into shreds. Only the cat is inside me, ripping at me. I cannot accept failure from myself. If it is the fault of some external factor, like a broken leg or someone skiing faster than me, then it is okay, because I have no control over it, but I can't have it be my fault.

When Marc and Adele return, Adele has to quickly re-pack and head out to Great Britain where she has many Olympic preparations and commitments with the media and the rest of the team to take care of there. Marc and I start work on our training program and the other commitments that I've agreed to help him with.

I feel a great kinship with Marc and a new chapter of my life beginning. A fresh approach to mental and physical training. Although Marc is helping me with making calls to dignitaries to help me with my situation, he knows that I am confused within myself about the word "failure." My work with him is cross-country specific and I feel nothing but excitement and joy to begin a new ski training plan.

Even though Marc is still on the national biathlon team roster as a coach, he is now training for cross-country skiing. In the early years of his career Marc competed in FIS ski races, then turned to biathlon and was on the British National Biathlon Team for 10 years.

He retired two years ago as a biathlete and is now acting as a coach and support staff for the national team. He also coaches an army regiment of biathletes assigned to him as the National Development Team. His performance as an athlete is unrivalled in British biathlon. No other British biathlete has placed better than him in the past 10 years.

Last season, at the British National Championships, he decided to compete for fun and won two national titles. Convinced he no longer wants to compete in biathlon, he (at age 37) has found motivation to compete as a skier and the British Olympic Committee is supporting him to pursue FIS races and World Cups.

Marc has asked me to help him prepare for the season on multiple levels. He will continue to coach the army regiment assigned to train in Ruhpolding. For my time and efforts he is able to provide me with the things I need to continue living and training full time in Ruhpolding. As I join the mix, training his team, it will allow him to delegate some of the extra stuff that he must do to train properly. Also Marc wants a training partner who can keep up with him and who is able to sustain the long and intense training sessions. I am happy to accept the challenge and the need for my involvement with his team comes at the most opportune time.

There are a few weeks before Marc's team arrives so we make a training plan for ourselves for the meantime. To begin, Marc and I separately write down the things that we individually know we need to achieve during a week to train the best we knew how. Then, after we are done, we compare lists and formulate a plan that will best accommodate both our needs. Writing the lists separately eliminates any factors of holding back or forgetting. After we discuss and finalize the plan I think it is excellent. I don't know about Marc, but I know I am in for a challenge.

In the first two days of our plan we rollerski over 130 kilometers; that's 85 miles! 50k of that is during one workout at the rollerski track, which amounts to a lot of elevation gain. There is one particular downhill on the course called 'The Cannonball' that accelerates you so fast you feel like you're going to crash any moment. Even coming to a near-stop at the top doesn't help. The combination of the heat on the pavement and the little rubber rollerski wheels cause an instability that makes your feet move sideways and it's hard to keep them pointing straight.

Marc seems so confident and determined that I can't help but think the same and become more motivated as a result. His reason for doing longer, faster kilometers in the beginning of our plan is to *"get the muscles awake and going fast."* I've never heard of that before, but, even though I feel exhausted, I do feel like I can maintain a faster pace leading into the rest of the week.

Near the end of the first week of our training I receive a letter in the post from the United States Anti-Doping Agency (USADA).

They state the dates they received notification of my "coming out of retirement" and under normal policy I would not be allowed to compete for 12 months, but they would send a petition request to the directors for an exception of 6 months.

I read the letter, sit and think, fire burning inside me like a raging dragon. A moment later, I stand up, look straight into a mirror and acquire a mischievous grin, thinking to myself, *"I'm just an average guy, doing the right thing. It's time to release a loose cannon filled with positivity and optimism.*

These USADA folks will never forget me after the emails I'm going to write as a response. What have I got to lose? I've already bailed on the sport, so I'll be doing it for fun. I don't think their policies are athlete-friendly, and they are more negative than positive in promoting sports. I feel obliged to represent myself and any other athletes (past, present, and future) and to stand up for what I believe is right. And I'll give it all a positive spin!"

The emails to the USADA representative raise the question of my whereabouts, as they need to know every hour of every day where I can be found for possible testing. Although I am staying at Marc's place now, when I travel I disclose that I will be unable to give a physical address to places like "in my van down by the river." He sends me a YouTube video link of the famous "Matt Foley" SNL sketch and indicates that I have become the weekly joke at USADA. I have to admit, it's comical.

After an entire year of dealing with ever tougher and tougher bureaucracy about rifles, and with the background noise of the USBA, I've been keeping my time and energy focused in more productive directions. What will they try to do next? Strip me of the bronze medal from the Austrian National Biathlon Championships, and of my gold and bronze medals from the British Biathlon/Ski National Championships? It's hard enough enduring the day-to-day training in the sport and competing in the races, but to continually have all these additional issues, one after another, is ridiculous.

Not only do I have to compete for a position in the races, but I have to implore USBA to allow me an opportunity to represent the U.S. to even be eligible to compete. I've never experienced more set-backs in anything else in my life. I write that letter to the USADA, filled with positivity and optimism. ...Amazingly, they respond and eventually grant me an exception to the 6-month special request.

All I need now is my name cleared from any law infractions and the return of my rifle. So, when I received word that my petition letter was approved and I was cleared to compete by USADA, I wrote the USBA Development Director about my rifle situation and mentioned that if I did not get any help, I would soon be forced to retire again. He notified the High Performance Race Director (HPRD) for the U.S. National Team, who is a German citizen, who contacted some of the board members within the International Biathlon Union (IBU). The results of this action have been interesting. It is like an avalanche of people began calling the police, speaking on my behalf, debating the issues of my case.

Luckily for me, USBA has a strong influence in the IBU and so does the German Biathlon Federation. The German Summer Biathlon National Championships are being held in Ruhpolding in less than two weeks. The chief at the Biathlon Center and chief for the event has invited me to participate. He works in the weapons control department for the Bavarian region of Germany. Marc talks to the Ruhpolding Biathlon Center Chief and he is outraged to hear about what the police have done and that they have refused to return my rifle. The Chief cited the exact documents that Americans are required to carry with their rifles and I had adhered to those rules.

While all this is taking place I continue to train with Marc. I am pouring my frustration into physical effort and transforming it into sweat at the Ruhpolding rollerski track doing threshold intervals of 6x3.6k. While we are flying around the course, powering up the hills and swiftly shifting techniques over the flats and graduals, we pass Tobias Angerer who is doing some easy Level 1 training. This will probably be the only time Marc or I will ever be passing him that easily! He's one of the best skiers in the world and for a brief moment I feel a strong connection with him, as he is a skier not a biathlete.

Other athletes who have been training here are Kati Wilhelm, who won two gold and two silver medals at the 2009 Biathlon World Champs. She also has six Olympic medals (three gold, three silver), so she is currently the best female biathlete in the World! Daniel Graf and the rest of the German men's biathlon team have been training here the entire week. It's been good to have them around to train alongside, acting as a gauge. We've recently seen them out on the farming roads in Siegsdorf rollerskiing, too.

Because of the popularity of biathlon and cross-country skiing in Germany, the Ruhpolding venue serves as a tourist destination year-round. There are tour busses that pull up and fill the stands on a regular basis. On any given day there will be between 25-200 fans that come just to watch these world-class athletes train and often in less than desirable conditions. In the United States, there are venues similar to this, where elite athletes train every day, but there are no fans. The level of respect for athletes in Germany is noticeable among all sports.

Marc and I are also going into the gym and have combined our two lifetime's training knowledge to devise the most productive routines I've ever done in the gym. He's been showing me interesting running routes in the mountains. This is just what my mind has needed. Ruhpolding even has a nice orange rubber running track and two rivers, one of which is deep and flows very slowly. I have found it to be great for swimming and cooling off after training in the hot sun. The water is a bit cold, but it feels so good and is beneficial to our muscles for recovery.

Andy and Marc overlooking Ruhpolding.

Our training sessions have been very solid, intense, and ending with the satisfaction that another quality workout has been completed. Most of our rollerski hours are spent on the Siegsdorf farming roads that are less used and have many long hills. We are usually out there from 2-3 hours each session and have specific drills that we implement in a continuous manner. I feel strong training out there and find it to be a sanctuary of quality. I experienced a similar situation while undergoing a poor season at my former University. After weeks of mental battles back then, I decided to just train and race with the intent of helping my teammates and to feel good about their success.

Here I'm doing the same thing. I'm no longer struggling with myself over the concept of failure and seeing my training as a battlefield against the forces opposing me. Instead, I see my role as being a support for Marc. He has explained that the only thing he needs to achieve the best training is to have someone to train with and push through all the workouts. By training with him I've regained the enjoyment and enthusiasm that has been so variable and fragile over the past years. The pressure is off and I'm training for the pure fun and challenge of it, rather than attaching a goal that I need to achieve that hangs like a guillotine over my head.

On the final day of August, Marc and I join the British Biathlon National Team for their uphill rollerski training. They use this same course every few weeks and always do the first one skating and the second one classic. Walter Pichler (the head coach) drops us at the bottom then drives the van to the top and waits for us to arrive then returns us to the bottom in the van to ensure a safe descent. The mountain that the course road follows up is a neighboring mountain to the Eagle's Nest—Hitler's hideout and where he died.

This long, curvy and steeply-inclined trek is rarely finished in under an hour. But Marc and I easily drop the entire team skate rollerskiing and finish together at the top in 53 minutes! It is a new record overall, and a personal record for Marc by over six minutes. Then, after starting again at the bottom, this time classic rollerskiing, Marc and I try to pull more of the team with us along but the same thing happens. Marc and I clock in at the top in 55 minutes. Walter is very surprised since Marc had done this with the team six weeks ago and finished behind most of his guys and over 20 minutes in total slower than he was today.

Andy (on left) and Marc (on right) near the top.

It shows great improvement and provides reassurance that our training plan together and high motivational levels are achieving even better results we'd hoped for. Marc and I have developed a strong friendship these past weeks that will last a lifetime. We train twice a day except on Wednesdays (only once) and Saturday (our official recovery day). Today has been a big showing for Marc, as the athletes and Walter comment, *"He's back!"* Marc had asked Walter weeks ago about taking some of the better guys on the team with him during some important training sessions. Walter didn't want any part of it, but after this display, who knows what he is thinking.

On a tangent, I'd always wondered if it was possible for the brute force of a human arm to generate enough pressure to make a ski pole explode. Well, in one of the interval training sessions with the British National Team Marc and I were just starting our 5th 3k uphill lap, doing V-2 over everything when it happened. I was mid-stride executing a forceful pole plant and my left pole exploded right out of the center. The combination of my arm forcing the pole down, and the energy returning from the hard tarmac, caused the release of energy to blow the middle of the pole into tiny pieces. So the mystery was finally solved!

At 4:30 am in early September Marc and I pack his car and roll out of the driveway heading north. Seven hours later, we arrive at the gate of the British army base that Marc is officially attached to. He doesn't go there very often and so is very busy for the two days we spend there. I come along to get out of Ruhpolding for a few days and see some of northern Germany.

It's the largest of all British Army bases, larger even than those in Great Britain. While Marc is busy with exams and meetings, he has me working in the gym testing a young guy that the Army is interested in advancing his athletic talent. He shows above-average ability and, most importantly, is highly motivated to train hard and compete.

When we return, the German Summer Biathlon Championships are about to commence in Ruhpolding. Marc and I are given coaching credentials to assist the British National Team for the events. There are over 2,000 spectators and the event is broadcasted on EuroSport TV. Other national biathlon teams that attend besides the Germans and British are the Austrians, Chinese, and the United States. USBA has added me to their short list of competitors and I have been invited by the German Biathlon Federation to compete. I have been added to put pressure on the police station to release my rifle, but it does not work and I am unable to obtain it or compete.

I take the opportunity to visit the U.S. Biathlon Coaches. The USBA Performance Director is the one who sent a copy of my team credentials and race invitation to the police station where they are holding my rifle. He called the station again right then out of frustration to tell them that none of the other U.S. athletes in this event have waffenpasses. This coach is also a German citizen from the same region, speaking the same dialect, so there is little chance that the police do not realize they have made a mistake, but they still won't return my rifle.

A few weeks later as my time in Europe is coming to an end I am happy to get a visit from my mother and show her around during a lower intensity and resting period of training. First I take her to the Deutsches Museum, and spend the entire day there.

After that I take her to Ruhpolding, then down into Slovenija to visit one of my favorite towns, Beld. From there we head into Austria, to Ramsau.

In Ramsau I am able to connect with Sylwia Jaśkowiec who is there as part of the Polish Ski Team for a ten day training camp. It is good to see her again and introduce her to my mother. The eventful trip gets even better as Sylwia and I rollerski together. On the highest loop she whooshes past me on a long, steep, downhill corner. That is the fastest I've ever seen anyone go around that part of the course and after I catch up to her I tell her why. It is the very corner where Bjorn Daehlie (the best skier in the World of all time) crashed, which led to his early retirement due to the trauma and back pain from the crash. The corner is in the shade and the track acquires a slippery, wet, mossy film.

From Ramsau we meander our way back to the Munich airport for my mother's return trip. We have planned to fully load her bags with my stuff to make my return to Alaska easier. We pack those bags to the max and send them down the Lufthansa conveyer belt without any problems. We say our goodbyes and she boards the plane.

During her connection in Frankfurt she has to go through another security checkpoint. It is there that she is detained for two hours, being questioned about the large crystal cup that she is carrying. It is the trophy from my Polish Worldloppet, and they are suspicious of its natural elements as many people smuggle drugs by shaping, polishing, and glazing them into the surface materials of cups like these. It is large enough to hold a basketball inside. Since all the writing on the cup is in Polish and the German Police don't speak Polish either, my mother cannot verify exactly where it has come from or where it has been prior to the last evening of me giving it to her. In the end, they release her and allow her to continue her flight with the cup to Alaska.

CHAPTER ELEVEN
New Horizons

After my mother leaves I return to Ruhpolding to train but decide to make one more trip to Ramsau to spend time training and catch up with Sylwia before her training camp finishes. The weather is sunny as usual in Ramsau and makes for a beautiful time. We train together in the day and at night, walk under the stars in the moonlight talking.

One evening Sylwia reads some of the positive and inspirational coaching tools that I've been preparing to help teams and individuals become better athletes within themselves. I also open up to her about some of the visions and ideas I have for the future, beyond skiing. At one point she becomes very serious and says: *"Andy, you have all this stuff about pursuing goals, unlimited abilities, and discovering success, but you, yourself are not doing what you are fully capable of."*

It hits me like a bolt from the sky. She is right. I've lost myself in the hassles around biathlon, and in a way this has dragged me down, blinding me from what is really important. This single moment allows me to gain clarity and start to focus on the future and how I can use all I've learned and all the ideas I've gained over the past ten years and I become excited about the future once more. Her words are exactly what I needed to hear, we continue to keep in touch.

The Rifle That Just Won't Go Away

It is the beginning of October and we are about to start the second block of training for Marc's team, when the native-German U.S. biathlon coach calls me. He says that he had multiple conversations with the officer in charge of my case who said that I must at least try to get a waffenpass. This would be my 4th attempt. The police officer does not believe that I have previously tried three other times.

To respect the coach, I go to the office near Ruhpolding to 'try' and get the pass they are so persistent on me acquiring.

I find the office, knock on the door, walk in, am invited to sit down and began with an introduction. *"I am an American"* to which I am interrupted by one of the ladies working there with: *"Oh, you must be Mr. Liebner, we know all about you."*

They already know the document that I need and their attitude is very helpful and keen to get things moving. I try to save them the time and energy by informing them about the German law that will not allow foreigners to be issued these passes, but they think differently, so I say: *"Okay! Let's do it! Sign me up! Let's get a waffenpass today!"*

Like so many times before, after a half hour of trying to process the forms, they find that they are unable to issue me the pass, due to my American citizenship. At that point I suggest that it is very important that they call the main office in charge of my case and explain to them the reasons why I cannot get the pass they are prosecuting me for not having.

Then the phone calls begin. Both ladies in the office are working on my case and over the next two hours calling everyone involved with this, including the U.S. coaches, directors, chief of the biathlon stadium in Ruhpolding, chief of the German Biathlon Federation, chief of the British Biathlon Union, coach of the British biathlon team, board members in the International Biathlon Union, the police station holding my rifle, and the main government office for the federal state of Bavaria overseeing of my case. The value of my rifle with the mags exceeds $4,000 USD and leaving them in Europe when I return to the U.S. does not appeal to me.

After spending nearly three hours in that government office, they concede that there is nothing they can do and they are going to wait and see what the prosecuting office will say given the documents I have, which means that I am back to the same place I was before.

After another day of extreme frustration I write a letter and send it to the police station holding my rifle:

> Attention Freyung Police,
>
> I, Andy Liebner, would like to ask of your department to contact the Staatsanwaltschaft Passau and explain to them the situation so my biathlon sport rifle that is being held in your possession can be released.
>
> I explained over and over to the field officers and your office that there is no way that any Landratsamt will issue me the passes you require for my rifle to be in my possession. For some reason the people at your office continue to deny that fact!
>
> The Freyung Police Department and the Staatsanwaltschaft in Passau has been provided all of the following documents:
> - Receipt of purchase proving it belongs to me and the rifle was purchased in the United States.
> - Invitation to a biathlon event within the federal state of Bavaria, Germany from two different National Governing sport bodies (one was the German Biathlon Federation).
> - Proof of my Active status as a U.S. Biathlon Member.
> - Letter from the Official State Police Department in Alaska authorizing that I am a legal citizen to be carrying weapons.
> - Invitation for a training camp in Ruhpolding as a member of the U.S. Biathlon Team.
> - A letter from an Alaskan Senator providing diplomatic power.
> - Weapons permit for the same rifle issued in Australia.

The declaration papers when I arrived in Stuttgart on 27 JUL 2009 were accepted by Customs but they did not provide me with a copy. But I do have a copy of declaration with the same rifle brought into Frankfurt, Germany on 05 JAN 2009.

I was invited to compete in the German Summer Biathlon National Championships held in Ruhpolding, but since the Freyung Police holds possession of my rifle, I was unable to compete. None of the other U.S. Athletes who did compete have the German Waffenpass, or Waffenbezitkarte, that you continue to require me to obtain.

The United States of America is not a part of the European Union and therefore the weapons permits that are required by European Union citizens are not authorized to be issued to foreign visitors to the U.S.

In 1787 The Constitution of the United States was written. The Second Amendment of the Constitution states that all American citizens have the right to bear arms. This means that we are not required to have permits or licenses to buy, and use, certain weapons. We cannot get a weapon registered in America or provide such documents to you.

Many members within the International Biathlon Union (IBU) have been involved with this incident and all have acknowledged the fact that Americans have not been held to the German standard with regard to weapon permits.

The former trainer of the U.S. Biathlon Team of eight years (a German citizen and former German Customs Officer) has called your office on my behalf and explained the situation and stated the requirements of American biathletes, but your office has failed to appreciate his knowledge and wisdom.

This incident has been very stressful and the repercussions I have been threatened with have been

> *difficult to accept, which have caused me to quit the sport of biathlon. And why? Because one German police office is not willing to create a solution.*

I am at the end of my tether. Judgments, some of them reasonable, others irrational, about the nature of Germans arise within me. I would like to think that I was using this letter as a means to release some of the frustration, rather than reflecting a deeper judgment within myself. But I am not sure which is true. Emotional threats aside, when it is expressed like it is in the first part of the letter, the absurdity of the situation is hard to miss.

All through this year-long journey I have bumped up against structures that seem to be inflexible and set against my forward progress. It started somewhat subtly with the USBA and has slowly escalated in intensity to this final point. Surely, this is not a normal situation!

British Army

In mid-October the Commanding Officer and his support staff from the British Army Base show up at one of our training sessions. We do some quick planning to engage them in our training routine to ensure they will be satisfied with the time and efforts that the 1LSR Team expends. The majority of the team funding comes from budgets that these officers control and so it is most important to show how professional we are and how beneficial our time spent here is.

They show up at the range in Ruhpolding and it is dumping rain. Right away, as has been planned, one of our best guys (Pete Bayer) takes the group and begins demonstrating the shooting process and details of a biathlon rifle. During that process, all the other guys follow the routine by shooting 20-40 rounds and I spend the time looking through the scope, as I usually do, calling out the corrections to make on their sights.

The rain has reduced and is now coming in sporadic showers. Pete does a great job by letting three officers shoot his rifle in both standing and prone positions. That's always a good thing to do so they realize how difficult the sport actually is. Then the CO asks if he can try rollerskiing. Marc happens to not have his boots on yet, so the CO borrows them and gives it a go. While Marc works with the guys I take the CO into the flat penalty loop area to teach him some basic technique so he won't be frustrated. He does quite well for never having done anything like that before in his life—and in the pouring rain! From the overall experience, he sees the challenge of biathlon and will continue the team's funding.

Until a few weeks ago we have been training outside in shorts and t-shirts, but on October 13 we wake up to find snow on the ground. I am on a deadline, knowing that I have to leave Germany before November and I was hoping to make it out of Europe before the snow hits, but I just missed it. The entire day is swept by constant rain, sleet, and hail, but we keep to the training plan of outdoor workouts because it was raining hard the entire day before and we'd done two sessions in the gym.

As we walk onto the running track we find that a few lanes are covered in snow. I don't think much of it, since half of the Alaskan track season operates with snow on some portions of the track as the season begins. But some of the guys find it a bit intimidating. The wind, rain, sleet and hail persists as we power our way through the workout. The back stretch has a headwind the speed of which I have only experienced in Palmer, Alaska, but after we endure a workout in such conditions we are all mentally tougher. It is one of those days where the weather is over-the-top and ridiculously miserable, yet we look at it with humor and train really hard anyway.

The Rifle Saga ...Ends!

It is more than two months since my rifle was taken away by the police, and due to the limited amount of time I am allowed to stay in the European Union for this trip, I am running out of time for the police to return my rifle back to me. On October 14 I go into the Ruhpolding town hall and wait in the lobby to speak with the town Mayor. I work mostly with his secretary and explain the situation and the urgency of getting my rifle back soon, because of my required departure date.

Ruhpolding has a reputation of being a highly popular biathlon-supporting village—the best in the world—and therefore wants no negative publicity with foreign athletes. Thanks to the combination of all the previous calls from other agencies over the past two months and now this addition of political power from German officials, I am finally able to get approval to pick-up my rifle!

But to do this I have to drive three hours north to a larger police station that ranks above the one that originally took it away. At the time I'm scheduled to pick it up I am supposed to meet with a doctor. The doctor is going to ask me some questions and if he deems me a 'fit' person my rifle will be returned. I arrive, pass through three security gates and once on the inside manage to locate the room for the evaluation. The doctor doesn't speak any English and they didn't realize that I am not fluent in German so they skipped most of the technical questions.

Basically, once I make it clear that I am going to be flying back to America with the rifle in another week they apologize and wish me a safe journey while opening the door for me on the way out. I am quite surprised to see how apologetic they are as they hand my rifle to me with the bag and all of the itemized things inside.

It's cheesy to say that everything happens for a reason, but these past months it's almost been too perfect. The German police taking away my rifle (removing the most stressful aspect in my life), reading the book *"In Search Of...,"* and Sylwia's comment about my life direction have all been part of a larger unfolding. I recognized the signs and see that it's time now to finally pursue skiing in a more serious sense and develop a series of inventions that I've had in mind for some time doing what I enjoy most in life. Since my decision to no longer improve as a biathlete, I've been offered three paid positions by different nations to work from now until the 2010 Olympics and one offer to coach a national team with a 2.5 year contract. I'm honored to have been offered them but I've turned all the offers down.

On October 16 I pack the van, say goodbye to Marc and the team, and leave Ruhpolding.

Driving to the Wunderle's house, which will be my base for preparing to leave Germany, I reflect on the past two months' training. The first 3-4 weeks of training with Marc at his house were the most confidence-building in my life. We worked hard two times per day and it felt great afterwards. Even after the first three days when I was tired and would have normally backed off the intensity, I just followed Marc and went for it. I found that my body could handle more and adapt to the training better than I expected. I've trained all these months injury-free and am feeling stronger and fitter than ever. I really feel ready to put the rifle aside and give the U.S. Ski Marathon Series my best effort.

Since Marc's team arrived it's been nice leading the "morning mobility" at 7:00 am starting with a run, then some sort of technique exercise or mental imagery, and then a quick stretching routine. Coaching and training, I've found is a comfortable fit to my happiness and lifestyle. I felt a sense of belonging and really enjoy it.

This spring and summer, I learned more about myself than I'd ever dreamt. While coaching the British Army guys I would create their training plans. I would ask myself key development questions on both physical and psychological fronts. From where they are now and what they have done, what is the next best appropriate training activity for them? What muscular systems and what muscle groups do we want to focus on this week, next week, and so on? What would be a self-esteem strengthening aspect we can improve on during all of these physical trainings? What are a few different mindsets, tips, and changes that might help keep them fresh and to optimally perform? If they begin to give up or shut down mentally, what key words would help revitalize their hard work ethic, and how can I help them make the necessary lifestyle changes within their program to keep them in a progressive and positive state? What does each person need to succeed, both physically and psychologically?

Andy (top left) and the British Army's I LSR Biathlon Team of 2009. Behind us is Hitler's famous hideout.

By me driving at those questions to help them, I found it absolutely fascinating, motivating, and at times inspiring to redirect those questions at myself, judging how I do my training and what I think about during my sessions.

I spend my final weekend in South West Germany at the Wunderle's house. For the 15 months I have been traveling, Bubenbach has been a 'safe haven' or 'second home' and now it serves as a real nice place to get all the final things prepared to move back to the U.S. Raphael and I go for some nice runs through the endless thick forests of the Black Forest and find some good fresh snow. During this time I reflect and realize that upon my arrival to Europe I'd planned for a 15 month trip and my return flight will cap exactly 15 months. Also during the entire time, I'd only seen Raphael at the very beginning and at the very end.

It is really great to visit and hang out with Raphael again after he had become my best friend in college. I have forgotten how nice it is to have quality conversations with old friends. We talk a lot about ski team stories and racing mishaps that occurred the two years we were teammates. He just graduated and at his final (2009) NCAA Ski Championships finished 2nd in the 10K Classic and 3rd in the 20K Freestyle.

After a weekend at the Wunderle's it's time to say goodbye, finish loading the van, and drive north to the Stuttgart airport. I have to stop at the airport to check-in and notify British Air that I am traveling with a rifle giving them the appropriate 1-2 days' notice prior to departure. I remember from flying to Australia that those were the rules.

To my great surprise, the rules have changed less than two weeks ago and I am now required to give 72 hours' notice and at the time I checked in it is exactly 40 hours. The flight agents are very sure there is no chance that I am going to be able to check my rifle on my scheduled departure date. I ask them if I can use their phone to call the London airport (the airport that grants the approval of processing the request). They are very stout in not letting me use their phone for such calls because they know the rules and are not going to stand up against what the law states.

By this time it's only getting later and I am beyond sick of dealing with rifle issues. I am at the point where I no longer care. It is so many levels beyond the beyond that I can't express it. I've long since let go of my rifle and I know I'm getting on that plane;

the only question is whether it will be with or without my rifle. I leave the airport and drive straight to the Holmenkol home office and spend the next 90 minutes on the phone with the London airport and my travel agency doing everything I possibly can to expedite the process. The final word is that my request is being processed, time unknown to confirmation.

During the remaining time in the work day I meet with Christian to finalize all my dealings. He is keen to keep me on board with Holmenkol in some capacity and we discuss some possibilities for the future and I promise I'll keep him at the forefront of my mind. I also agree to keep monitoring the situations in Greece and Australia that I have established for the company.

The final job is to sell the van. I've arranged to meet a guy from Lebanon and he duly takes my beloved transport/home off my hands and provide him with a hammer to hit the starter. He plans on driving to Lebanon and I hope he makes it!

The next morning I arrive at the airport around 5:00 am. The first thing I do is go to the British Air customer service desk and inquire about the status of my request hoping for an approval. In the system it says it is still being processed. Conveniently, the same ladies that helped me in June are working this morning too and I remind them of that incident. They remember me and I explain the problems I've had in Germany with my rifle and inform them that, because of this experience, I will probably never be coming back to Germany for biathlon again!

They call up London right then and explain the urgency to approve my baggage. Michael from Holmenkol, who had driven me to the airport, has kindly waited to see what will happen and I am ready to leave my rifle with him to keep in a safe place for the chance that I will return someday and can hopefully fly with it back to America in some future years. But, within an hour of my flight taking off, the rushed approval comes through and I am allowed to check it on the plane. Deep down I knew my energy and efforts to motivate others to get it approved in time would work, which it did.

After a nice non-eventual flight, I gather my strength to travel with my heavy luggage from the international baggage claim to the Alaska Airlines check-in. I have to carry my many bags through three terminals and my bags weighed more than 200lbs in total. It becomes the most difficult transport I've ever undertaken in an airport.

I am only able to use a cart during one stint. Going up and down escalators and in and out of the monorail is a nightmare. I have stuffed my rifle case into my ski bag and filled the ends with extra stuff, so I have one really long, really heavy bag, one big fat duffle bag, and two 'little bricks' as I think of my carry-ons.

As I approach the Alaska Airlines ticket counter sweat pours off my forehead and I am breathing heavily. There are no other customers checking in and both ladies behind the counter see the state I am in and are more than kind and helpful in checking my bags. I think I am supposed to pay another overweight baggage fee, but the ladies say nothing of it and check them to Anchorage, no questions asked.

Standing in line for security, I remember that I have forgotten to tell them about my rifle inside the ski bag. I go back to the ticket counter and tell them. They only have to call the X-ray guys and all is done. God bless America and the 2nd Amendment!

But despite the sense of belonging and the satisfaction of achieving so much I know it is time to go and continue my life and the plans that I am working to achieve. All the things I've wanted to do for all these years are finally falling into place within my own mind as I am starting to see which direction my life will go. For the past six months I've been assailed with an inner conflict about whether to keep pushing down the one track I was on or concede that I need to change direction. Now that the decision has been made I finally feel a sense of peace. On the flight as each minute becomes one less minute to landing in Anchorage, I know my life is about to change again. I also feel more complete as a person and ready for the next chapter of my life.

There is a section in Alastair Smith's book *"In Search Of..."* that resonates with me regarding what inside me holds me back in contrast to what lets me move forward:

> *"Fear gets called guilt, doubt, insecurity, and anxiety, but in the end, they are all emotions that are invoked through an underlying fear. Similarly*

for love. When we express emotions of joy, beauty, and peace, we are experiencing life through a state of love...You can only get to God through a state of love, not fear.

People get so caught up over which great teacher is right ... which one can take you further. There is so much conflict in the world because humans try to separate everything and put a structure around it. The truth is that the messages of all the great masters, both past and present, are the same. They all talk about love and the need to approach God through love. When groups of people get together, they place their own interpretations on the teachers' words. They start to erect their own structures, constraints, and limitations. As this continues, fear starts to creep in, and as the constraints grow, it becomes increasingly difficult to maintain a state of love and hence to approach God through love. It has happened to all religions, a natural imposition of fear develops." –Alistair Smith

Upon my arrival to Alaska, I am asked to give a speech at a school to a few hundred kids, many of them athletes. I prepare and finalize a document and thoroughly enjoy giving the presentation. Below is the document I still use today.

How do you mentally prepare for a competition? Do you fail to prepare or prepare to fail? If you have failed to prepare, you have prepared to fail.

We all can do the physical routines of warm-up, exercises and drills of the sport, and cool-down, but have you learned any tools that establish that same routine of warm-up, exercises and drills, and cool-down of the mental side? Most of us have never been introduced to this aspect that is so critical for success! I want you to be fully capable of performing at your most optimum levels physically and mentally, so this is why I am here.

Discovering a love in the sport will enable you to give your absolute best effort and no one can ever take away that feeling. Let's see a raise of hands of how many of you have heard, *"It's not about winning or losing, it's how you play the game?"* What does that statement really mean to you? Why does that statement stick around? [ask a few of them what it actually means to keep them engaged and involved so they remember]

Guidelines to help gain the mental edge in competition:

1. Strategies of a Good Routine
2. Love of the Sport
3. Mental Rehearsal
4. Get your Focus through Breathing
5. How to obtain an unshakable self-belief in your abilities
6. Best Effort Attitude
7. Compete Big!
8. Questions

I. Strategies of a <u>Good Routine.</u>

- Know how this performance will contribute to your short and long term goals.
- Check all equipment before each event.
- Always use positive self-talk.
- Eat specific foods that you know your body performs well with to maintain blood chemistry.
- Be aware and ready for any last minute program changes for the event.

2. Love of the sport

Through positive thoughts, images, and attitudes you can generate a greater energy, emotion, and direction that will help you perform at your best. Thoughts and images are energy. You have a personal connection to an unlimited source of energy in the form of powerful words, high-performance images, and video that you can use to enhance your mentality. Fear is the most limiting emotion known to mankind and people continue to let it manipulate their mentality, which directly effects their actions and reactions. Fear can cause stress, reduce breathing depth, stop energy flow, and limits performance. Love is more powerful than fear. Love is endlessly expansive leading to new possibilities. Although fear can motivate a good performance, <u>love can inspire greater performances</u>. To help grow your passion for sport, choose something to love in every event.

Q: What are the most common feelings that limit athletes?
A: Fear, anger, fatigue, and pain. Examples include:
Fear (of failure) - "I haven't trained as hard as I could have or should have to reach my goals this year."
Fear (of injury) - "Be careful." "Take it easy." "I don't want to get injured or burned out."
Anger - "Something is wrong." "It's not happening." "There's no way." "What's the use?" "I'm sick of this."
Fatigue - "I'm beat." "Not now, not today, maybe later." "I feel too tired from this week."
Pain - "It's going to hurt too much, so I'll go easier." (usually comes mid-end of season)

One of the qualities necessary to being a star athlete is mental consistency of stability and control. This can be done by attending to your best effort attitude by remembering goals and personal commitment. Loving your sport will also help you gain the confidence necessary to pull off a great performance.

3. Mental Rehearsal

Mental rehearsal is visualizing things you want to do competition. This includes seeing both your technique and your responses to your body with each motion. Mentally rehearsing technique is imagining, seeing or feeling yourself performing with speed, power, and with the right energy. Mental rehearsal is like a creating a blueprint that strengthens and clarifies intent and, in doing so, increases the probability of success! Many sport psychologists believe that it's more important to think of the process of how you are going to get there (that is, mental rehearsal) than it is to focus on the end result. Think about the successful end result you want to achieve, but remember without the journey to get there, the end will only remain a dream.

How to mentally rehearse:

- Eliminate all distractions; this is easily done by focusing on you and your physical technique.
- Get comfortable, relaxed, and control your breathing to clear your mind.
- Visualize yourself going through the race course 1-2 nights before each race. Corner by corner, every up hill and downhill, think about how the land comes in front of you.
- Next visualize yourself making crisp and precise movements with your technique as you compete.
- Experience the feeling of how you want to feel in a great performance.
- Next visualize yourself from your view (in motion) and from sideline views. (Internal and external)
- Use all of your senses.
- Make the imagery realistic and precise.
- Think about your breathing with each action.
- Acknowledge your weaknesses and have mental strategies planned for to do your best at them.

4. Get your Focus through Breathing

Sports demands energy! All athletes use many ways to energize before a competition, some listen to music, some exercise, some visualize themselves competing in the way they would like to perform, and some talk positively or aggressively to themselves. In many cases they use breathing to help direct their emotions into the mentality they want to be in. This will significantly help getting refocused moments before a performance that will help bring the right feeling you want and a best effort attitude to perform with.

Focus   Distraction and Fear   Performance

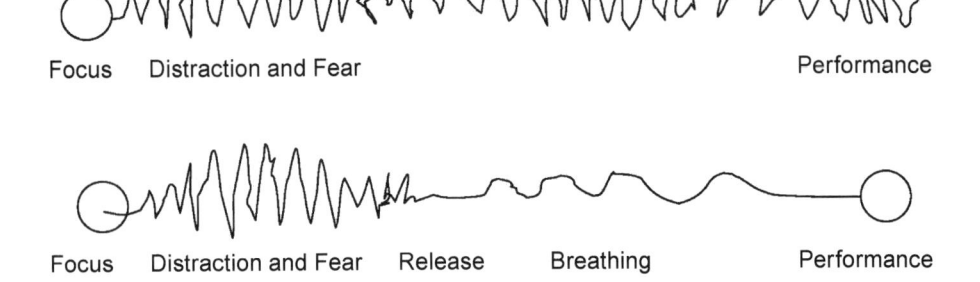

Focus   Distraction and Fear   Release   Breathing   Performance

5. How to gain an unshakable self-belief in your abilities:

- Recite to yourself aloud, *"I am ready for this competition."* And maximize your belief in your abilities.
- Focus on your strengths and how it will help you succeed.
- Spend more time thinking about what's important, what you <u>can</u> control.
- Imagine yourself going through the competition the way you want to perform.
- Be around people who make you feel confident. Confident athletes try harder and focus better in training and competition. They also try even harder when they don't reach their goals.

6. Best Effort Attitude

A **best effort attitude** is a way of thinking that helps you become more successful and allows you to enjoy the sport much more. Motivation is a key to success as it's what moves us to action. Having the drive from motivation in combination with, goals, and commitment for some athletes is an excellent mesh to ensure they will follow through with the day-to-day action necessary to turn their goals into a reality. Commitment is the willingness to do what's necessary to get the result you want. Success than, is getting what you expect instead of a surprise. *"You gotta want it. If you don't want it bad enough you shouldn't be here. If that's the case you don't need me."* –Sten Fjeldheim (Head Coach, NMU Ski Team)

Confidence and **Identity** are also very important in a best effort attitude. What is confidence? Confidence is you internal view of yourself. A confident person believes they can do the job without question. What are some aspects of identity? Who you think and feel you are and who others perceive you to be are all aspects of identity. Successful and stable athletes have some identity or image of themselves as effective competitors. It is definitely something <u>you</u> shape and control. If you have a poor performance, don't latch onto that disappointing perception and keep rerunning it as an identity program of who you are. Instead, use it. Say to yourself, "That's not who I am." Then imagine performing with speed, power, and performing well. Remember, to improve your performance identity (and increase your confidence), think about and visualize yourself at your best.

7. Compete Big!

"Our deepest fear is NOT that we are inadequate. Our deepest fear is that we are powerful beyond measure. It is our light, not our darkness, that most frightens us. Playing small does not prove anything. There is nothing enlightening about shrinking your abilities." -anonymous Get out there and give the sport your best effort. In every competition after giving 100%, you will always feel good and naturally acquire a sense of accomplishment.

The mind is always on, thinking thoughts, reviewing images, and creating feelings. Understand you control what is on your front view. Responsible means *response-able*. You are *response-able* for leading yourself to optimum success through loving your sport and *response-able* for creating feelings and focus that will help you excel and perform to unknown potential. *"You cannot control your competitors, but more importantly, they cannot control you."* –Andy Liebner

8. Questions

Q: What is the purpose of the following questions?
A: To build leverage on yourself and bring the priority of your goals to the surface.

Q: What do you really want to achieve within this sport?
Q: What will it take for you to achieve that?
Q: What will it feel like facing the challenges along the way?
Q: What will it feel like to achieve your goals?
Q: At what point in a competition do you back-off or give up?
Q: What causes you to do this?
Q: What are you afraid of, which may be part of the cause for this?
Q: What will you <u>lose</u> by working harder for longer? (list 5 things)
Q: What will you <u>gain</u> if you work harder for longer? (list 5 things)
Q: Why race/ compete and not just continue with training if you're not ready or willing to give your all?
Q: How much time and energy do you spend thinking about our most vulnerable point/ weakness?
Q: What thoughts do you plan on using to ensure you have strength when you get to our vulnerable point?
Q: Make a list of feelings and great moments in the same athletic discipline. (if possible) This will help you build confidence.
Q: To you, what is the most important aspect of competing in athletics?
Q: What do you get out of participating in solo activities?
Q: What do you get out of participating in group activities?
Q: Do your daily habits hinder or help your success?
Q: What could or should you be doing differently?

CHAPTER TWELVE
Follow-up

My plan for the winter is to run the Seattle Marathon then compete in the U.S. Ski Marathon Series, in hopes of winning it.

The Series consists of 13 total races held between January and March. Most races are a weekend apart but sometimes two marathons occupy the same weekend in different regions of the country so I have to plan well to optimize my travel and performance. I sign up for seven marathons, held seven consecutive weeks.

Not many skiers compete in more than a few of the events and you never know who is going to turn up on any given weekend. What this means is that the winner of the overall series is not necessarily the best skier, but the guy who can accumulate the most points. That said, points are only awarded for the first three positions, so the winner of the series needs to finish on the podium consistently. In addition, the series winner must compete in each of the three regions—East, Central, and West.

The Seattle Marathon is run on November 29th. I run a strong, steady pace and finish in 7th place overall, completing the course in 2:43 and my feet are covered in blisters.

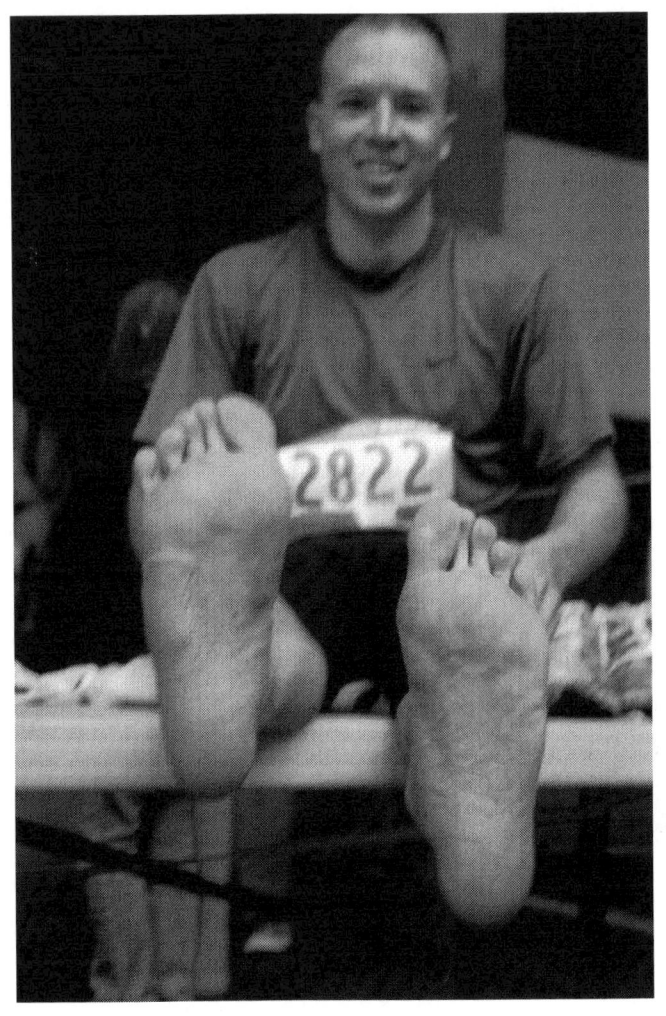

(Photo by Cheryl Brown.)

The U.S. Marathon Series was once highly competitive, with many professional teams and athletes battling every weekend in pursuit of points, prize money, and glory. Since the economic crisis, sponsorships have dried up, the marathon teams no longer exist and only a few of the elites turn up on their own, unannounced, competing as unattached individuals. This has created an opening and I feel it is my chance. I am going to hit this series full force using all that I have learned in Europe with the highest level of confidence.

The catch is that I have completed only one 50k ski marathon in my life and now I am attempting to knock out seven in seven weeks. It is quite a step up and the greatest challenge is likely to be recovering between races. Rest will require almost as much effort and focus as racing. But after all I've been through around the world within the last two years I have the confidence, not only that I can do it, but that I can do it on my own. This challenge of strength and endurance is something I have always wanted to take on and feel it will be a great opportunity to become an even stronger athlete physically and mentally.

My positive empowerment winds blowing in my favor is not enough to escape an emergency root canal to my top front left tooth. It is so painful before and after the operation that I am incapable of any physical activity for 3 long days. I'd choose the pain generated in a marathon over the tooth pain any day, and can't believe the intensity. Then a short time later, within a few weeks of the first race, I am in a car accident and my car is totaled. The other party visits the hospital with minor concussions and I am fine, but now without transportation. It takes weeks for the claim to process and I get a car just in time for the first Ski Marathon.

Pepsi Challenge

The Series kicks off each year in the small northern Minnesota town of Biwabik. The event is the Pepsi Challenge and consists of two 24k loops. The day is cloudy and the trails are fast. An hour before the start the officials delay the start another hour because it is so cold. Such a long race burns a lot of calories but I have no other food with me except a large cinnamon roll that I had bought to eat afterward. Now I am concerned that waiting around for an extra hour will diminish the optimum energy levels I've worked to achieve for the start of the race. With limited options I eat the cinnamon roll and settle down to wait.

My warm-up consists of a jog across the stadium, and when the race starts I quickly find myself in a good position. By 10k I am feeling awesome, gliding well, and find myself in the lead so I put on a surge, hoping to drop the big pack of about 30 guys on my tail. I surge for about 5K and look back to see only 10 guys remaining, now in a long string. Backing off the pace a little I allow the nearest racers to catch me and ski behind them so that I can catch a draft and recover.

The bigger hills commence and I begin to struggle a little bit. Adam Swank, Bjorn Batdorf, and Matt Weier are now putting on their little surges trying to drop me and the rest of the guys. I hang on and one by one we drop more guys. Skiing though the stadium at the end of the first lap we are on a course-record pace, and nearly 20 minutes faster than last year.

In the second lap I put on a surge at the same place as the first lap, as my skis are gliding really well and this section is gradual downhill and flat. The lead pack is only 4 guys and soon it's just 3. A race for the podium! We switch our order often, as our individual energy levels surge and recover. This is a real race here! With 10k to go Adam Swank puts the hammer down and nearly drops me and Bjorn completely. He breaks away and we are struggling. I keep pushing, gliding, and churning with every muscle and every bit of energy, trying to catch Adam.

Finally Bjorn and I succeed in reeling-in Adam just before the course enters a downhill nearly 2 kilometers long. I take full advantage of my top-quality self-applied wax service and tuck as close to the ground as possible, flying past Adam just after the top of the long downhill. By the bottom I have a several-second lead and with only 1.5k to the finish I start sprinting right then and there. My legs are cramping, my lungs are maxed out, and my heart is beating and feels like it is going to explode. The adrenaline rushes, I swiftly ski as hard as I possibly can and never look back. Coming across the line I am 5 seconds ahead of Adam. I have won and now hold the new record on a 26-year-old race course.

Noquemanon and City of Lakes

I compete the next week in the Noquemanon Ski Marathon in Marquette, Michigan and finish 3rd in the 51k Classic, another tough and grueling race all the way to the finish line. The third week I compete in the City of Lakes Loppet held in Minneapolis, Minnesota and win the event by over 4 minutes.

North American Vasa

The fourth marathon on my schedule is being held in Traverse City, Michigan, and I am welcomed by the officials and organizers, as they know about my dominance in all the events so far. Warming up for the Vasa I don't see any guys that look to be a threat, but you never know how good anyone really is until the race starts. I lead the first 2 kilometers with a solid train of several hundred skiers directly behind me. Then I pull to the side and let one guy ahead out of courtesy in case he wants to go faster but also to let him break the wind and open the trail for a while. It had snowed the night before, dropping about 2 inches on the course, so we are breaking trail, which slows the skis down significantly.

The guy in front of me is skiing in a V-2 so erratic that I can only take it for a half kilometer. His stride is so disruptive that I cannot focus or even think of anything else besides how strange, short, and high-impulse it is. I wait until a short gradual downhill and blast by him. I ski away easily and never look back as I race away with the event. I find the course to be very entertaining and enjoyable to ski, with its rolling hills and thick-wooded ski loops.

The rest of the race I break trail, being the first one to ski on the fresh snow, and win by 5 minutes and 29 seconds. It is nice to really relax and glide out without worrying about out-sprinting anyone. What makes it even nicer is that the Elmore family (second cousins of mine) lives in the area and comes to watch the race and see my largest victory yet.

A day following the race, I compete in a 16K classic race. I win it also, and at the same time lead a new friend/ competitor (Denny Paull) to have a peak performance.

I am now leading in points, but there are contenders who have competed in other races out East, and I am unsure whether they have registered in the Central and Western events still to come.

Minnesota Finlandia

My fifth ski marathon of the season is the Minnesota Finlandia, in Bemidji, and it is a race I will never forget. The previous event had not contained any real big names and it looks as if this one is going to be the same. I arrived 2 days before the race, booked into a hotel for the first night but not the second, as all were full because of a snowmobile convention in town. So here I am again, sleeping in my car, just like the van in Europe and in the morning it is -4° F. I warm up by testing my skis, sizing up the opposition in the process. I don't see any serious contenders, but keep to my normal routine. I'm actually a little disappointed but that gets turned on its head about ten minutes before the race because Andrew "AJ" Johnson and Zach Simons come into view and start testing their skis. *"This race just got a whole lot tougher,"* I say to myself.

Zach Simons is a well-accomplished and recognized skier and 2007 American Birkebeiner Champion, and Andrew Johnson is a 2006 Olympian and 4-time National Champion. They are two of the big names in American skiing and now I'll get the chance to test myself against them. For the first few kilometers Simons hammers and Johnson follows along with two other guys. I am 100 meters behind all of them at 1k and feeling okay. I see Simons looking around and starting to slow the pace as he realizes the competition is not real tough. This allows me to close the gap and catch up.

Over the next 30K we drop the other two guys and so it is just the three of us—AJ, Simons, and yours truly! I do not believe they know who I am, as I am wearing no sponsorship affiliated gear, only black spandex bottoms and a blue/white training jacket. Also, I'm listening to my MP3 player with earbuds. It is not common to wear training jackets in races, or to listen to music, although I do this in all of the marathons, as it reminds me of my progressive training with Marc Walker. That always takes the pressure off as I'm lining up at the start and during the races.

For the rest of the race AJ and Simons seem to be putting on little surges to try and drop me. On one occasion, when they saw I was taking a few gulps out of my drink bottle they sprinted away, making me sprint after them to catch up. They know how to ski smart, but I am also on top of things and am using my experience and knowledge to match their pace, conserving energy when I can. With 5k to go AJ really takes off and he nearly gaps Simons and me. After some serious effort we catch back up, then he just starts skiing real easy and we do the same, knowing it is just going to be a free-for-all sprint the final 200 meters.

For a short time Simons takes the lead then he acts like he doesn't want to keep breaking the wind and pulling us and AJ waves me forward. I sense this is a tactic they are using to get to sit behind me so they can slingshot past me at the end. With this in mind I take the lead they so generously offer but I immediately hammer away, pounding through the final 2 kilometers as hard as I can go. After going through the tunnel and into the final 200 meters I feel awesome, adrenaline rushing. I am unstoppable. I never look back and fly across the line 8/10th of a second ahead of Simons, with AJ a second behind him. 7 minutes later 4th place finishes. This win really adds to the positive flow of my marathons so far. I feel alive, progressive, and satisfied.

Top of the Podium at the Minnesota Finlandia.

American Birkebeiner

The following weekend is the American Birkebeiner, the 6th marathon. I must compete in this race as it is the largest and most popular skiing event on the North American continent. Unfortunately, I eat at a Thai restaurant in Duluth a few days before the event and endure a 24-hour period of vomiting. I feel death knocking at my bedside as my body recovers. This is followed by 4 days of diarrhea leading up to the race. During that week I stay with some of my former Alaskan coaches (Sarah and Jesse) in Duluth, and one evening during prayer time their daughter asks, *"Mommy, is the guy in the basement going to die?"* I lose 10 pounds due to an inability to retain food, water, or electrolytes and have no realistic chance performing optimally, but I go to the race anyway.

I notice a big drop in my strength and endurance after less than 5 kilometers. It wasn't hard to predict I would feel this way and I've taken the precautions to prepare myself as best I can, carrying two drink bottles filled with a high-electrolyte mix. After 10 kilometers, the front pack has formed and I can only watch them ski ahead from about 200 meters behind. It is difficult mentally to be physically incapable of hanging with them so early on, but I do my best to ski conservatively and efficiently taking electrolyte feeds every few minutes. Surprisingly, at 20 kilometers I manage to catch them, either by skill or their slowing the pace or a combo of both. Once in the pack I make an extra effort to get right behind the leaders. By placing myself in the mix of the pack I get more protection from the wind and in my condition this is a tactical necessity.

Over the next few kilometers I can hardly believe that I have caught them (there are about 25 in the group) and there is a lot of shifting going on within the pack itself. To maintain your personal space within a pack requires extra energy, whereas being directly behind the leaders allows me to ski 'best line' (the most inside route around the corners) and glide longer, thus conserving as much energy as possible. Through the famous OO checkpoint ("Double O") at 22.8k I am struggling to keep my top-ten position. It isn't long until I find myself drifting off the back of the pack and getting dropped fast.

For the remaining 27k I do my best to move my fatigued and

exhausted body along the rolling terrain with my eyes fixed far down the course to see skiers ahead who have also fallen off of the pack. There are soon only a few within my line of vision, some ahead, some behind. It feels like the final miles of a botched running marathon, a "death march" some call it. Any way you think about it this is the toughest thing that can happen in these races. I am doing the best I can given the illness I'm recovering from and, knowing that my vision of success in this important race has skied away right from in front of my eyes, my energies are now fixed on maintaining the will to merely finish on my own two feet.

With 5 kilometers to go I experience the first signs of passing out. When the bright lights form in front of my eyes, followed by loss of hearing, and lack of cognitive recognition, I force myself to slow down. I am excited when the marker indicating only 3K left appears and shortly after that I become blind altogether for brief periods. With my drink bottles depleted and both arms and legs cramping I have no other option but to ski for a while using only my legs until they also cramp so badly that I cannot control their locking and spasms.

At that point I switch to double-poling, which works for a short time until my triceps cramp to the point of locking and spazzing. I endure this cycle of trauma until I am finally able to struggle across the finish line in 30th place before laying in the snow for 20 minutes. The support staff feeds me snacks and drinks, helping me regain the ability to see clearly, hear, and stand with coordination. This is the most exhausting ski race I've ever completed.

West Yellowstone Rendezvous

The final race of the series is the West Yellowstone Rendezvous in Montana. This will be my only qualifying race in the West and I have scored enough points by this time that all I need to do is start and finish. To score points in any of these races you must be within the top 3, but you do not need to be in the top 3 in all the regions. There are a few good race contenders, one of whom I recognize right away as Leif Zimmerman, a 2006 Olympian and multi-U.S. National podium champion. We competed against each other as juniors and he acknowledges me before the start.

The race starts and I feel the mental fatigue, *"Here we go, another 50k for the 7th week in a row."* I ski near the front of the pack, in about 5th place over the first few kilometers. Leif, meanwhile, flips between first and second place over the first 10k. Soon the long string of guys dwindles to 4 and we press on. Leif puts on a few surges and so do I. Then one of the other guys in the pack surges and we all hang on. This goes on for the majority of the race until the 40k mark and that is when Leif surges and only I am able to hang on. We drop those other guys without even realizing it. *Bam!* We are out ahead!

It is Leif and I for the next 5k and I am feeling pretty tired physically as well as mentally. A great feeling though, as I know that I am getting bonus points because I really wasn't expecting to finish in the top 3 out here after the past 6 weeks and 6 marathons. Add to that the extra elevation of West Yellowstone at 6,666 feet of altitude, and I have a few things against me. Over the final 5k Leif kicks it up a notch or perhaps I slow down, I don't know which because I am tired and still skiing as hard as I can. I know Leif has great sprinting ability as I have witnessed him winning the final rounds at the U.S. National Championships. At this point in the season and in this race I am proud to finish 2nd place behind him. I ski to the finish with a smile and know I have successfully captured the U.S. Marathon series.

So, I led the Series in points from beginning to end. This was only possible because of all that I have learned, trained, and reflected on over the past few years, particularly the time spent in Europe. My journey has led me to this success, how small or big it may be.

To give my best effort through every marathon was satisfying enough that I did not even need outside recognition to feel successful. I felt accomplished from within which reinforced my positive image and self-belief.

The season has come to an end and my nerves are settled and, as I reflect on the endless challenges I've faced, I am happy that I kept believing in myself when others doubted. The results do not matter as much as the fact I have proved again to myself that I can succeed at whatever I set my mind to.

Summer Begins

The day following the final race I drive to Bellevue, Washington and spend two weeks there with my father. I also meet up with Roberto Carcelen, who I'd met at the World Championships and had just returned from the 2010 Olympics in Vancouver. We ski nearly every day at Snoqualmie pass. Before I return to my home in Alaska, I finalize a summer job as the Nordic Holmenkol representative in Canada. On my return trip to Alaska I stop at many Nordic ski shops handing out catalogs and speaking with retail store owners about contracts. I spend the majority of the summer training in remote areas of Alaska and communicating with Canadian retailers.

Mt. Marathon

On the 4th of July I compete in Alaska's most famous and prestigious running race, known as 'Mount Marathon.' This being my rookie year in the event, I am challenged by all the top Alaskan mountain runners and past mountain running veterans and finish in 6th place overall. The race is only 4.2 miles but takes the leaders about 35 minutes to go from sea level to the halfway point at the top, at 3,022 feet, then turn around and run back down in less than 15 minutes to the bottom. It is the most extreme and dangerous race I have ever competed in.

The first half begins with a half-mile gradually uphill run through the downtown streets of Seward to the base of the mountain. The first section of the mountain is a near-vertical 100 meters of climbing, requiring the use of all four limbs. This is followed by mud-slick single-track paths winding up the spine of the mountain through the thick green bushes, alders, trees, and Devil's Club. (If you don't know what Devil's Club is, you'll know after you grab one, as the spines on both leaves and stems release a venomous fluid which causes swelling and itching.) When we break out above the tree-line it reminds me of the significantly diminishing oxygen level and also marks the half-way point of the uphill section.

The remaining trail to the top consists of loose shale, steep climbing on the mountainside, random snow and ice, and enduring either scorching exposure to the sun or clouds that commonly come with cold rain and high winds. At the peak of the climb is a large boulder that each athlete runs around as the half-way checkpoint.

While the uphill climb is exhausting, the downhill is a free-for-all survival descent to the bottom. From overhead racers can be seen in fully-extended running strides, cautious downhill running strides, climbing backwards down cliff-sides, and flat-out falling every which way. The loose shale at the top acts as a nicely absorptive running surface since your feet wallow in up to your shins in the skin-piercing rock. The shale can break ankles, catch your feet to flip you on your face, and also has been known to become flying projectiles harming other parts of the body that have not been damaged yet and/or others around you.

The top runners sprint down the mile of dangerous shale in less than 10 minutes, while others take 30 minutes or more. After the shale there are three cliffs (or little water falls) to master. Some, like myself, take the risk in launching over the top and pray that we don't shatter our ankles at the bottom, since they're between 2-4 meters in height and the uneven, rocky, wet, slippery surface is never guaranteed to be safe. From there only one large drop remains and those runners who have not yet hurt themselves often acquire their wound here. In my race, I trip in the middle and fall flat on my face against a sidewall of a sharp rocky platform only to bounce off and continue my adrenaline push down to the road and the final half-mile run, passing thousands of fans cheering so loud you cannot hear yourself think.

After enduring such steep climbing followed by steep running-descending in deadly terrain, your legs feel like they have been hit thousands of times with a meat hammer and are incapable of a normal running cadence. The delight comes after rounding the last corner in downtown Seward when your eyes can fix on the finish-line banner at the end of the street. The fun comes later in reliving the experience with other Mt. Marathon warriors, friends, and family.

Northern Michigan University

All this prepares me for the next step in my journey, which begins mid-July. I enroll as a NCAA student-athlete at Northern Michigan University and overload my Subaru to drive 3,500 miles of the AlCan (Alaskan-Canadian) Highway for the 3rd time this year.

Andy loading the car for college. No room for the snow tires. Invention! Tire holder for the front of cars, made of two 4X4's.

At NMU I find my place on the team and take full advantage of the knowledge and wisdom that Sten Fjeldheim and Jenny Ryan, the coaching staff, have and are willing to share as a result of their lifetime of involvement in skiing. In the classroom I find it difficult to sit in rows and take notes as a student again. Overall my fall season at NMU is tough athletically and academically. The team trains hard and I put in my best effort to perform well and contribute to the team's training sessions.

At the 2011 U.S. National Championships held in Rumford, Maine, I do not have any one race that is excellent, but all my races are pretty good and consistent. In the end I am awarded the "2011 U.S. National College Cup Champion" although I did not know such a point system and title existed until the awards banquet. During the season I finish every Central Region College race in 1st or 2nd place.

My ability to efficiently classic ski has significantly improved, which was very enjoyable. I cannot thank Sten enough for his relentless examples and patience in explaining the timing of the arms and when to implement overall power. At the NCAA Championships I earned my 3rd and 4th All-American Certificates by placing 9th in the 10k Skate and 8th in the 20k Classic. After the season I was awarded Central Collegiate Ski Association (CCSA) Skier of the Year.

The experiences away from the U.S. resided within me as lessons and maturity landmarks. My ability to improve as an athlete both physically and mentally were significantly increased. While, as an athlete, I am always trying to win, I now had a better reason to compete. I solved the mystery in my wondering mind as to why the Europeans consistently perform better than the Americans and that is simply that they love the sport. They truly love the sport and when I can embrace this love, it seems effortless and always enjoyable.

Although I have balanced academics and skiing all year, the inner voice calling out to me to get my inventions moving forward has been growing louder and louder. I left NMU after only completing one year and moved to the Western United States to begin a business venture involving the development of my own inventions as well as supporting the development of others' inventions.

NMU was the right place for me at the right time in my life and I promise to return at some future time to finish my degree.

Andy #3 and Martin Banerud #2 leading the CCSA Championships in Ishpeming, Michigan, February 2011 (Photo by Dennis Loy)

CHAPTER THIRTEEN
Epilogue

Since my return from Europe I have continued to maintain contact with Alistair Smith, the Australian author of the book *"In Search Of..."* that so captivated me. I have not yet met him or even spoken on the phone—all our communications have been through email.

Nevertheless, his support has become important to me. When I finished writing this book I asked him if he would look at it for me and he agreed. After reading it, he wrote the following email, which puts into words some of the things I had felt during my journey but could not fully grasp.

Dear Andy,

First of all, congratulations on your journey! You have truly engaged in a modern quest which is worthy of the attention of the Greek gods, should they exist in some realm and be looking down upon us. I am sure your perseverance, courage and honesty will serve as an inspiration to others, be they skiers or people with a more general interest in confronting themselves.

Having said this, there are a few observations I'd like to offer, not so much about what has been written, but more about what has not been said and what is yet to come.

In the past, every culture had a mythology and they used this mythology as a foundation for maintaining harmony between their own existence and the world around them. For the first time in history, our modern civilization finds itself without a prevailing mythology to guide its interactions with the world at large. It is no small coincidence that this coincides with a period where we are having a rapid and destructive impact on our beloved planet.

Many people, especially the young, sense this loss and are searching for it in many places. This is why so many movies revolve around the theme of mythology: Star Wars, The Chronicles of Narnia, Lord of the Rings, The Matrix and more recently, Avatar and Battle of the Titans, to name a few. It is also why so many computer-video games have a mythological theme embedded within them. Deep down we know we are missing a critical ingredient and we yearn for a way to connect to that missing component of life.

Do not misunderstand me. In speaking in mythic terms I am not suggesting a return to the old days of superstitions, gods, and demons. Our modern scientific world has shed too much light for that to be useful, nor would it be an evolutionary step forward. When I speak of the mythic I am referring to the ability to connect ourselves to something larger than our individual quest and our individual outer circumstances.

Humans evolved from biological life through a long and well-tested process. It is well known that life, in the animal realms, evolves at the level of the species, not the individual organisms. It is the same for humanity. We are somewhat unique in our ability to perceive ourselves as a separate entity of consciousness, independent from our tribe, but this capacity masks the deeper reality that we continue to evolve at the level of the species. This, my friend, I believe to be important to you and your future pursuits.

Science has demonstrated that we live in a holographic reality of some form and while this is not fully understood the implications are profound. Each life acts as a microcosm of a larger whole of our society and our world. When one embraces the mythic quest they enter a reality in which they understand that their personal journey is, in some way, a reflection of a larger journey being undertaken by mankind, or at least a portion of mankind.

I believe, Andy Liebner, that the quest that dragged you through Europe, throwing up continual challenges at the hands of authoritative, inflexible structures, is a microcosm of the quest that your great nation, the United States of America, is confronting as it tries to demonstrate global leadership in the world. This is a young nation, filled with passion, enthusiasm and vision, but it has not yet found its place as the global leader and, dare I suggest, it will not until enough of its citizens enter into a deeper level of mythic understanding that will open the door for a new sense of wisdom to emerge on how to interact with the world at large.

It is clear from your story that you did not find this connection or this wisdom during your time in Europe and I daresay you were never meant to. The quest always begins at the surface level where we see the opposition as enemies and as obstacles to be battled and defeated. In this you showed admirable resolve, but, finally, you were worn down, suffering the failure that every young hero must endure if he is to make the transition into the realms of deeper wisdom. Lord knows, I've suffered a few myself!

If I may be so bold, I would like to offer a small piece of advice for you as you embark on this next stage of your journey. Well, two pieces of advice, actually!

First, those events, people and institutions that you draw to you and that appear to be obstacles and enemies are actually your friends. The universe has an innate intelligence, one that does not have to be attributed to any God, or Goddess, but that is inherent in the natural forces of life. This intelligence is driven by an over-riding impulse, and that impulse is to continue the evolutionary process we are so deeply engaged in. In order to do this, when one offers themselves in service to the greater evolutionary good of humanity, the universe will move mountains to bring to you the challenges that will reflect back the aspects of your own being that need to be embraced and healed.

Now, make no mistake, young man, for although your story may appear as if you were driven by your own goals, perhaps even selfishly pursuing your own endeavors, it is clear to me that beneath this is an over-riding force that is attuned to the evolutionary good of the people of your nation and this world.

It is only in confronting those things that we judge and hate about our collective society, that the new wisdom needed to support a more flexible and harmonious collective space can emerge. To that end your continual conflict with the structures of government and the sporting hierarchy has a purpose.

The second thing I will suggest is that it is, ultimately, impossible to continue to outrun our own shadow. You show an admirable *capacity to turn negative emotions and thoughts around and use them as fuel to drive you on. This is a wonderful capacity, but as with most things, the greatest gifts usually carry the greatest challenges as well. You may notice, if you read your story from outside the living of it, how you have to keep running harder and faster to stay in front of the darkness that lurks within you. Even with all your best efforts, ultimately, most notably in Australia, when your running stopped, it was still there waiting for you.*

One secret that I have learned is that our darkness is not our enemy, but is in fact the source of our greatest evolutionary wisdom. It is easy to say this and even relatively easy to comprehend it at an intellectual level, but it is a completely different matter to truly grasp and integrate it. Yet it is an essential part of the greater quest.

In many ancient stories of mythical quests the young warrior meets the dark knight, or something similar. Always he tries to slay his adversary, but, in the end, he must come to realize that the dark knight is a reflection of himself and then he must embrace it. There is no recipe on how to do this, but I am sure that the universe will guide you if you should be willing to continue deepening your journey.

Oh, and I should add, that I will be around somewhere on the planet, to help out should you need me and should it be appropriate.

All the best and much love,
Alistair

If you have been inspired to support Andy please contact:
wildshot@live.com

If you would like to find out more about Alistair and
his work in the world he can be reached at:
unifierhypothesis@gmail.com

I'd like to thank to the following people for their
support and suggestions for improving this book:
Alistair Smith, Jeff Potter, Sue Whitney, Sue Liebner, Roger
Liebner, Bob Gregg, Denny Paull, Ben Hugus, Jenny Ryan,
Matias Sarri, Sten Fjeldheim, John Morton, Janet Conway,
and Sawyer Gordon for making the maps (illustrator).

If you'd like to donate and support the NMU Ski Team please contact:
Sten Fjeldheim at: sfjeldhe@nmu.edu

To support the U.S. Ski Team please send contributions to:
U.S. Ski Team Foundation
1 Victory Lane
Box 100
Park City, UT 84060

Contact details for Obertilliach aka "O-town":
Hansjörg at the community information center:
obertilliach@osttirol.com   www.obertilliach.at

Contact Ingrid and Hans for nice, friendly, and
reasonable accommodations in Obertilliach:
hausgatterer@aon.at
www.haus-gatterer.com

Haus Gatterer
Ferienappartements
9942 Obertilliach 82
0664 4147152

Made in the USA
Lexington, KY
15 August 2015